ANOTHER DISASTER

ANOTHER DISASTER

Hong Kong Sketches

Denys Roberts

The Radcliffe Press
LONDON • NEW YORK

Published in 2006 by The Radcliffe Press
6 Salem Road, London W2 4BU

In the United States and in Canada
distributed by Palgrave Macmillan, a division of St Martin's Press
175 Fifth Avenue, New York NY 10010

ISBN 1 84511 112 5
EAN 978 1 84511 112 0

A full CIP record for this book is available from the British Library
A full CIP record for this book is available from the Library of Congress

Library of Congress Catalog card: available

Typeset in India by Digital Publishing Solutions
Printed and bound in Great Britain by T.J. International Ltd, Padstow, Cornwall

To Fiona with love

Contents

ABBREVIATIONS

A.D.	Armistice Day
A.G.	Attorney-General
C.J.	Chief Justice
6C.L.C.	Sixth Commonwealth Law Conference
7C.L.C.	Seventh Commonwealth Law Conference
C.S.	Chief (and Colonial) Secretary
D.R.	Denys Roberts
D.P.P.	Director of Public Prosecutions
Ex. Co.	Executive Council of Hong Kong
H.K.	Hong Kong
H.K.C.C.	Hong Kong Cricket Club
H.H.	Hulme House
Leg. Co.	Legislative Council of Hong Kong
M.M.	Sir Murray MacLehose
N.T.	New Territories
S.C.	Supreme Court
S.G.	Soliciter General

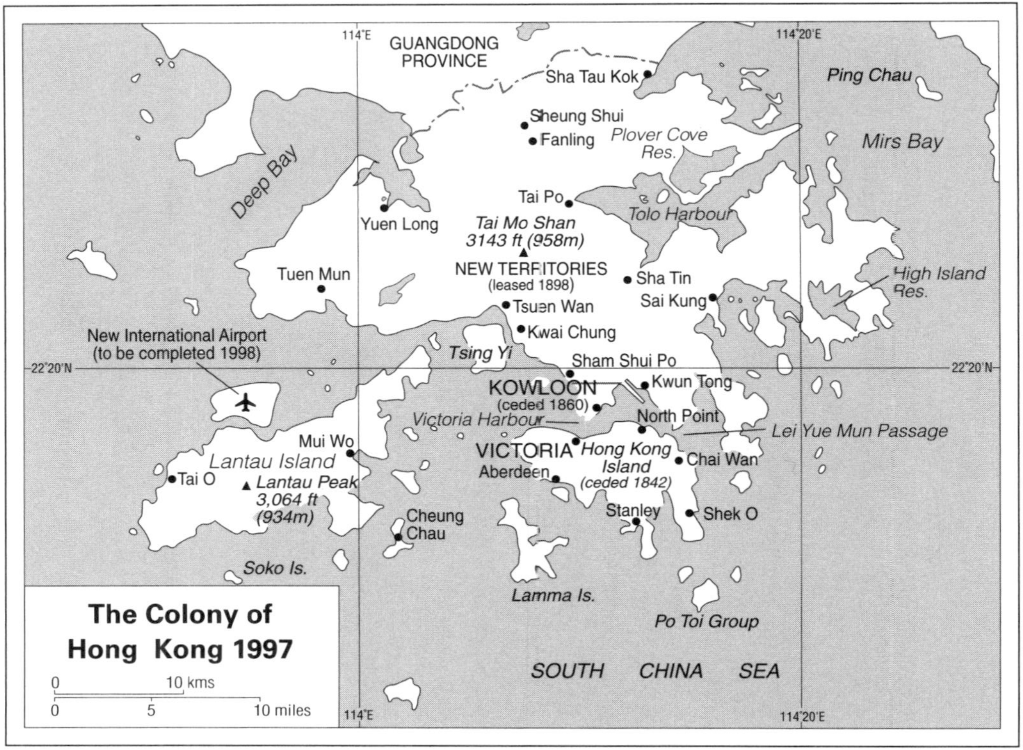

The Colony of
Hong Kong 1997
0
10 kms
0
5
10 miles
114°E
114°20'E
22°20'N
GUANGDONG
PROVINCE
Sha Tau Kok
Ping Chau
Sheung Shui
Fanling
Plover Cove
Res.
Mirs Bay
Deep Bay
Tai Po
Tolo Harbour
Yuen Long
Tai Mo Shan
3143 ft (958m)
NEW TERRITORIES
(leased 1898)
Sha Tin
High Island
Res.
Tuen Mun
Sai Kung
Tsuen Wan
Kwai Chung
New International Airport
(to be completed 1998)
Tsing Yi
Sham Shui Po
KOWLOON
(ceded 1860)
Kwun Tong
Victoria Harbour
North Point
Lei Yue Mun Passage
Mui Wo
Lantau Island
VICTORIA
Hong Kong
Island
(ceded 1842)
Chai Wan
Tai O
Lantau Peak
3,064 ft
(934m)
Aberdeen
Cheung
Chau
Stanley
Shek O
Soko Is.
Lamma Is.
Po Toi Group
SOUTH CHINA SEA

Chapter 1

Where are you going?

By the beginning of 1962 I was starting to enjoy life in Gibraltar. I lived in an early nineteenth century house, which was slowly sliding down the hill towards the barracks, and provided a romantic view in the sunset. The garden, long and thin and containing a variety of dead or dying plants, was supposed to be kept in order by Flores, a retired pastry cook, who dozed quietly in the gardener's hut for two hours twice a week.

Carmen, the housemaid, called me Caballero, which I thought was appropriate, as I had not been on a horse since I fell off one in 1946. She kept the crumbling house neat, except when she was in love, when she was likely to burst into tears and not be seen for several hours. Shortly before we left Gibraltar, she grizzled all the way to the frontier where she was greeted by an equally miserable Spaniard. They lived happily ever after.

I had discovered a shop in Spain where I could buy sherry and Spanish wine cheaply. I was thus able to see my friends and acquaintances become incapable without having to worry about the expense.

After a burst of misplaced energy, on my arrival, during which I redrafted a number of statutes that did not need redrafting, I was able to rely on the absence of any qualified help to farm out all the prosecutions to members of the Bar in private practice.

My predecessor as Attorney-General had been provided with an assistant, who was a Gibraltarian. The latter, when acting in my predecessor's place, is said to have enlivened a dull morning by walking up and down beside the convent, as Government House was called, raising a hat to the sentries, who were obliged to salute in reply. Shortly afterwards, the assistant's post was abolished.

I had been transferred to the Rock late in 1959, after representing the Government of Nyasaland in a disastrous enquiry, at the end of which a report highly critical of the Government had been issued. Following the usual bureaucratic principle, a debacle was presented as a vindication, and those held responsible were promoted.

I had also been appointed because the Gibraltar Executive Council members had resisted the appointment of the first choice of the Colonial Office, an able and charming Turkish Cypriot, because he came from Cyprus, where there was thought to be a lot of disloyalty to the British Crown. The latter was much in favour in Gibraltar, because it was beastly to Franco.

In addition, I had been attached to the Colonial Office for three months in 1956, when I had gone to a lot of trouble to conceal my deficiencies from the legal staff, whom I plied with toffees. It is better, I have discovered, to be remembered for something, provided it is not too disreputable, than to have my superiors ask who the hell Roberts is and what about Smith, who was here last year and kept picking his nose – wouldn't he do for Malta? Besides, one of the legal advisers had been a pupil of my father in the Temple in 1920 and owed him a favour.

Much of the work in the chambers in Gibraltar was done by Louis Saccone, a short-sighted man who wore glasses for everything except close reading, for which his sight was excellent. He was a solemn man, who regarded life as a serious matter. He had worked in the chambers for thirty years. I had learned not to contradict him. When I did so, I was usually wrong.

When the letter about Hong Kong arrived at the chambers in Gibraltar, Saccone was asking me about a bill that was intended to amend the legislation dealing with companies. As I did not understand it, I was following the English Act, a useful expedient if you do not know what you are doing. Even if the English draftsman did not know either, he was at least able to cloak his ignorance in persuasive language, making full use of archaic terms and sentences that led nowhere.

'You've put down a plural for "company",' he said accusingly, laying the offending bill on my desk.

'Where?' I asked aggressively. I often started like that.

'Here, here, and there, and more than once on the other pages.'

'Then I've been consistent.'

'Consistently wrong,' replied Saccone. 'Company should be followed by a singular, not a plural.'

'Fowler says I can use either.' I had not looked at *Fowler's*.

'Not in an amending bill when you have used the singular in the principal one,' he retorted.

'Oh,' I replied. I wasn't going to let him get away with it that easily.

'I'll alter it,' he replied, with one of his rare smiles, which he reserved for moments of triumph.

I read the letter, while he mangled the bill in the next room. It offered me the post of Solicitor-General in Hong Kong at a salary of $5,600 a month, which was the equivalent of £4,200. I showed Saccone the letter when he brought me a cup of lukewarm tea.

'It's a bit early,' he said. 'They usually leave the A.G. here for three or four years. Have you upset anyone?'

This had been my reaction too. I supposed that it was possible that a vacancy had arisen, which they wanted to fill in a hurry, but Saccone's explanation was more likely.

'The Governor got annoyed at me last year, when the Colonial Secretary was away and I was acting in his place,' I admitted.

'What did you do?' Saccone asked.

'He said I interfered with a military parade and shouted at his ADC.'

'Did you?'

'Well, yes, I did. You see the soldiers wanted to close off Main Street for a march and I thought I should have been told.'

'Should you?'

'Yes, but it is better not to remind generals of this. So I shouted at his ADC, who naturally went to the General, who chewed me up.'

'Were you in the right?'

'I suppose I was. I shan't make that mistake again. In future, the Governor will always be right.'

'That's the system I have adopted with you,' Saccone explained. I looked to see if he was joking, as he had been putting me right ever since I arrived. He was not.

'What would you do, Saccone? I rather like it here.'

'Is the money good?' asked Saccone, who was a very practical man.

'About double.'

'You'd better take it,' Saccone sighed. He would have to break in another A.G., who would be his eighth. 'There was a Mr Kees here before the War. He refused a job in Ghana. He wasn't offered another one. Died in the General Hospital here as an alcoholic some years later. Shows how dangerous it is to say no.'

At lunch time I consulted my first wife, who usually made up my mind for me when I was faced with a difficult decision, though we both pretended that I had decided myself.

'How would you feel about going to the East?' I asked her.

'Have you done something dreadful, which you haven't told me about?' she asked.

'No, no, I assure you I haven't. I upset the Governor last year, but that's all I can think of.'

'That's quite enough too. Apart from that, why should they want to get you out of here?'

'Possibly', I replied diffidently, as I did not believe this, 'they want me badly in Hong Kong.'

'That would be splendid,' she agreed, with a lack of conviction in her voice, which I resented, even if this was what I thought too.

'The salary is much better.' I thought I should emphasize the advantages.

'That will enable me to replace some of my pre-War clothes,' she agreed. 'I've never been closer to the East than South Africa.'

'I don't suppose Hong Kong will be much like the nightclubs in Cape Town.'

'You enjoyed India, didn't you? That is Far East, according to my school atlas.'

'Yes, but I expect Hong Kong is different.'

'How?'

'I don't know, but it must be.' I began to wish she would not ask me so many irrelevant questions.

'Have they sent you any notes about Hong Kong?'

'There was a printed sheet in the letter, dated 1948, saying that housing was short and that they hoped to eradicate malaria by 1950.'

'Your trouble', she said, 'is that you don't want to move.'

'I have', I replied stiffly, 'a certain duty to the people of Gibraltar.'

'If you had,' she replied, 'you would probably leave at once.'

'It is not fair on you to move, just when you've settled in. And Mandy is happy at her nursery school.'

'Don't shelter behind us. Just remember your friend Jack Holt in Zanzibar. He refused a post in the Solomons and was never offered another.'

'That was not because he turned the job down. It was because he drank too much on the Queen's birthday, and knocked out his pipe on the Governor's wife.'

'I've told you that we are willing to go. I'm sure you will make up your own mind as usual.'

I decided to go, in spite of her wish to do so. Nobody could say that I could not make my own decisions, when I had to. Besides, I had persuaded myself that, after all, they needed me in Hong Kong.

It was not long after I had arrived in Hong Kong that I was told that the vacancy which I had filled had only arisen because a man from Uganda had refused the job of A.G. because he preferred to remain in Africa.

I explained to my daughter Mandy, aged 4, that we were all going to Hong Kong. She was used to her parents moving, for what seemed to her to be inadequate reasons.

'Where is Hong Kong?' she asked. She had long, blond hair, which was odd, as she had been born in Central Africa.

'It's part of China.'

'I know about China, Daddy. It's full of people with yellow faces, who all look the same.'

'Where did you learn that?'

'My teacher, Mrs Grimes, told me. Will there be lots of dolls there?'

I told her that Hong Kong was awash with dolls.

'All right, Daddy. We can go. Shall I take all my toys?'

'A good idea.'

'Is it a secret, or can I tell them at school that we are going to Hong Kong?'

'You can tell anyone you like.'

'I think Charlie Posso will be sad. He kicked me in the weewee, because I made him fall over. But he likes me very much.'

The following day, when I arrived home for lunch, my wife was there with Mandy, whom she had fetched from the Scud Hill Steps Nursery School.

'Mandy got into trouble today at school,' she told me.

'What has your daughter done this time?'

'Mandy was on her way to the lavatory.'

'Do you think she needs an operation?'

'Not at her age. Do let me finish. As Mandy had not asked for permission to go, the teacher was not sure where she was going.'

'Just a minute, Mandy,' the teacher asked. 'Where do you think you are going?'

'I'm going to Hong Kong,' she replied.

'What did the teacher do?' I asked.

'Made her stand in the corner for being rude. Whenever she tried to go to the lavatory she was told to stand still. So she did it down her leg.'

'Is she all right now?'

'She's fine since she got some dry knickers. She complained about you on the way home, saying that you did not warn her that it was rude to tell people that she was going to Hong Kong.'

I gave Mandy a cream chocolate bar, from which I had only eaten one segment, to compensate for the injustice. I did not attempt to explain to her that life is very unfair.

Chapter 2
The oily man

One of the more bizarre results of a long cruise is that people become more attractive by the day.

My daughter, who is now a psychologist in New England, tells me that, if you lock rats up in cages, the females will start eating the males within a week. I would have wrongly attributed this to hunger; but she assured me that it was lust and that the same thing would happen to human beings who were thrown together in a cruise ship.

I have a different theory. I believe that the motion of the ship is responsible, so long as it is not violent. The slight movement and the sound of distant water produce in many people an almost uncontrollable urge. Plain people become more beautiful, and those who are already attractive are chased vigorously round the boat deck.

I was, of course, immune to this sort of thing myself and regarded it with a cynical detachment. However, during the voyage from London to Hong Kong, which took about a month, I saw at my table an example of what might happen when the usual social barriers were removed.

On my left sat a retired Brigadier, a widower who, I assumed, had bored his wife to death. Next to him sat a woman with fuzzy blond hair, thick glasses and the sort of complexion which you sometimes see on a teenager who is under medical care for psoriasis. For the first few meals they were polite but somewhat distant, their exchanges limited mainly to the passing of the salt and the vagaries of the weather. About the fourth day out of London, the Brigadier started looking at the woman, who remained aloof. As far as I could tell, she was still not attractive, though her complexion seemed better. After a few more days, I began to suspect that something was going on. It was not so much the fact that she was using lipstick and powder or that she breathed rather more noisily when she sat next to him. It was their conversation.

'Pass the salt, darling?' the Brigadier asked.

'It's in front of you,' she replied.

'What about the pepper, then?'

'You don't take pepper. You told me so yesterday.'

'I did? Well, I do now.'

'Would you mind passing Gerald the pepper?' she asked the man on her left. Gerald had been 'the Brigadier' at first.

She passed the silver-plated pepper shaker to Gerald, who closed his large hand over her fingertips, which I saw were bandaged.

'Ouch,' she said, 'you're hurting me.'

'Oh, good,' said Gerald. Flavia, which was her improbable name, gazed at him and gnawed at her lower lip.

'Tell me', I asked Flavia, 'how you managed to hurt your hand.'

'It's Gerald, you know. He is such a strong man.' The Brigadier coughed modestly.

'Oh,' I said. I did not ask her how she knew Gerald was strong. There were various intriguing possibilities.

There was no doubt that, by the tenth day out, Flavia was far better looking than she had been when we sailed. By the fifteenth day, she was most attractive – so much so that the Brigadier ate very little, which was not surprising, as he seldom let go of her hand during the meal. I dropped my napkin once to see what he was doing with his knees and was not surprised to see that his left leg was locked with her right one. If they had to rise in a hurry, as they did one evening when the fire alarm went off by accident, they were likely to fall over.

This was about the time, though the ship was having no effect on me, as I was much too sensible for that, that I first saw Mary.

I had spent the last hour in the library, looking for something suitable. Because I was on holiday, I had borrowed one of Barbara Cartland's romances, which were packed with heaving bosoms and untouched virgins. I did not, of course, enjoy the book, but thought I should take out a couple more of her works, to see if her plots varied. Although they did, there were still villains and unsullied girls. I found them refreshing.

I started to wander back to my cabin when I found my way blocked by a bottom. There are many kinds of bottom, some large and unattractive, like my own, some slim and probably dimpled, like the one in the corridor, which was covered in slacks.

'Hallo,' I said. I was seldom at a loss for a witty phrase.

The slacks turned towards me. About two feet above them was a charming face.

'At least you didn't pinch it,' she said.

'I never thought about it.'

'Then you should have done.'

'I'm really very sorry.' I felt quite inadequate.

'Are you queer or something?'

'Certainly not.'

'That randy old Brigadier can't keep his hands to himself.'

'I thought he was keen on a lady on my table, named Flavia. She must be keen too, as they keep passing the salt backwards and forwards.'

'He'll chase anything,' she said. 'It's being on a boat. He was quite all right when he was in command of a battalion in Singapore.'

'I expect it is the male menopause,' I replied, in some disgust. I was not yet forty and could afford to be acid about it.

'Don't let me keep you,' she said. 'I can see that you are reading only serious books.' She pointed at the romantic novels and giggled.

'Huh!' I replied as I passed her. That should have silenced her. She continued to giggle as I walked along the companionway. As I later discovered, she did this rather a lot. It was rather an attractive sound.

Two days later, I was playing deck cricket with a group of men who had clearly not played the sport before, in any of its forms – not even French cricket. I was doing well, until one of my opponents, who was undisputedly throwing the ball, hit me on the instep. I was carried to the cabin of the ship's doctor. He gave me some painkillers and assured me that nothing was broken. I did not believe him.

As I was waiting for the X-rays, which he had taken to be developed, Mary entered the cabin with her throat covered in a scarf.

'I'm hoarse,' she explained, 'but I don't think it's contagious.'

'If it were, that would not prevent me,' I replied. I had learned what to say in the romantic novels.

'Shouting at me, you mean, thinking that I couldn't answer back?'

'That is not what I meant.'

'What did you mean?'

'I'm not at all sure.' I had lost my nerve. She giggled at me again.

After this encounter, which seemed to strengthen our relationship, as there is nothing so powerful as a shared misfortune, I became steadily more attracted to her. I think she may have sensed this, as she refused on three occasions to walk with me on the lifeboat deck, which was said to be the best place to go if you wanted to avoid the Brigadier.

The ship was within a day or two of the coast of Malaysia when Mary invited me to her cabin. I met her outside the cinema, where they had been showing a film which I had seen before. However, as the sound was not working, it had seemed quite different as a silent film.

I hurried back to my cabin to shave. I was not in the least bit affected by the ship. There would be no shipboard romance for me. But I might as well shave, just in case something happened. As it did, though hardly what I had hoped for.

I had not realized that her cabin was close to the cinema and that the lights in the passage were attached to the same circuit as the sound in the cinema. It still does not make sense to me. Whatever the reason, the companionway leading to her cabin was dark. I made my way cautiously along it. As I did so, a figure emerged from another dark passage on my right and bumped heavily into me.

'Mind where you're going,' shouted a voice, which I recognized as that of the Brigadier. I apologized, in a stage whisper.

'Damn disgrace,' he said. 'Can't do a bit of private business without stumbling over someone out to do some poodle faking.'

I heard Flavia's voice from the dark.

'What have you found, Gerald?'

'A fellow out on the prowl, Flavia. It's a damn disgrace. What on earth do you think you're doing, sir? Just you wait till I get you in the light. Then we'll see who the peeping Tom is, eh?'

I lost my nerve and hurried back along the corridor. I did not try to find my way to Mary's cabin that night.

Two days later, she asked me if I knew Malaysia.

'I have never been there,' I admitted. 'I was sent to India to take part in the invasion in 1945, but that was cancelled a month before I was sent out.'

'It shows how important they thought you were.' She might have said this without a giggle.

'That is a consolation,' I agreed. 'But it was really because the War Office decided that it was too difficult to change anything. Several people on my boat went straight home again in a couple of weeks.'

'I thought you might like to spend the night with some friends of mine in Penang. They will be in their bungalow for a week's rest.'

'I suppose you will be there?'

'Certainly. Is that a disadvantage?'

She knew that it was not. I had been most attentive to her for a week. I admitted to myself that it was the ship's fault and that whatever I did was not, consequently, to be judged by ordinary standards. It even justified the Brigadier's extraordinary behaviour.

'I'll come. I promise not to behave myself properly.'

'Don't carry it too far', she said. 'Jimmy and Wilma, who are my friends, look on me as a member of their family. They are very protective.'

The bungalow was on the top of a cliff, overlooking a long sandy beach, a few miles out of Penang. It had a splendid view. It also had electric light from a generator which was out of order, hot water from a tank heated by the generator, and toilets which did not work because the sea water, which was meant to flush them, was pumped up by electricity.

Jimmy and Wilma put me in a room across the hall from that occupied by Mary. I assume that, when I arrived, they had decided that I was not to be trusted and did not give me the one next to hers. They were both very pleasant to me, even if they had little confidence in my ability to behave myself with Mary.

We spent the evening in candlelight, which is flattering and makes everyone look better than they are. By the time we all retired for the night, I had to keep my hands in my pockets to avoid emulating the Brigadier by pawing at Mary.

'Is there anything either of you wants?' Jimmy asked. I thought it unwise to tell him.

'Just a glass of water,' Mary replied. 'Perhaps Denys can bring it to me. Preferably without spilling it,' she added. This was unnecessary as she had only seen me knock over two drinks on the ship and neither accident was really my fault.

'Not at all,' I muttered, doing my best to sound reluctant. I think I may have overdone it, as Wilma offered to take it herself.

'Let him do it,' said Mary. 'The lecher has been trying to get me into my nightdress for weeks.'

'There'll be nothing like that in this house,' said Jimmy. 'I promised your father I'd keep an eye on you.' He looked at me severely, as if he meant what he had said.

When I took the glass of water, which I had overfilled, he was standing in the hall, making sure that I did not try anything. Mary was sitting up in bed in her nightdress. This did not seem to fit well round the chest, as half of it was outside the dress. I decided not to offer to replace it. She thanked me for the water, which I had slopped all over the bed in my excitement.

'I hope you will sleep well,' she said. 'Knock on my door if you can't.' She winked. I walked quickly from the room into the hall, where Jimmy was waiting for me.

'I will wake you in the morning,' he said, as he ushered me into my room. I thanked him as he closed the door behind me. At least, he didn't lock it, like my father did when he did not approve of one of my fiancées.

I thought that it would be wise to wait a while before I returned to Mary's room. I sat on the edge of my bed and dozed off. I awoke with a start when I heard a scream. It seemed to come from Mary's room. I opened my door and hurried across the hall into her room. She rushed at me and took me by the arm.

'Don't just stand there. Do something.'

'No need to get too excited, old girl,' I replied. 'Better make sure that the others did not hear you shouting for me.'

'Shouting for you!' she exclaimed. 'I saw a hideous face at the window. Was it you, then?'

Jimmy entered the room behind me, looking angry.

'You ought to be ashamed of yourself,' he said, 'bursting in like this and frightening Mary.'

'Dreadful,' added Wilma, who was behind him.

'But I did not,' I protested.

'He's telling the truth, for once,' Mary explained. 'There was a face at the window. Even uglier than his,' she added unnecessarily.

'Are you quite sure?' asked Jimmy, who asked as if he did not believe what he was being told.

'The man', Mary went on, 'was covered in oil. And he was stark naked. When I woke up, I saw him standing by the window. I thought for a moment it was Denys, until I saw the oil.'

'I wouldn't put it past him to pour oil over himself,' Jimmy commented. 'But it sounds more like an oily man.'

'What is that?' I asked.

'The burglars round here take off all their clothes and cover themselves in oil. Then if a victim catches one, he can't hold on to him.'

'Couldn't I grab him by the testicles?' said Mary, who seemed to be taking an unhealthy interest in oily men as a class.

'Not if they have oil all over them, Mary. You'd never get time for a proper squeeze. The only thing to do is to impale them. Come on,' he said to me, 'there are some spears on the wall outside. Follow me.'

He took a spear from the wall and handed it to me. Underneath was a plaque, which said, 'Used for Pig Sticking in 1932'.

'I don't think it will work very well on people,' I suggested. I did not tell Jimmy that I didn't like going after a burglar with a spear. The burglar might have a weapon too.

'Nonsense,' he replied. 'I've seen off a lot of Communist terrorists who were scaring my workers, so I don't mind an oily man or two.' He flung open the front door and ran to his left, telling me to go the other way round the house.

I went cautiously, holding the spear in front of me. This route would take me to Mary's window, where the oily man was last seen. As I did so, I heard a shout from Jimmy of 'Tally-ho. Stop him.' This was followed by a pounding of feet as a naked man ran towards me, his oil glistening in the moonlight. He disappeared into the jungle.

'You should have stopped him,' Jimmy complained. 'Could you recognize him again?'

'Only his genitals,' I replied. 'I've never seen any unstrung before and thought they were fascinating.'

'We shall have to report this to the police,' said Jimmy. 'Not that they will do anything about it, but if I don't tell them they will be annoyed.'

An hour later, a police sergeant arrived. He spent the next hour taking measurements. He dusted Mary's window for fingerprints and insisted on examining the spears for blood.

By the time he started to take statements, it was after one in the morning. He wrote them in a slow longhand which took two hours. We signed the statements. He drove off in a police jeep, having assured us that the police were not likely to do anything, as there were a dozen or so oily men operating in the area and nobody had caught one yet. As we had not lost any property, there was nothing for us to identify. So, unless somebody confessed, it was unlikely that we would hear any more. We never did.

'The least we can do', said Jimmy, after the sergeant had left, about half past three, 'is to stay and look after Mary for the rest of the night.'

'I'm quite all right,' she said. 'I'm so tired now I shall sleep very well.'

'I will take my turn,' I volunteered.

'Nonsense. You are a guest,' Jimmy replied. 'I shall watch Mary's room till the morning, just in case the oily man comes back.'

Chapter 3
The first morning

The staff captain of the *Cathay* looked doubtfully at me during dinner, the evening before the ship was due to dock in Hong Kong. His name was Peter Love. He had cheerfully borne bad jokes about it for years, but was nearing the end of his patience.

'I suppose you won't be up at six in the morning?' said Love, who knew something of my habits.

'Why should I be awake at that hour, apart from the fact that I can't sleep on that dreadful bunk in my cabin?'

'About that time, we should be coming into Hong Kong harbour. It will probably be the only time you'll see the place at dawn.'

'I will do my best to get up.'

I did not commit myself. I was in the grip of shipboard inertia, in which it is no longer possible to decide on anything. A fellow passenger admitted to me that he had given up coming to breakfast, because the waiter asked him every day if he wanted his eggs boiled, fried or scrambled. When he was unable to answer, the waiter brought him all three, which ensured that he would not be able to eat any of them.

I did not sleep well. I kept waking up in order to tell myself that I had no intention of getting up so early. At a quarter to six, I shaved, using a new blade for the occasion. It cut me in several places, which I tried to staunch with pieces of cotton wool; these hung limply from my face as I walked from my cabin to the bridge. On the way I met a man in a track suit, who was jogging round the deck, looking red faced and healthy. I was much cheered later to hear that he had turned his ankle and was carried ashore on a stretcher.

'Morning!' he shouted. 'Bit early for you.'

I nodded in reply. I did not want to speak to him. He made me feel unfit, overweight and puffy. The fact that I was made me even more reluctant.

'Don't often see you up this early.' I muttered my agreement.

'Glorious day, what?' I nodded. As I walked, he trotted alongside me, exuding good health. I began to hate him.

'Getting off today?' he asked.

'Yes,' I replied, hoping that he would now be satisfied, as he had wrung an answer from me.

'Me too.' He added, 'I'm the new fitness man for the British Council.'

'The what?' I asked.

'The Council has decided to modernize its image. It's going to have keep fit classes, as well as run a lending library.'

'Good Lord,' I said.

'See you later. You look as if you could do with a bit of exercise yourself. I must do my thirty circuits now. It was nice talking to you.'

'Even if you couldn't get a word in,' I added, making sure that he did not hear me.

When I reached the bridge it was light. Peter Love was at his most cheerful, which was not attractive at that hour. I greeted him with a grunt, which was a triumph of good will over sense.

'I've been sailing in here for fifteen years,' he said. 'I never get tired of the view. It's splendid when there aren't any people to spoil it.'

It was. On each side of the ship were rocky slopes, with the walls of old forts, which had once dominated the channel, still to be seen. In front of us lay the main harbour, where the new airport pushed its main runway into the water.

'You will like it here, I'm sure.'

'Not if I have to get up at six to enjoy it.'

'How long do you think you'll stay?'

'Not long. As soon as you start to be useful, you get moved.'

'That's to stop you becoming corrupt, I expect.'

'That may be the reason for changing the auditors but it hardly applies to lawyers in the service, Peter.'

'You mean they're all too honest?'

'They don't get a chance to be anything else. Some of them may be drunk or incompetent or both. But they're all poor.'

Love concentrated on trying to prevent the ship from hitting one of the other vessels which were crossing the harbour at high speed, apparently intent on self-destruction. He did not seem to be having much success, to judge by the number of clenched fists that were shaken at him as the *Cathay* made its way towards the berth. I did not understand what the other boatmen were shouting, but the meaning of their gestures was unmistakable.

I contented myself with the conviction that I had made a bad mistake leaving Gibraltar. How could I have done such a thing? It could only have been for the money. I should regret it. I wondered what percentage of Solicitor-Generals of Hong Kong had committed suicide? As I ate my breakfast, I was trying to decide if I wanted to be buried or cremated.

I thanked the Indian waiter, who seemed to be delighted about arriving in Hong Kong. I asked him why.

'It's the girls,' he said. 'There are many pretty girls. Your very kind gift will give me four.'

'Four! Then I'd better have half of it back for myself.'

'You are jesting, sir. I wish you a good time here and lots of happy girls.'

I did not tell him that it was probably illegal to run a brothel, even in Hong Kong. He would not have believed me and I was not too sure myself. When I enquired about it, a few weeks later, everybody said I was right but there were more serious crimes to deal with, like spitting and dropping litter.

I returned to my cabin to pack, and to prepare for what I was sure was going to be an awkward day. I picked myself up from the floor, as the ship lurched into its berth, and began putting things into my suitcase, which was held together with string. It was still only eight o'clock and it was unlikely that anyone would come to fetch me yet, though I had been warned that someone would.

I answered a tap on my door. In the corridor was a red faced man with a mop of black hair which did not look as if he had combed it. I later discovered that it always looked like that, even when he had. He was dressed in a black jacket and striped dark grey trousers. He looked like the man from the tax office in London whom I had dodged about ten years before, not because I was earning anything taxable but as a matter of principle.

'Are you Denys Roberts?' he asked. I nodded cautiously.

'I'm Michael Morley-John. I've come to meet you.'

'Oh, good.' I thrust out a hand which he looked at with distaste and did not take. I decided that he must be a member of the English Bar, as they never shook hands with a fellow member. However, I had not heard of him before. I was not good at remembering names, but I would not have forgotten anything as odd as his.

'I'm acting as S.G. until you arrived,' he added with a wince. 'So I've been sent by the A.G. to welcome you.'

'I haven't quite finished packing', I said. 'Would you care to wait in the lounge?'

'No, no, I'll just squat on your bed.'

He cleared a space for himself by dropping a pair of unmatching socks with holes in the toes into my half packed suitcase.

'I say,' he went on, 'do you play that?' He pointed at the guitar, which was standing against the wall in a canvas case.

'Not very well,' I replied. 'I am still having lessons.' I thought it better not to tell him that even my teacher, who was paid to be optimistic, did not foresee a great future for me with the instrument.

'I'm sure you are just being modest. Why not come and play at one of our church evenings? They are very informal. My daughter plays the recorder there.'

'Before we land, I must finish packing, Michael. If I don't, I'll have to leave my clothes here and they are all I've got.'

'I'll give you the name of my tailor,' he replied, handing me a card which said 'Ah Mee. Tailor for Mens and Womens'. Within a week I had a dozen tailor's cards.

I hurled the rest of my clothes into the suitcase and tied it tightly with string.

'Before we go ashore, would you mind having your photo taken?'

'Upstairs, you mean? In the light, where everyone can see I cut myself shaving at half past five?'

'It's not my idea,' Michael replied hastily, having decided that I was easily upset in the mornings. 'It's the *SCMP*.'

'What is that?'

'It's the *South China Morning Post*. It's the main English paper. It's very influential. I expect you've heard of it?'

'No,' I replied. 'And I don't think I ought to be photographed with plaster all over my face. It looks as if I've just had a fight.'

'I'll tell them you refuse, if you like. Of course, they'll say that you were not helpful and they will catch you as you go ashore anyway.'

I thanked him for putting the alternatives to me so fairly. As I did so, he opened the cabin door and shouted 'Please come and take your pictures.'

I had expected one photographer. The cabin was filled with small men holding large cameras and light meters and shouting at anyone else who got in the way.

'Where did the others come from?' I enquired, though it didn't matter.

'I don't know. I expect they saw the *SCMP* chap and came on board and followed him, in case he had got someone important to photograph.'

'Then they will be disappointed,' I replied tartly.

One of the photographers pulled a curtain across the window. There was an unpleasant struggle as it was pulled back again.

I did my best to fulfil their requests, though these seemed, on several occasions, to be in conflict.

I thought I had finished, until one of the photographers noticed the guitar. With a grunt of pleasure, he thrust it into my hands, upside down, and pointed his camera at me. Before I could protest he had taken a picture.

'That's it,' Morley-John shouted. 'No more pictures. Everybody out, please.'

'I always say please to journalists,' he assured me out of the corner of his mouth. 'Then they eat out of my hand.'

The eating was not obvious, as most of them remained in the cabin and took out their notebooks.

'Mr Roberts is tired,' Morley-John shouted. 'Just look at him.' This seemed to me to be exaggerating a perfectly normal shipboard dyspepsia. 'No interviews, please.'

'Not an interview. Just a few questions,' one of them replied. It was a distinction without a difference that several journalists used on me in the future.

'Are you happy to be here?'

'Of course. I'm delighted.' I couldn't very well tell them that I'd rather be on the Rock. I realized, as soon as I said this, that I was caught. Once you begin to talk, the reporter has won. You only stop when you have made an ass of yourself, to his satisfaction.

For the next twenty minutes I told them how pleased I was to be in the Far East. I mentioned my cousin, who had been in the Royal Navy and had contracted an unpleasant social disease when he was ashore in Hong Kong. He spoke enthusiastically about the place.

They left shaking their heads in disbelief when I said that I knew nothing about the Walled City of Kowloon and had never met the Governor. I was described in some papers next day as 'tight lipped' on these important subjects.

'Sorry about that,' said Morley-John when they had left. 'I didn't expect any questions. They must be very short of news.'

The following morning, he brought me a selection of papers.

'It might have been worse,' he said. I looked at what he had brought, and did not see how. The photographs showed a man of 60 or so, his face festooned with cotton wool, which I had not removed. The bags under my eyes were deep and my double chin large. My hair, disarranged by my visit to the bridge, looked wild. The guitar, upside down, was draped untidily across my breast. The headlines were no better.

'Guitar-playing law officer arrives.'

'Rock on the Rock?'

'Roberts prefers music to law.'

'Roberts refuses to disclose views on capital punishment.' This was correct. I had not been asked about them.

In the text of one article I was described as in my early fifties, plump, bald and casually dressed.

'Pretty friendly stuff,' Morley-John commented. 'You should see what they write if they don't like you.'

A first impression is hard to dispel. It was some years before I was able to persuade my colleagues that I was not 200 pounds, not well over fifty, not wholly debauched and not interested only in the guitar. They seemed rather disappointed.

Chapter 4

The first evening

Morley-John took me to the Gloucester Hotel in Pedder Street, which was thought in the early 1960s to be the best hotel on the island. My suitcases were placed disdainfully in my room by a Chinese room-boy, who was not impressed by their condition or by the tip which I gave him in Singapore dollars. When he had left, Morley-John handed me an unsealed envelope, in which lay a single red Hong Kong hundred-dollar note.

'I have heard about corruption here,' I observed. 'But isn't this a bit early?'

'It's not that at all, S.G.,' he said stiffly. 'It's an advance in Hong Kong money to help you out. The A.G. sent it, with a letter of welcome. That is in the envelope too.'

I read it. 'Doesn't say anything about the note. Does he want it back?'

'Sometime, I think.'

'But I can't do that until somebody pays me.'

'I expect you can get an advance.'

'A loan you mean, so that I can repay this loan?'

'You're forcing me into a corner,' Morley-John protested. 'I suppose that's why you were sent here.' He was, I thought, mildly upset because the job had not gone to him, as no doubt it should have done.

'It's nothing to do with merit,' I assured him. 'I had made such a mess of the Gibraltar job that they had to find somewhere else for me in a hurry.' I was aggrieved when he nodded his head in agreement.

'I'll tell you what I'll do,' he said in a moment of kindness that I am sure he regretted later. 'I will lend you the money so that you can repay the A.G. We do this for everyone who arrives in chambers from abroad.'

'That's very decent of you, Michael.' He looked pleased, though why anyone should be happy at lending money to me I did not know.

'We ought to go and look at the flats next.'

'What flats?'

'The ones the Government has kept empty so that you can look at them. Didn't you get the letter we sent on to you?'

I shook my head. I did get it a month later, sent on by the ship, to which it had been forwarded. It contained no mention of the flats which I was shown, though it was full of praise for two others, which I did not see. The first flat was on the ground floor of a block called 'Queen's Gardens'. Morley-John thought it was named after Queen Victoria.

'Good location,' he said. 'You would be able to walk to the office. Though not back, as it's uphill then.' This did not seem to me to be in its favour.

The other was even larger, was in the floor above his own on the Peak and close to the cable car, which went to within a hundred yards of my office.

'You can come home for lunch here. I always do.'

'Isn't it a bit of a rush in an hour?'

'It's quite comfortable in an hour and a half. I usually go back late, because anyone I might want to talk to isn't in his office before about half past two anyhow. So you might as well be at home yourself. We are', he added, 'very punctual here. It's the Hong Kong work ethic.'

I took the second flat and moved in when my baggage arrived, as it did at about the same time as a typhoon. This was the only occasion on which I saw a TV set float past a second floor window. It was not switched on.

For the next year or so, I had lunch at home. Nobody seemed to notice that I was not available for an hour and a half in the middle of the day. I found it somewhat disconcerting that nobody minded.

I was due, on my first evening in Hong Kong, to meet Maurice Heenan, a soft spoken, good humoured and thoughtful New Zealander. He had only become A.G. shortly before my arrival. For four years, until he went to work for the United Nations, he bore my mistakes with patience and good humour. Maurice was married to a beautiful Czech, who had made many enemies by refusing to age. She had escaped from Prague by going through a ceremony of marriage with an American consular officer, whom she divorced as soon as she got to New York, in order to marry Maurice.

It was not my fault that we arrived late. My driver did not know where it was, in spite of his assurance, when I entered the car in Pedder Street, that he knew exactly where Mr Heenan lived.

'Mr Heenan lives on Peak side,' he explained. 'Never mind blood.' He pointed at the white cover, spattered with brownish stains, which concealed the upholstery. 'Small accident,' he went on. 'But only when this car was a taxi.'

'Isn't this a Government car?'

'Drivers are very badly paid. So we have to make money some other way. I use the car as a taxi. Not when it interferes with any official work, of course.'

'Naturally,' I agreed. 'But don't you need a meter for a taxi?'

'That's a European law. We Chinese don't follow it.'

'Don't the police enforce the law?'

'Some of the police are very bad and take you to a court, where the magistrate talks about justice and makes you pay a fine. Sometimes you pay the fine to the police officer instead and you hear no more about the case.'

The driver took me to Severn Road, in which the Heenans lived.

'What time is your dinner?' he asked.

'I was told to be there at eight. What time did they tell you?'

'Eight. But they mean nine. It's always dinner at nine at Mr Heenan. At eight, Mrs is still in the bath.'

I rang a bell marked 'Heenan'. The notice attached by string to the bell clattered to the ground. I bent to pick it up. When I straightened, I saw that the door had been opened by a trim figure in a well fitting suit and a dark moustache.

'I'm Maurice Heenan,' he said. 'But there's really no need to kowtow. Just call me "lord".'

D.R. with Maurice Heenan

I handed him the notice. I thought of a devastating reply the next day.

'Claire will be here soon. She's in the bath.'

'My driver told me that she always is, at this time.'

'He's right. I must get her to change it. I'll get the notice fixed too. We've been here two years and it falls off whenever anyone rings the bell.'

The Heenans left four years later. When I called on the man who took over their house, the notice with a new name painted on it fell off the bell.

'Claire will be late,' he told me. 'She keeps her mid-European habits. In Prague it was not polite for a woman to be on time.' He drew on his pipe, which spluttered alarmingly, as if it was full of water.

'Please smoke if you want to. As you can see, I am trying to give up cigarettes.'

'So am I.'

I had little success either, until five years later, when I was so badly poisoned by food in Beirut that I could not smoke for a fortnight. It is quite an effective method. Probably any strong poison will do. I ate a quantity of raw meat in an Arab house, though I concede that this method is not available to everyone.

As Maurice began to talk about Hong Kong, I started to feel uneasy. I had been up at five thirty and been hurried around most of the day by an ebullient Morley-John, who seemed to be full of unnecessary energy. At first I thought I was just tired. I then began to feel ill. It would be better, I decided, if I was going to lose my lunch, if I did not do so in front of my new superior. This would not create the correct first impression. I wanted him to believe that he had acquired a smartly dressed, well turned out, carefully controlled and clever man, upon whom he could rely with confidence in any crisis which might arise. I did not want him to think I was a drunk. The service was reputed to have plenty of those already. I stood up from the sofa and looked about me desperately.

'If you want the cloakroom, try the second on the right down the corridor.'

As I hurried towards it, I recalled my failure to find one in Washington airport, where I had asked for a cloakroom repeatedly and been greeted with the sort of puzzlement which anyone talking Turkish in Alaska could reasonably expect. Only when my predicament became obvious and people began to wonder why I was standing with my legs crossed was I offered a choice of eight toilets.

I hurried through the door on my right. It was full of household equipment. In spite of the bucket, into which I placed my foot, I was sure that this was not the place Maurice had indicated. I backed out into the corridor where a man in a long white gown, carrying a plate of peanuts, looked at me in surprise.

'The place is next door, sir,' he said. 'Shall I take the mop?' He had seen the head, which had somehow found its way into my pocket.

I handed it to him with relief and scuttled into the cloakroom, in which I lost my lunch. It is not easy to do this quietly, though I did my best, faking a loud cough after each eruption.

I did not want my host to know what I had done, although my pale face cannot have left him in much doubt. He was too polite to mention it.

In the drawing room, Maurice was sitting with a much younger woman, whom he introduced as his wife. It seemed somewhat odd for a man to marry someone much younger than himself. When I did so myself, it seemed entirely sensible.

'Are you feeling all right?' she enquired, after we had been introduced. 'It takes some people a while to get settled.'

Her English was perfect and without any accent. In view of her Czech origins, I found this disturbing. If you are not born in Britain you should talk broken English, like they all do in war films.

'Good heavens, yes.' I was feeling much better without my lunch. I did not need it anyhow, as I was about to have an excellent dinner.

'The water here sometimes makes visitors quite ill, until they get used to it,' she went on. 'So please let us know if you don't feel too good and Maurice will run you home.'

I promised to let her know if I felt off colour, though I was determined to make a good impression on the Heenans, especially on Claire. She would decide, if she was like other wives, whom her husband should befriend.

It would not help me if I were to lose any part of the dinner, which she must have supervised. The most equable wife involves herself in the dinner and regards each course, even if she has done no more than order it, as a personal challenge. If a guest enjoys it, he rises in her estimation; if he does not, there is a black mark against him. Whatever Claire may have said about the water, she might well decide that my stomach had been upset by one of her dishes.

The first course was a prawn cocktail covered in a rich and elegant pink sauce. I had eaten half of it, when I began to feel odd again. I hurried to the cloakroom, blaming my visit on a weak bladder. As I lost the prawns, I wondered if I should have mentioned my bladder.

I don't suppose Maurice would be at all impressed by an S.G. who had a weak bladder.

I felt a great deal better after losing the prawns. I tackled the next course with more enthusiasm. It was chicken, plain, well cooked and recognizable. My confidence was fully restored. I took a large mouthful of the lemon mousse which came next and wished that I had not. I hurried from the dining room again, not pausing this time to offer some improbable excuse. I consoled myself that it didn't matter what I did, so long as I did not do it in front of the Heenans.

I can no longer remember clearly what we discussed that evening. I would like to think that I was as modest, patient and restrained as they were, though I doubt it. It was more likely that I sat uneasily on the edge of the chair, so that I could get to the basin quickly, looking dreadful and sounding half witted.

At about ten thirty, Maurice looked at his watch. I must have said something particularly irrelevant. He seemed to have a watch that told the correct time, unlike mine, which only went when it was shaken and was always wrong.

'You've had a long day,' he said. 'You must have been up very early.'

'I assure you, I feel fine,' I replied.

'You'd say that however you felt,' he said. Claire made kind and unidentifiable noises in support.

I thanked both of them for their kindness. By summoning my last reserves, I even told them what a pleasant evening it had been.

The driver, who was snoring noisily in the front of the car which had brought me to the flat, took me back to the hotel. I was sure I had made a poor impression on the A.G. and his wife. I supposed that there was still a job for me in the Solomon Islands. There had been a vacancy there in 1959. Perhaps there still was.

Four years later, when the Heenans left for New York, he asked me if I remembered my first evening in Hong Kong.

'Vividly, Maurice. I managed to do everything wrong. I was convinced that you must have thought either that I always looked dreadful or that I was a drunk, or both.'

'We thought you managed splendidly. We knew you were feeling ill and would much rather have stayed in your hotel and rested, instead of trying to eat all that rich food and entertain us.'

'I had to rush out three times. I was sure you would never forget. What a way to start!'

'You should have seen the Crown Counsel who came off a ship the year before you. He was so ill, I had to send him home half way through dinner.'

When the driver stopped the car outside the hotel in Pedder Street, I felt ill again. I ran from his car to the refuse bin which stood on the pavement. I deposited in it the Heenans' coffee. There was nothing else left. I walked slowly to the lobby, assisted by the driver, who was used to Europeans who were well past their best. I was greeted by the doorman with a broad smile. Chinese seldom wink. If they did, he would have.

'Plenty to drink, sir?' he asked. 'Must have been a good evening.'

Chapter 5

A Chinese dinner

K. Y. Chan was a fairly rich Chinese. Probably not very rich, as I doubt if his fortune was worth more than ten million sterling or so. He lived in a brick house, which had been built in what was considered to be a traditional Chinese style, with long corridors, which were cool in summer and cold in the winter, and tiled black roofs that went up at the ends.

It was unusual to be asked to dinner at his house, especially as he was a magistrate and I was in the Legal Department, the members of which did not think well of those who sat on the bench. The latter were continually acquitting people who were obviously guilty.

K. Y. Chan apologized deeply for the awful meal, of fifteen courses, which he was inflicting on me. He did this about half way through it, when I was already feeling distended by his excellent food.

'Not so, K.Y.,' I insisted. 'The dinner is first class.'

'Alas,' he replied, 'I only wish it were. You are only being kind.'

'Nonsense,' I said, 'I'm telling you what I think.'

'More fish?' he suggested. I did not want any more fish. I was full of fish. But I could hardly refuse, after what I had just said.

'I suppose', I asked him after I had forced down the fish, which consisted largely of bones, 'that it must be a dreadful nuisance, having caterers in your kitchen?'

'I suppose it would be if I had them. In any case I would not bring them in for a simple meal like this.'

He waved an elegant hand at the fish. This was rare and expensive, as his wife had told me at least twice.

'Rather,' I agreed. I was not really listening. I was trying to locate the fish bone, which had lodged in my teeth, before I swallowed it.

'I have a fish cook from Shanghai. The best cooks come from there. So did my father. Not that he could cook. The next course is a double boiled melon soup, with sesame seeds.'

I nodded vigorously. This made me swallow the last of the fish, with no ill effects. When my mouth began to bleed in the middle of the night, I woke my wife and asked her if she knew whether there was a TB hospital in Hong Kong.

'Probably,' she said in what I thought was a very unsympathetic way. 'But I don't think you will qualify.'

'I'm bleeding,' I protested. 'Look at the sheet. It's covered with blood!'

'You just spat out a fishbone, Denys. That's why you are making such a mess.'

'It's all K.Y.'s fault. If he'd entertained us in a restaurant, this would not have happened.'

'What has that got to do with it?' she asked.

There is nothing I dislike more than an unanswerable question. Not that I was bereft of response. I sulked for the rest of the night.

It was, however, unusual for most Chinese hosts to entertain at home. They preferred to do so in a private room at a restaurant. Here guests could drop food on the floor at will; at home the host would have to face an angry wife, who would inform him that Roberts had ruined the blue carpet by tramping noodles into the pattern.

The usual method of seating differed from the Western system. Under the latter, it was thought wrong to seat husband and wife together. They would either have nothing more to say to one another, in which case there would be an area of silence, or they would be in the middle of a row about something important, like who left the light on when they came out, so that their corner of the table would be noisy with snarls. The Chinese host, however, often put husband and wife together. This suited those who had been recently married, as it gave them a chance to tell one another how gifted they were. The other guests knew that on one side of them at least there would be someone who would reply, even if this consisted only of agreement with whispered criticisms of the other guests.

It took me some time to realize that many Chinese wives preferred to leave the talking to their husbands. On such an occasion, it would have been obvious to anyone with the slightest sensitivity that they would much prefer to be left alone. I felt, nevertheless, a compulsion to try to make them talk. It was a challenge.

The woman next to me was wearing expensive jewellery, not only half a dozen rings but earrings, a bracelet and a choker. They all sparkled with diamonds. I was sure that they were real, not because I knew anything about precious stones, but because one of the other women present, who could have spotted paste at fifty paces, would otherwise have congratulated her on being clever enough to find some fake jewellery.

'I could not help noticing your lovely rings,' I said to my neighbour. She favoured me with a blank stare. No doubt she had been valuing the earrings worn by Mrs Chow, who was sitting opposite to her. I tried again, pointing at her fingers, which were covered in them.

'The rings are very good,' she agreed, unleashing a smile which revealed about a hundred thousand Hong Kong dollars' worth of implants and crowns. She was a well preserved woman of fifty. She looked about thirty-five, as she would do until she reached sixty or so, when she would age fast. Until then, she kept out of the sun and controlled her emotions as these produced lines.

'Must be very valuable,' I commented.

'Not really. Only half a million dollars.'

'For one of them?'

'No, no, the lot. They are cheap rings.'

'The one on your little finger does not look cheap.'

'That was given to my grandmother.'

'Who gave her that?'

'My grandfather. Just before the Japanese came for him.'

'Did they – er – get rid of him?'

'He was not there. He came back later. He was eighty-four when he died.'

'What about the next ring?'

'Came from my mother.'

'Did she get that from your father.'

'Just before the Communists came to look for him, as he was a landlord.'

'But he was not there?'

'He was not. He was here. He sent for the rest of the family afterwards, when he was doing good business.'

'What about the other rings?'

'One from my first husband, one from my second husband and the rest from the one I have now.'

I did not like to suggest that this could only be a temporary arrangement and that she could look forward to other rings in due course.

'I know what you are thinking,' she said. 'You are wondering why I have so much jewellery and are saying that you could not even afford the insurance.'

'Oh no, I assure you.'

'It is because you can carry it with you when you have to leave in a hurry. You can live off it, if you have to sell it, for a long time.'

'I would not like you to tell my wife that. She keeps saying that diamonds are an investment.'

'That is what she said to me before dinner.'

'We can't afford them,' I replied defensively. 'I'm a poor Government servant and I have a son at boarding school in England.'

'Does he like it?'

'Not at all. He keeps running away. Unhappily, someone finds him each time.'

'I have two sons and two daughters.'

'Are they still at school?'

'Of my sons, one is a solicitor. The other is a doctor. They were both at boarding school in England. They were happy to get away from home.' I did not ask why.

'What about your daughters?'

'One is an accountant. She keeps her father's books.' I assumed that this meant one set for the Inland Revenue and another for him giving the correct picture.

'What about the other?'

'Very rich. Her husband is an undertaker. He has a very good business. Are you thinking of dying soon? I can give you his card.'

I could not think of any plausible reason why I should not need his services. I accepted the card which she produced from her handbag, which was covered with pearls. The card read 'Ho Ha Yau, Undertaker. All you have to do is die. Leave the rest to us'.

'Also,' she said, 'my son-in-law will provide mourners, for a very low price.'

'Mourners?'

'Certainly. If you are going to have a proper funeral, you must have a lot of unhappy people in the funeral parlour. For a few dollars a head, he will provide you with plenty of mourners.'

I went to several funerals. All of them were attended by a large number of mourners. I wondered how many of them had been provided by her son-in-law.

On another occasion, I found myself next to an English wife who believed that she must make plenty of noise; otherwise, it would be assumed that she was not enjoying herself. It was not an accident that she had been put next to me. It was carefully planned by my host.

'I think we ought to have the Roberts,' he said to his wife.

'She is very nice. Why do we have to ask him? He does not say much and he can't manage his chopsticks.'

'I've told you before. He is the Attorney-General and he is in charge of prosecutions. Any member of your family is likely to get into trouble and need his help.'

'What about your family?'

'That is beside the point. I am thinking of you, as always.'

'Roberts won't do anything. He has this ridiculous idea that the Legal Department is honest.'

'It will do no harm to keep in with him. The question is: how shall we make sure that he has a good evening?'

'I could get my cousin to send a couple of girls from the Baretits Bar in Wanchai.'

'But we are asking his wife.'

'Sorry, I forgot that. She might not think that was a good idea. I expect Roberts does what she says, just like you do. What about Mrs Turvey? She never stops talking and we owe her a dinner.'

'Her husband works in the Rating and Valuation Department. We may need him.'

'She will upset Roberts, I expect. Does that matter?'

'Well, can you think of anyone else?'

'There's Mrs Krantz. But she slapped his face in the Hong Kong Club last week.'

'Really? I didn't hear about that. What had he done?'

'Nothing. She thought he'd interfered with her daughter. It was a mistake. I mean somebody had, but not him. It was a man called Robinson.'

'Perhaps we should not ask Mrs Krantz.'

'She shouted "filthy beast", "lecher" and "paedophile" at him when she hit him. So even if I've got the words wrong it would be better to have Mrs Turvey.'

We had not been seated for long before Mrs Turvey spoke.

'Are you a member of the Executive Council?' she demanded.

'What if I am?' I knew already what was likely to come; not that an evasive answer would obstruct her.

'You are? Then you were one of them. You put up the ferry fares.'

'Yes, but –'

'It's a disgrace. How can the poor people manage another ten cents?'

'I don't know, Mrs Turvey.'

'There you are. You just put up the fares without thinking.'

'We only put the ten cents on the first class. The fare for the other class was not affected.'

'It's a matter of principle, isn't it?'

'Well, I'm not so sure.'

'Not sure! How long have you been in Hong Kong?'

'Only about ten years.'

'Then you have no excuse for refusing to do anything. And what about the wages I have to pay my cook?'

It was rather like being a doctor. If you are, a man will sidle up to you on social occasions and ask you to have a look at the lump on his ankle. If you are unwise enough to do so, he will demand an instant opinion as to whether or not it is cancerous. If you refuse to do so, you are considered incompetent.

So I was becoming accustomed to being attacked for any unpopular decision of the Executive Council, of which I was a member, and of the Director of Public Prosecutions, who came under me in theory, though in practice he did not refer anything difficult to me, as he did not trust my judgment.

'What about the wages?' I asked.

'You've just specified a minimum. It's a disgrace.'

'I'm sorry if you have to pay more,' I replied.

'I don't. My cook gets a lot more than the minimum. It's the principle. You should not interfere with a free market.'

'I'm sure you're right,' I agreed.

'You are supposed to be in charge of prosecutions, aren't you?' I nodded cautiously. 'You're not doing much of a job,' she went on. 'I've been burgled twice.'

'Actually, I don't investigate. That's for the police. Why not have a go at the Deputy Commissioner?' I had no compunction about diverting her to him. He was more skilful than me at listening with a wealth of sympathy and understanding, and doing nothing.

Two of the ingredients which are widely used in Chinese cooking caused me discomfort. I therefore tried to avoid both garlic and monosodium glutamate. Garlic was used in many dishes. I ate these with pleasure if I did not know that garlic was present. If I could smell it, I did not eat it, as it would make me feel sick. Monosodium glutamate was used to make meat, and sometimes vegetables, more tender. It did not affect the taste, so that I took it without knowing. It produced an unpleasant headache, which remained with me for several hours. I was not able to persuade my colleagues that my hangover was due to food. I acquired an unjustified reputation for taking too much brandy at Chinese dinners, in spite of the fact that I had not drunk spirits since 1946.

I was not unacquainted with garlic before I came to Hong Kong. It is widely used in Spanish cookery. For this reason, I did not find it hard to resist the few Spanish women who appeared to have an interest in me. On warm, tropical nights, a thick wave of garlic would escape from their unshaven armpits, which might otherwise have fuelled my somewhat abnormal tastes.

In Hong Kong, garlic assumed some importance when I met Jean, an American woman of great charm. She was visiting Hong Kong to shout at the manufacturer of clothing for her firm in California. As usual he had not adhered to her specification. As he explained to her, with a cheerful smile, she could not expect anything else for such a low price.

Jean had married twice, each time to a man with the same surname. I thought this showed an undesirable degree of uncertainty. She told me that this proved that she was not superstitious.

I took Jean to a Chinese dinner at which she ate her way with enthusiasm through every course. I avoided taking any dish in which I could detect garlic. At the end of the meal, I thanked the host, who protested that it had been such a third rate affair. We had an argument about how poor the dinner was.

I took Jean back to her hotel. Perhaps, I thought to myself, this was the moment. Jean had drunk generously. With luck, she would not know what she was doing. She was staying at the Mandarin, a hotel of such high standards that the front desk refused to send strumpets to your room, so that you were obliged to rely on room service instead. I offered to show her to her room. She did not object when I entered the lift with her. The attendant gave me an unjustified leer as the doors closed behind me.

'Twenty-second floor,' she muttered. 'This belt is killing me. I shall be glad to get into something more comfortable.'

I could only think of one thing more comfortable. She pouted her lips in what I imagined to be a gesture of encouragement. I moved towards her in the lift, convinced by now that I had become irresistible. As I did so, she sighed deeply and a cloud of lukewarm garlic filled the lift.

'Yuk,' I shouted in dismay. 'You've been eating garlic.'

'I know,' she agreed. 'It makes me sexy.'

'Perhaps you also feel ill?' I asked, looking for a way of retreat. 'Shall I get the doctor? I always do when I've eaten garlic myself.'

The lift stopped at her floor. She preceded me. I followed with my handkerchief to my nose. This was not the right moment for tact. If I displayed too much of it, I should find myself in her room, as I had hoped to be a few minutes before.

'Someone', she explained after trying vainly to insert her key into the wrong door, 'has moved the lock while I have been out.'

I took her key and opened the door of her room.

'Are you coming in?' she said. 'Did you fall over or something? I see you've got a nasty nose bleed.'

'My driver will be waiting downstairs. Thank you for a splendid evening. I really enjoyed meeting you.' I bolted for the lift. The attendant was clearly impressed, as I left, that I had taken such a short time. I have not seen Jean since then.

Something similar happened after I had taken monosodium glutamate. I had been asked to take a partner to a Chinese dinner. I had taken Grace, a woman of charm. By the end of dinner, my headache had begun. We left together in my car, in which I had brought her.

'Would you like to come up to my place for a drink?' Grace asked.

'I don't think I'd better, Grace. I am starting to get a headache.'

'We are not an old married couple,' said Grace rather sharply. 'You've been trying to get into my flat for weeks. Now that I ask you in, you produce a transparent excuse. Or are you gay?'

'No, no,' I replied. 'It's just that I have this dreadful headache. I can see two of you. Which is the real Grace?'

'Whichever it is, this will be the last time you are invited to my flat.'

Grace slammed the door as I left. The pain in my head was excruciating. Six months later, she married George Wagley. I had not seen her again. It is no consolation to me that she has three children and is very content.

Chinese cuisine is catholic. Anything which moves, or has moved, or grows, may form part of it. If there is resistance to it, for emotional reasons, or because it tastes awful, it is explained to the guest that it is good for his health.

This was the justification for serving snake soup, in which pieces of the reptile floated. It tasted just like chicken and was agreeable so long as you did not know what it was. If you did, you began to imagine that the snake had come to life in your stomach.

'Are you enjoying your soup?' my hostess asked.

'Rather,' I replied, raising a spoonful to my mouth. I had been pretending.

'It is expensive,' she added. I knew that chicken soup was not.

'You mean it is not chicken?'

'Certainly not. I would not insult my guests by giving them chicken. It is snake.'

I put my spoon down.

'Snake is very good for you. It stops you getting colds, rheumatism, tuberculosis and piles. Have some.'

'I don't really have any of them.'

'I know what you need,' she added. 'The snake soup will make you strong.'

'I am strong,' I replied. 'I can even lift my wife's suitcases.'

'I mean potent,' she whispered. 'If you take plenty of snake soup, you will be able to satisfy any woman, even your concubines.'

The only time I enjoyed drinking snake soup was when I found myself next to a European woman who had not had it before.

'Is it true', she asked me, 'that we are having snake soup later?' I looked at the menu and nodded.

'Isn't that a disgrace! Poor thing.'

'The snake was probably a cobra. Anyway, you've just had shark's fin soup. The sea must be full of finless sharks, swimming at half speed.'

'Killing any animal for food is dreadful,' she answered. Her mouth was full of beef as she spoke.

'Are you a vegetarian?' I asked.

'That is different. I was brought up to eat lamb and chicken and so on. It's my parents' fault, not mine. But they did not eat snake.'

'It's very good for you,' I explained. 'It cures all sorts of things. Like piles,' I added helpfully.

'I do not have piles.' She sounded quite indignant.

'It's also said to be very good for male potency.'

'My God,' she muttered.

'Is your husband here? He won't be able to contain himself after a couple of bowls of snake soup.'

'Rupert,' she shouted to her husband across the table. 'You must not eat the snake soup. It will be far too rich for you. It'll upset your stomach.'

I noticed that Rupert, who was sitting near his hostess, emptied his bowl of soup as she watched him, explaining to him the many benefits which would follow. As he left, an hour later, I saw his arm go around his wife's waist and a thin line of saliva coming from his mouth.

One of the advantages of a Chinese dinner is that it is friendly. It is difficult to remain aloof, even if your wife is sitting next to you, if others at the table are shouting cheerfully at you, your bowl and glass are constantly filled without you asking for it, the cloth, once white and untarnished, is covered with spilt food and one of the other guests is making an even worse mess than you with his chopsticks.

One of the difficulties of a European dinner is that, when you have fed your guests, they settle down again and refuse to leave until they have been plied with more liquor. One hostess, in despair, left the room and reappeared half an hour later in her nightdress. This did not work either.

There is, however, no doubt when a Chinese dinner is finished and the guests are expected to leave. Tea is served to the diners, fruit is brought to the table, and a bowl of flowers is placed on the table, on the revolving platform in the centre of it. The flowers are the signal to leave. There is then a rush for the door, the host being left to wrangle over the bill with the restaurant, which has charged him for various things he has not ordered.

Chapter 6

The geomancer

The Chief Secretary lived in an elegant house on the Peak. This was called Victoria House, because it was built on a site formerly occupied by the Victoria Memorial Hospital for Women. The latter, the result of subscription by members of the public, who appear to have considered that sick women should be carefully segregated from men, was finished early in the century. After a short life, and no doubt a happy one, in spite of the name 'Memorial' in its title, the hospital closed before the Pacific War when the more modern Queen Mary Hospital, which restricted itself to segregation in its title, was opened instead.

After the war, one of the committees, which any Government establishes if it wishes to do something but hopes to cloak its action in respectability, recommended that houses should be built for the Chief Secretary and the Chief Justice.

The latter's house, which was designed by an architect in private practice, was unattractive, inadequate and inconvenient. Everyone except lawyers, whose taste in such matters was thought to be

Victoria House

unreliable, thought that the house was suitable for the holder of an office which carried considerable prestige but was not thought to be of much importance in the business community.

The residence of the Chief Secretary was designed by an architect employed by the Public Works Department, since it was considered unwise to entrust such an important project to anyone who was not a government employee.

I have referred to the Chief Secretary, although he was known as the Colonial Secretary before 1976. In a burst of modernity, which I later regretted, I presided, with firmness and skill, since the result was of little importance, over a series of meetings of increasing bitterness. At the end of them, there was no agreement. In spite of this, I took the wise decision to change the name, thus, as I said at the time, removing from us all the shackles of colonialism. Nobody bothered to alter the laws which referred to the former title. At least the initials remained the same.

The house for the Chief Secretary was well designed, finely built and impressive, with a good garden and a splendid view of the harbour. The architect was subjected to constant interference by the wife of the Governor. An American by birth, she believed that an impressive house should look as much as possible like the Spanish style residence in which she had been brought up.

Due to her influence, since she believed that the C.S. should be properly housed, the architect found himself left with an area on the upper floor which had not been in his original designs. He described it to anyone who enquired as a storeroom, which appeared to silence criticism. Nobody seemed to realize that it was a mistake, leaving an area virtually unusable. In spite of this, the house remained warm and handsome, surviving well the alteration to which it was subjected in the 1980s to make it more suitable for large scale entertaining.

After a few years, during which it was inhabited by couples who indulged in no more than the usual marital warfare, the house fell on harder times. It was occupied for some years by a C.S. who was a bachelor and preferred the lads.

He was succeeded by a man who was married but preferred other people's wives to his own, simultaneously if temporarily. The wife remained unsuspecting until a close friend informed her of the husband's adventures because she thought that the wife ought to know. How the knowledge would be to the wife's advantage was not stated. The wife, having considered the matter at length, tackled the husband in the middle of a supper party which he was giving for senior government officers. He replied, in rough but definite terms, that it was none of her business. Although it was, as could be expected, intended to be a dull evening, it is debatable whether she should have attempted to enliven it by emptying a tureen of spaghetti, which was happily lukewarm, over her husband's head and leaving.

The next C.S., who had a pleasant wife, worried greatly about doing the right thing, a fault which he should have eradicated during his many years in the service. After his wife had found him in the study early in the morning with his head in his hands, muttering about the difficulty of deciding which side of the bed to sleep on, she persuaded him to retire early. He did not stay long enough in the house to enjoy it.

After him, the next C.S. was unmarried and apparently neuter. It was a great surprise when he became married soon after he had left. He was followed by a C.S. who was married to a wife who, except for a short period in Hong Kong, preferred to live in England. When I entered the house, in 1973, I had recently been divorced.

About two years later, I found myself, after one of the unexciting dinners which I felt obliged to give to justify my generous entertainment allowance, sitting next to the wife of a clever, if mildly eccentric, Executive Councillor named T. S. Lo. I believe that her first name was Tierney, though I was never sure of how to spell it.

We were sitting on one of the handsome but uncomfortable sofas which was stationed in the drawing room, beset by the kind of uneasy silence which arises when nobody can think of anything to say. We had already discussed the weather. I saw Tierney's face break into a smile.

'I suppose', she said 'that you have had a fung shui man to look over this house?'

'Good heavens, no,' I replied. 'He might want me to do something.' I had heard of the importance given by many Chinese to the fung shui expert, or geomancer. It was common for an office or a house to be rearranged to accord with his findings. I did not think that the PWD would react well if I informed it that I wanted to convert my study into a bathroom, because I had been advised to do so by a geomancer.

'Do you realize', she went on, 'that there have not been a couple living here for about ten years? And just look at you! Why have you not married again?'

'I've only just been divorced for a couple of years,' I protested. 'Besides, nobody will have me.' This objection, in which I did not believe, seemed to work well.

'Nonsense. That is only an excuse. The real reason is because the fung shui at Victoria House is bad. Why, the last C.S. is living happily in England with his wife and the one before that has married since he left the house. You see, that proves it!' she added with that lack of logic to which there is no rational reply.

'Naturally, I have thought of getting an expert to come,' I replied, making it up as I spoke, as I had been doing with mixed success for years, 'but I decided against it because I am told that it is very expensive.'

'That is not so,' Tierney replied with enthusiasm. 'It will cost you nothing. The fung shui man owes me something. I bring him a lot of business. I will get him along next week.' I could not think of any objection at the time, though a number occurred to me after she had left.

The following week, she brought to the house a charming old gentleman who was wearing a dark grey cheongsam. In his hands he carried a round wooden object which looked like a compass. As he carried the instrument round the house, the needle in it pointed to one of the Chinese characters round the side.

Tierney introduced him as 'Mr Lam' in the loud voice which Cantonese use when talking to one another. He spoke no English himself but smiled benevolently at me.

'Please tell him, Tierney, that I am glad that he has found time to visit the house and much honoured that he has done so.'

'I already have', said Tierney, 'on the way here. But I'll do it again.' Mr Lam inclined his head in a regal manner, when this was translated to him.

'I will take him round the house and garden,' Tierney went on. 'I have told him about your problems.'

'Which ones?' I asked. I had had a lot of trouble that day with the Governor. He had refused to follow my advice on three occasions. The fact that it was not very good advice made no difference.

'Your domestic problems.'

'I have a selection of them, you know. Some of them won't really be improved by a geomancer.'

'I have explained that it is not your fault that nobody loves you and that you are really a most likeable man.'

'I've tried that, Tierney, and it doesn't work at all.'

'Mr Lam knows', she continued, ignoring me, 'that this house is bad for women. He will tell you what to do if you want to put matters right.'

Mr Lam nodded his head at me and made for the staircase, holding his compass and talking to Tierney. As he went, he peered at his instrument and clucked dismally.

I let them go upstairs on their own and concentrated on the heap of annual reports on individuals which lay on the floor. The rule was that, if you intended to say something critical, the subject of it must be told. This was supposed to give him an opportunity to correct his error. What it usually did was to convert a pleasant colleague into an enemy. The only way to avoid this was not to be critical, which is no doubt why such reports were carefully neutral, even when directed at someone who ought not to be where he was.

I have on one occasion been spoken to about my own annual report. The Attorney-General, in Africa, asked me into his office.

'This is very embarrassing, Denys,' he said, after making sure that all the doors to his office were shut.

'I beg your pardon, Basil?' He was talking in a whisper, which I found difficult to follow.

'I have to ask you about Mrs Arthur. Have you finished your affair with her?'

'But –,' I began.

'I'm not just prying,' Basil went on hastily. 'It's these annual reports. I thought I ought to mention it, if it's affecting your work at all.'

'Is it, Basil?'

'Of course not, my dear fellow.'

'If it will console you, Basil, I have no idea who Mrs Arthur is.' Zomba was well known for unsubstantiated rumour, but I had not heard of her before.

'She is the wife of that chap who runs the Central Stores,' he explained. 'I'm afraid that she doesn't speak very well. She has a strong South African accent.' He wrinkled his nose in distaste. He came from Trinidad and spoke faultless English himself.

'I can assure you', I said, 'that I have never met Mrs Arthur. And if I had, I certainly wouldn't have had an affair with her.'

'Oh, excellent,' he replied. 'I knew I could rely on you. I need say nothing about it in your annual report. And the next time anyone repeats the rumour to me, I will be able to say that I asked you about it and you denied all knowledge of it?'

I nodded. It was just as well that he had got the wrong name. If he had questioned me about Mrs Crain, it would have been more difficult. At that time, extra-marital conduct was not fashionable. Only later did it become a matter of suspicion if you refrained from it.

'I am afraid', Tierney said a few minutes later, as she ushered Mr Lam into the study, 'that the root of the trouble is that the house is the wrong way round.'

'If that's all, it shouldn't be too difficult to rebuild it correctly.'

'There is no need for anything as drastic as that. Mr Lam has some easier solutions for you.'

Mr Lam tapped his compass and spoke in solemn tones. He was used to being taken seriously. This was not surprising in view of the fees he charged. For that amount of money, you would listen carefully.

'The garden is too flat,' he began. I did not tell him that I had just removed the last of the lumps in the lawn, so that a mower could operate more effectively. 'You must put rocks there. I will tell you where.'

'Have I got to put them there anyhow, or only if I want to try out my climbing kit?'

'Anyhow,' Tierney replied, 'the rocks won't been enough, either. Mr Lam has some other things which you must do, to ward off the evil spirits.' 'I haven't seen any.'

'That does not mean they are not here. You are probably insensitive. Mr Lam is worried about the bad influence of the mountain behind the house. He thinks the spirits get into the house through your bathroom.'

'What do they do then?'

'Women, who are much more acute than men, begin to feel uneasy. That is why they want to leave the house.'

'Perhaps I could just block up a window in the bathroom?' Mr Lam thought that would not work, as the devils would come through the glass.

'In your bedroom,' Tierney continued, 'you have a large mirror on your dressing table. You can see your own reflection from the bed. Mr Lam does not like that. He says that any woman who sees her image there is sure to leave at once.'

'If not before,' I suggested and was ignored.

'So you must move your dressing table, or cover up its mirror. You should read a love poem which he has composed.'

'If it's in Cantonese, it won't be much help.'

'Mr Lam knows that you can only manage English. So he has had a translation made.'

'That is a relief. Can I use it on anyone?'

'Certainly. You need not have the girl present. Place a photo of your beloved on the table, making sure that the table does not reflect your own face. You repeat the poem to the picture on three successive nights. The next time she sees you after this, she will fall deeply in love with you.'

She passed me the translation, which seemed rather extravagant for my taste, though as I was to repeat it to a photo this did not matter.

Oh beloved, oh beloved, oh, oh, oh,
How I miss you, how I miss you, oh, oh, oh,
Make my nights and make my days,
Hours of happy passion,
Do not let me live alone,
Come and share my humble home,
Oh beloved, oh beloved, oh, oh, oh,
How I miss you, how I miss you, oh, oh, oh.

'It's pretty raunchy stuff, Tierney. But as the girl is not here, that won't matter. I rather like the chorus. Is there any music?'

'You can sing it to 'Swanee', if you must,' she replied sharply. 'Just let us know if you would like Mr Lam to come again. If you do what he says, we shan't have to.'

I did not ask Mr Lam to revisit the house. I was uneasy about my failure to follow his advice and make the structural alterations which he had recommended.

I did, however, make full use of his poem, which I placed on a table in the study beside a series of photos of different women, one of whom, I discovered later, had been dead for some years. On each occasion, I confidently expected the woman concerned to hurl herself into my arms, when next we met, making the sort of moaning noises which I had heard on confiscated tapes smuggled in from Denmark and seized by the police. The girl in one of the photos screamed 'Stop looking at me like that' and insisted on going home early by herself from a dance to which I had taken her. Another called me a dirty old man and said that she would never trust me again.

The head houseboy, Ah Lo, entered the study one evening. I had decided to try the poem once more. I was reciting it to a photo of a rather unattractive girl who ought to have been delighted by my attentions. I was beginning to lose confidence in Mr Lam's poem.

'Master all right?' he asked, which was his usual enquiry when he thought I was behaving oddly. He must have heard me talking loudly to myself, as there was nobody else in the room. I had just declaimed 'Oh beloved, oh beloved, oh, oh, oh' in what I thought was a very persuasive manner, when he came in.

'Certainly,' I replied haughtily. 'I was just trying out a speech.'

'Master make a good speech,' he agreed. 'But the words are no good,' he added, pointing to the love poem which I was trying unsuccessfully to conceal with my elbow.

'Why do you say that?' I asked.

'Fung shui man gave me no lai see when he came.' Ah Lo shook his head. 'That is bad.'

'Why is it bad not to give you a tip?'

'If many things have to be changed, I will have to do it. If he gave me a big tip, I would see that you followed what he said.'

'So what do you suggest?' I was prepared to listen to other advice after several clear rejections and no successes.

'I will take the poem,' he said. 'Perhaps I can make it work properly.'

'You'd better take the photos, just in case.'

Ah Lo left the room with several photographs and the love poem. I did not think he would get any better results than me. The following week, he returned the poem to me.

'No good,' he said. 'I tried it on several pictures. The ones you gave me and some others I found in your drawer.'

I did not complain about the drawer. I kept locking it because it had personal papers like my will, which I changed every few months when I had a row with some member of my family. As Ah Lo had a duplicate key, the drawer was insecure. I continued to lock it because the principle of privacy was at stake.

'How do you know the poem will not work?' I asked him.

'I know it in here.' He tapped his head.

About a week afterwards, I went to the retirement party of a divorced woman of fifty-five who was about to leave for England. I had taken her out once, about three years before. She had thrown up into a pot of flowers and I had not asked her again. On this occasion, she hinted that she would not be averse if I made a proposal of marriage. I left hurriedly, as I could not think of a convincing reason for refusing, as merely not wanting to propose would have been insufficient. When I arrived home, I glanced at the photos which Ah Lo had found in my drawer. Among them was one of the woman who had asked me to propose to her.

Chapter 7
Dinner at home

During a quarter of a century, I must have attended about a thousand dinners.

When I was a child, I used to amuse myself, though not my parents, by working out how many garbage bags a month might be filled by my food, how many lorries would be necessary if I went on eating for fifty years, and the number of Carter Paterson vans which would be needed if the latter collected rubbish instead of moving furniture.

I realized that it did not matter what food was provided. One of the female guests would remember having been served by me with something similar many years before. Some of the guests were in the middle of a diet, which forbade them to eat anything except food which they were not offered. I noticed that none of the diets seemed to be free of alcohol.

It was important, I was told when I first arrived, not to ask to the same dinner those who no longer spoke to one another, because of a disagreement between them, or some real or imagined slight which had taken place years before.

I had heard from the A.G.'s secretary, who was an endless source of inaccurate gossip, that it was fatal to ask the Director of Water and Supplies and the Postmaster-General on the same occasion, apparently because the P.M.G. had made advances to the wife of the D.W.S., who rejected them indignantly, because she was carrying on a raging affair with a police officer at the time.

As it was too late to alter the guest list, I apologized to Smithers, the D.W.S., for asking him to the same dinner with the P.M.G. and his wife.

'No need to apologize,' he said. 'They are dull as anything but they mean well. Mrs P.M.G. is rather better value than he is, mind you. I rather like the look of her.'

'I suppose that is one way to get your own back, Smithers.'

'Why should I want to do that?'

'Well, I mean, I know it's all a long time ago, but don't you?'

'The post office has lost several of my letters,' Smithers agreed, though this was not an answer to my comment. 'I'm quite relaxed about it, though my wife wasn't very pleased because one of the letters which went adrift contained some dress patterns which she wanted for her daughter, who was pregnant.'

'I was told that you do not speak to the P.M.G. or Mrs P.M.G. because you had a row with him some years ago.'

'Can't say I remember it. Do you happen to know what it was about?'

'Not really.' I did not think I should mention what I had been told. 'Perhaps he was given precedence over you at an official function?'

'Ah, that would be serious,' Smithers conceded. 'But I don't recall it. Not that I mind about these things myself, but my wife is very sensitive about them.'

My secretary told me, not long afterwards, that it was the P.M.G.'s predecessor who had made advances to Mrs Smithers. However, she said, Smithers and the P.M.G. were extremely hostile to one another because the P.M.G. had been given undue precedence at a dinner given by the Urban Council three years earlier.

After this, I ignored my secretary and, in spite of her warnings, insisted on asking together couples who had been enemies for years. The fact that they did not talk to one another at dinner, except for an occasional acid exchange, did not seem to be noticed.

'It is about time you had another dinner,' my secretary would say. 'There are a lot of people you ought to ask to Victoria House.'

'Have I got to?'

'Yes,' she replied firmly. 'What about next week? You are not going out on Thursday or Friday.'

'If I asked them for Friday, some of them wouldn't be able to come. A lot of people go out on Fridays.'

'That would leave you with an unbalanced group, Mr Roberts.'

'Who cares about balance? I thought I was asking people I ought to ask. They're not supposed to enjoy themselves as well.'

The secretary ignored me, as she always did when I said something with which she disagreed. She could insist later that she had not heard what I said.

'So you agree, we'd better make it Thursday.'

'Oh, all right. I suppose you have got a guest list already?'

'It's only to save you trouble. You choose the guests.' This was not true, but I let it go. 'You really must have the Steins.'

'Oh, no,' I protested. 'He's a computer engineer. If he talks about his work and he doesn't talk about anything else, I shan't understand a word of what he is saying.'

'She's lively and talks about hairdressing.'

'Another of the subjects in which I am an expert, you mean?'

'They had you to dinner last year.'

'Why did I go? You must have made me.'

'You insisted on going, because you thought Miss Stable had been invited.' It was obvious that the secretary did not approve of Miss Stable.

'Nobody told me she had not been able to go. So I wasted an evening.'

'I will ask the Steins, as you insist. What about the Deputy Accountant-General, Scarman, and Kwan, the Assistant Secretary for Chinese Affairs?'

'Are you selecting guests by the length of their titles, or can I have someone I know?'

'There is Mr Justice Moult.'

'Not Moult. Surely I've fed him before?'

'Yes. But you failed to turn up for one of his dinners last year. He thinks you did it on purpose.'

'It was my sub-conscious. Because I didn't really want to go, I wiped it from my mind.'

'You can't expect him to know you have psychological problems. If you ask him to dinner, he may forgive you. Even if his wife won't,' she added unnecessarily. 'I expect the poor woman was preparing that meal for months.'

'All right, ask the Moults. What about an odd woman, to make up the numbers?'

'What about Priscilla Lyttleton?'

'I didn't mean that odd,' I protested. 'Besides, I asked her last month, surely?'

'You did. And she is a trained nurse, in case any of the other guests needs one.'

'If anyone is sick, they shouldn't be on my list. Everywhere I go, the unfortunate Priscilla is asked as my partner. She is a dear girl, but she is over fifty, she looks like a horse which is about to refuse to jump, and she drinks like a fish.'

'I will put her down then, as you like her so much.'

'She will get the wrong idea. She will think I am after her.'

'It's your own fault,' she continued. 'You were awarded a golden apple by that magazine as one of the three most eligible bachelors of the year.'

'Have you met the others? George Smith runs a hair salon and has a steady boyfriend. Waldo Gibson has not been sober since 1970.

He makes a living by riding a bicycle across a canvas and calling it painting. He has had four wives and is a sexual deviant.'

'No wonder you were included in the list, Mr Roberts. That gives you ten, including Priscilla. You ought to have two Chinese couples.'

'That will make fourteen. I haven't got room for that number.'

'They will have to sit close together. That makes them more friendly.'

'It's a bit more difficult to be remote, if you can't eat till your neighbour releases your elbow,' I agreed.

'I think you should have P. L. Shum from the Legislative Council and C. Y. Poon, the businessman.'

'P. L. Shum never says anything.'

'Isn't that why he was put on Leg. Co.?'

'Even if it were, that is no reason for me asking him to dinner. I don't know C. Y. Poon at all.'

'He is one of our many millionaires, the Secretary for Chinese Affairs told me when I asked him for a list of guests.'

'What did he make his money out of?'

'Night soil.'

'Out of what?'

'I think you heard me the first time. He collects it in buckets and sells it to China.'

'Will he wash before he comes?'

'He does not collect it himself. He would not be a millionaire if he did. That's economics,' she added.

'I get all my vegetables from China.'

'It does not matter what they are grown in, my doctor tells me. Your reaction is wholly emotional. That makes fourteen. I will ask them for eight o'clock next Thursday, black tie.'

'Do we have to wear a black tie?'

'Certainly. The Governor can get away with a lounge suit, because he can pretend that he has guests from London who have not brought a dinner jacket with them. You can't. What is more, if you don't dress up the guests will think it's a second class dinner. I have spoken to your cook about the food.'

'Soup, fish, meat and pudding,' I interrupted, as I thought it was time I contributed something.

'I'm sure he will be able to manage that,' she assured me.

'It'll all be overdone. He hasn't been the same since I found him chasing the houseboy with a kitchen knife and promising to cut off his member if he came into the kitchen again.'

'I expect he was drunk.'

'Probably. Cooks do their best work when they are. Since then I've had quite a job persuading the staff to go into the kitchen to fetch anything.'

'People do not go to your house to get a good meal, Mr Roberts. There are excellent restaurants for that. They go in order to be able to say they have been.'

On a small table, which stood in the hall of Victoria House on evenings when I entertained, was a plan of the dining table, showing where each guest was supposed to sit. The plan was carefully prepared in accordance with the precedence list. So long as you did not appear on this list at all, it did not matter where you sat, so that there was a reasonable chance that you would find yourself next to someone who was unknown to you and might be interesting.

As soon as your name appeared on the precedence list, it was another matter. It then became of more importance to be put in the correct place rather than next to someone who might be rewarding. For four years, as Solicitor-General, I was placed between Mrs Fire Services and Mrs Government Printer, both admirable matrons with whom I exhausted all possible avenues of conversation before long. It was probably during this period that I acquired a reputation for silence, which I eventually dispelled by talking too much.

At five to eight, I was trying to don a pair of evening trousers and tie a black tie simultaneously. This did not work well, as I kept having to start the tie again whenever I retrieved the trousers from the floor.

I knew that there were already some cars parked in the drive without lights, which contained guests. The Chinese, in particular, regarded an invitation for eight for eight thirty as meaning that they should attend at eight. Some of the others, especially the Europeans, regarded eight thirty as the time by which they should be there, unless they wanted to drink at the host's expense, in which event they arrived earlier.

I came into the drawing room at two minutes past eight to find that half of the guests had already arrived and been provided with drinks by Ah Lo. I made an excuse about being obliged to take a last minute phone call. Nobody believed this. I'm sure that nobody minded or had even noticed my absence.

Six of the guests were chatting to one another happily in Cantonese. Moult J. and his wife were not talking, save that he implored her, for once, to try to remain sober.

I discovered later that the Cantonese guests were commenting unfavourably on the furnishings, which they thought were anaemic and typical of a bachelor. No doubt they were correct, but the furnishings were years old and had been selected by the last wife to live in the house for a long time.

I left the six to criticize the décor and concentrated on the Moults. Fortunately, it was only necessary to ask him if he had heard any interesting cases lately. He would thereupon deliver a long narrative, which showed him to be a wise and good humoured man, which was more than you could say about some of his colleagues. He interrupted himself twice, to hiss at Mrs Moult that she had had enough to drink, apparently without success.

At twenty past, the Steins, the Deputy Accountant-General, Scarman, and Priscilla arrived, all with even less convincing excuses for being late than I had offered myself on previous occasions.

Stein had made a fortune out of computers, which at that time were relatively new. I welcomed him, asked him the difference between hard and soft discs and left him to explain this to Hanson, a quiet man with thick glasses and dewdrop trouble. I do not recall his wife. Priscilla bounded in like a stag and planted a kiss on my cheek before I could stop her.

I had asked Ah Lo to call us to dinner, assuming that it was more or less ready, at eight thirty, whether or not all the guests had arrived. This would save the cook from having to warm the food up again. It was not all that appetizing when it was fresh. This also shortened the time during which I had to make conversation with the guests, who seemed to think it was polite to let me speak.

The latecomers had not finished their first drinks when the dinner gong was sounded by the steward. He did this with some circumspection, as the string on which it hung had broken a few weeks before, when the gong had rolled into the garden and disturbed a young couple, who were courting before dinner and had been asked by mistake.

The steward stood in the doorway with the dinner plan in his hand, in case anyone had forgotten where to sit, which they usually had. There was also some confusion, when the guests sat, because some of them seemed to be unable to distinguish between left and right. Although each place bore a name card, not everyone had remembered their glasses, and some very short-sighted women preferred to grope about in the mist rather than don them.

I sat at the end of the table. On my right was Mrs Shum. On my left was Mrs Moult. I was at the end because, in theory, I was able to see all the guests better than if I had been half way down one side. What difference that made, I am not sure.

Mrs Shum, as I soon discovered, did not speak English. I did not speak Cantonese. I smiled at her a couple of times and received a nervous giggle in reply. I confined myself to matters which could be conducted by signs, like passing the salt, complimenting her on her dress and pointing at the other guests in a disparaging way.

It became obvious, during dinner, from the way in which she glared at Mrs Shum across the table, that Mrs Poon was not pleased to find herself half way down the table, while Mrs Shum was at the top. Mrs Poon was wearing so many diamonds that I wondered if she could stand without help.

I was later told that Poon had inherited wealth and had increased it. He regarded Shum and Kwan as persons of no importance since neither were rich. In addition, the Poons came from Shanghai and the others were Cantonese, whom those from the north of China regarded as uncultured country people, even if superior to most Europeans.

Mrs Moult, on my left, could at least have balanced the monolingual Mrs Shum. A thin lady, with thick spectacles and a face which reminded me of a mouse, she said very little either, though she seemed to have no difficulty in making the steward understand that her glass was empty, as it seemed to be for most of the time.

I asked her about her children. This was not a happy question, as she had no children and insisted on making it clear to me that Moult J. had not been understanding when he was told she was barren. I enquired about her amah, to be informed that she had to do everything herself, because Moult was too mean to pay for one. When I mentioned her next holiday, she replied that she knew nothing about that as Moult only seemed interested in putting her into some health place where she could dry out.

After a while, I tried to talk across them, to Mr Kwan, seated next to Mrs Shum, and Mr Scarman, beyond Mrs Moult. Mr Kwan was a happy man, who laughed at everything, whether or not it contained a joke, as he thought that this was what senior British bureaucrats liked best. Mrs Stein, who was sitting on Kwan's right, assumed that he was laughing at her and glared at him throughout dinner, by the end of which he was no longer laughing.

Scarman had been the target of bad jokes about his name for many years and was known to his subordinates (and to most others as well) as 'Scarface'. The deep pockmarks left in his cheeks by adolescent acne had made his sensitive to this. Mrs Moult had not spoken to him during dinner, except to ask him if she could have his sherry. He was delighted to talk to me about anything. I knew that he was an unusual man for an accountant and something of an expert on fishing, book binding and modern art. I knew nothing about any of them and agreed with whatever he said. The next day he told others what a lot I seemed to know abut these subjects. We talked across the front of Mrs Moult, who contemplated her empty glass sadly and did not intervene.

At the far end of the table Priscilla, the surrogate hostess for the evening, was half listening with a frozen expression as Moult J. described, in detail, a case in which he had been involved when he was a magistrate in the Solomon Islands. This involved ritual murder and cannibalism, which Moult was describing in some detail when the meat course arrived. On her other side, Mr Shum was silent and smiling, qualities for which he had been appointed to Leg. Co.

The stewards took a long time to serve dinner, assisted by Mr Kwan, who knocked a tureen of hot carrots to the floor. Kwan giggled loudly in embarrassment and was joined by the steward who had dropped the carrots.

At a quarter to ten, I led the guests to the drawing room. Some of the men seemed reluctant to come. There had been a time, when I first arrived in Hong Kong, when it was customary for the men to remain behind in the dining room and drink port. While they did so, the women guests were taken to one of the bedrooms, where they sat in a row on the bed waiting for the lavatory to flush, so that they could use it themselves. The older system was disrupted when two American women refused to leave the dining room after dinner. As the standard of conversation was much improved by their presence, I tried not to ask female guests to leave the men alone any more.

In the drawing room, the guests were offered tea, coffee or other drinks. Several of the women insisted on going to the bedroom to repair their make-up and to dissect the dinner, rather than because they needed the lavatory. On their return, they made for their husbands, not because there was much to say to them but because it was close to the time to leave.

I made little effort to cheer them up at this stage. I had decided that the dinner was a disaster. Priscilla's efforts to be jolly confirmed this foreboding.

After about twenty minutes, much of it spent in silence, Mrs Shum, prompted by her husband, shook my arm like a pump handle, smiled briefly and hurried from the room. The other guests followed soon. Moult J. was muttering at his wife for letting him down again.

'A fine evening you gave me,' I complained to my secretary next day.

'I'm glad it was a success. I thought it was a good mixture.'

'If you mean that there was a good balance between those who kept silent and those who did not like some of the other guests, I suppose you're right.'

'I've had three calls so far this morning, from people who say how much they enjoyed your dinner.'

'They'd say that anyway.'

'Maybe. But in a couple of months they will believe it.'

Chapter 8
The charity ball

During my last few years in Hong Kong, in spite of the fact that, as a civil servant, my salary was published so that everyone knew that, by local standards, I was relatively poor, I was asked to about twenty balls a year. Some of them were tribal, though the majority were charitable.

The English held their dance on St George's Day. The main course was roast beef, and the chef was paraded and made to drink ale. The President of the Society was expected to make a humorous speech about St George. This was not difficult as nobody knew much about him except that he spent most of his time in full armour, chasing dragons who muttered 'Tinned food again' whenever he appeared.

Those present were expected to dance something called the 'Sir Roger de Coverley'. In spite of its French name, this was supposed to be an ancient English dance, slow and decorous. Practice evenings were held for those who did not know the dance, or 'measure' as the

St George's Ball

committee members insisted on calling it. As these evenings were not well attended, the number of those who knew what they were doing was far smaller than the number of those who did not.

The English balls were well attended, admirably conducted and slightly dull. Nobody had to apologize to the owners of the ballroom next day. This was not the case with some of the others.

The Welsh, on St David's Day, talked volubly to one another in Welsh and lapsed into heavily accented English for the sake of those unfortunate enough not to understand them. The ballroom was prowled by girls dressed in mediaeval Welsh clothes, wearing black top hats.

A volunteer, and some people will do anything for acclaim, was made to eat a raw leek, a vegetable whose good properties are not obvious even when it is cooked. The soup was a form of broth, made from your neighbour's dead sheep if available, and the main course was lamb chops.

There were no Welsh dances, presumably because much of the principality is too uneven for that sort of thing. Instead, a Welsh male voice choir would sing and go on singing. It was difficult to stop them. They were eventually led away, after most of the audience was crying for their lost valleys with the grey slate glistening in the drizzle. The dancers departed and cried themselves to sleep. It had been an enjoyable occasion.

The Scots held their ball on St Andrew's Day. Many of them wore the kilt, from which the moths had been disturbed for the day. Practice sessions were held to instruct the ignorant in the Sword Dance and the Eightsome Reel. I assume that these were well attended, as everyone seemed to know what they were doing. As they leapt in the air, the Scots whooped, establishing their origins beyond doubt. Apart from them, only members of a small number of backward African tribes whoop when they are enjoying themselves.

During the evening, a man with the bagpipes was let loose in the ballroom. His playing of this tuneless instrument, which is very impressive in the open but much less so inside, was invariably greeted with rapture. I always applauded too, as it was something of an achievement to wring any sound from a selection of wooden pipes thrust into a sheep's stomach.

We were expected to eat only food from Scotland. This was fortunate as porridge and oatmeal would not have been suitable for dinner. It was enough to be confronted by cock-a-leekie soup and haggis. The former resembles snake soup in that it is excellent so long as you don't know what it is.

This was not a sober evening, as whisky and some of its derivatives come from Scotland. It was regarded as essential, if you wished to establish your Scots origins, to drink as much of this as was compatible with getting home without help. Happily, the natural disinclination of many Scots to be seen enjoying themselves prevented any display of emotion.

The Irish purported to be celebrating the day on which St Patrick got lost in Ireland, though few of them appeared to know much about him. There was no national dish, though potatoes kept appearing throughout the meal in various disguises, beginning with potato soup. The only Irish drink was whiskey, which was drunk, so those who took it said, for patriotic reasons and not because they liked it.

Although the President of the Irish Society made a speech about St Patrick each year, few listened to him and bursts of laughter punctuated his serious passages. The band played Irish jigs, which were danced by a few zealots, though the number of collisions suggested that not all the jiggers had been to the same classes.

Soon after dinner, the audience began to drift away to Paddy's Bar in which Guinness was available. It is more accurate to say that it had been available, as it ran out each year early on, even after the most ambitious estimates of the likely consumption of it. There was a general atmosphere of good will. Even the atrocities of the English in the seventeenth century were forgotten for a few hours. The Irish were determined that they and their guests should enjoy themselves, even if on the following day it was necessary to return to the hotel and apologize for disrupting the sleep of anyone there who had made the mistake of thinking that the place would be quiet at two in the morning.

A charity ball is a different matter. Unlike the tribal dances, it is held to make as much money as possible for a charity and to add greatly to the prestige of the chairman. This was usually a woman, preferably one with a rich husband who would contribute generously to the funds to ensure that the ball was a success.

It was customary for the Governor and his wife to attend. He seldom enjoyed himself and was happy to leave at eleven, though his wife was sometimes reluctant to do so. The chairwoman, who had sold a lot of tickets because the Governor had promised to attend, was happy to see him go, after she had danced with him, slowly and incompetently. She made no effort to argue with his protestation that he had to make an early start in the morning. His presence was worth a lot of money to the charity, which was why he attended, when he would have preferred to have a quieter evening at home.

The chairwoman usually nominated her friends as members of the ball committee, selecting them for their generosity, rather than for any other qualities. They agreed with whatever she said, as this was the way to ensure that their names, and a flattering photograph, would appear in the ball programme. One woman who argued found that her photo in the brochure had an unpleasant snarl on its face. The chairwoman had engaged a photographer to take her picture when another woman was talking to her husband.

The ball programme was a bulky and finely produced brochure, consisting mainly of advertisements by companies which had paid handsomely for them instead of sending representatives to the ball. The brochure also contained some excellent photographs of the other committee members and a full page studio portrait of the chairwoman. Somewhere in the middle of it lurked the menu. This was often in broken French, to make it look more impressive than it was. The hotel had been told that an inexpensive dinner was required, as the evening was intended to raise money for a desirable charity and not to fill a lot of stomachs.

Before the ball began, there was a period of drinking, included in the price of the ticket. Experienced attenders at charity balls knew that, at best, inexpensive wine would be served at the table, and that the only chance of drinking at another's expense would be permitted during the time before the ball. Consequently, many Europeans were punctual and some were already in poor shape by the time they reached the ballroom, as a significant quantity of drink can be absorbed in forty-five minutes.

Meanwhile, the principal guests, standing in a separate corral like prize bulls, were introduced to members of the committee and to others who had been asked in order to give the top table an appearance of importance.

'That dress looks lovely,' I would say to a Chinese wife who was so loaded with jewellery that she could barely stand. The dress bulged in a number of places.

'It is an old thing I have worn before many times.' We both knew that she meant once. If it was new, she would say that it was a cheap thing which her tailor had made for the evening.

At about eight o'clock, a quarter of an hour after the advertised time for dinner, the hotel dispatched a man with a gong to try to move the guests into the ballroom. He was ignored until his third appearance, at about eight fifteen, when there was a slow and reluctant move towards the ballroom. The principal guests were marshalled into two lines by the secretary of the charity. He did this from a piece of paper on which was a plan which had been altered a number of times, to try to meet the bitter complaints of those who were convinced that they had been put in the wrong place.

'No, no, Mrs Chan,' the secretary explained. 'You are supposed to be on Mr Yong's left.'

'Why so?' she asked.

'Because all the women are on the left hand side.'

'I prefer to go with Mr Chan.'

'He is going in with Mrs Ho.'

'He is my husband. I want to go in with him.'

'You are right behind him. I can't alter the procession at this stage.'

'Why not?'

'Because if I do, there will be a lot of other complaints. So please do as I ask you.'

The secretary, having assembled his flock, moved them to the door and waited for the others to sit. As soon as they had done so, he ushered the official party into the ballroom, while the band, which had not been trained for this, played an unidentifiable fanfare. On one occasion, it played the national anthem by mistake, thus freezing the official party as it was walking down the main aisle.

The theory was that, as the official party processed, the remainder of the guests would stand politely as they passed. In practice this seldom happened as many of the guests were too busy trying to find out where they were supposed to sit.

The official party was expected to divide into two before it reached the long table at which it was to sit. This worked well, so long as everyone remembered which side to go and the name cards were correctly stationed. On one occasion, the second couple went the wrong way. So did every other couple behind them. It took the members of the party some time to seat themselves, as everyone else arrived at the wrong end of the table. The secretary to that charity event resigned.

The ball began with a short speech of welcome by the chairwoman. It had been written for her by the secretary and was intended to remind everyone of why they had come, which a number of the guests had already forgotten.

'I thank you all for coming to make this evening such a success.' She did not look at the three empty tables, which had been paid for by those who had decided not to attend. 'I am especially grateful to our guest of honour and his lady and to the Director of Social Welfare and his lady for their attendance. The proceeds will be used to help our juvenile offenders to live happy lives in our homes. I know that many of you have visited them and been greatly impressed by what you have seen. Some of the inmates will dance for us later. I hope you will bid generously in the auction and will enjoy yourselves. I thank the ball committee for all it has done to help me and wish you a happy evening.'

The chairwoman, who had not allowed herself to be diverted because the microphone did not work properly, sat down with relief. She had not expected people to stay silent throughout her speech. She was not disappointed. I congratulated her on a fine address, full of humour.

'Nobody laughed,' she replied.

'I meant wisdom,' I said hastily.

'I remember now,' she said gloomily. 'I did not thank the hotel. I expect that is why the microphone was not working.'

'Nonsense. They couldn't have known in advance that you were going to leave them out.'

'We shan't be able to come here next year.'

'Does that matter? It won't be your worry.'

'Ah.' She cheered up at once. The idea of one of her friends being in difficulty was consoling.

I looked at the menu, which presaged a dreadful meal.

'The dinner looks excellent in the brochure,' I said. 'Did you try it out yourself? It would perhaps', I added, 'be wiser to spell "poisson" with a double "s" rather than a single one.'

'I had seven lunches here to try out the various meals. I am now very fat.' She pointed in disgust at the large tyre which was pushing out her cheongsam at the waist.

'Don't be silly,' I replied, hoping that the insincere note in my voice would be missed. I need not have worried. She wanted to believe me.

'My husband tells me I am fat.'

'I expect he doesn't like plump girls.'

'That is the trouble. He likes huge women. His mistress has a forty-four inch waist. I want to be thin but he will not let me. He is a pig.'

The schedule of events, contained in the brochure on the opposite page to the menu, stated that dinner would start at 8.15 and that the dancers would perform at 9.30, by which time dinner would be finished. It never is. The organizers are faced with an unenviable choice. Either they postpone the rest of dinner, or they put off the dance until the dinner is over. The latter is seldom a sensible option.

The dancers were already restive and had fused the arc lamps twice by playing with the electric wires which festooned the ballroom. The waiters were still serving the pudding, a colourful and inexpensive mousse, when the dancers appeared. It was a male dance troupe, which had been practising for weeks. There is little else to do in a borstal type institution. They danced well, and left to a round of genuine applause. They looked angelic. It was difficult to believe that any of them was there because he had committed some kind of crime.

Soon after the dancers had left, the members of the hotel band appeared, stubbed out their cigarettes on the players' platform and performed a slow foxtrot, designed for those who could not dance. The time had arrived for the chairwoman to take the floor.

'Should we dance now?' I asked her, if I happened to be the senior guest.

She nodded her head. 'I do not dance very well.'

'I don't either, so we should suit one another,' I replied cheerfully. This was intended to put her at ease, though she might have been happier if I had told her that I was very accomplished and would guide her if necessary.

'Please mind my feet. They seem to be very big when I am dancing,' she said. She was right. They were huge. They seemed to be everywhere.

I took her to the dance floor. Her friends at the other tables distracted her attention by clapping, so that her left stiletto heel penetrated my right shoe. We were soon joined by other dancers. Many of the men were as clumsy as I was. Most of the women were accomplished, which was remarkable as they had to walk backwards and guess what their partner, who had no idea himself, was likely to do next. The chairwoman began hesitantly. By the end of the dance, she was moving round the floor as if she had been doing so for years. My own dancing did not improve.

I had been taught dancing in 1942 by a female ATS sergeant who was on leave at the time. I paid her a guinea for six private lessons, most of which were devoted to the rumba, a dance she liked. It was, she explained, because she had Irish blood, though she did not tell me what the connection was.

We spent the last couple of lessons on the foxtrot, the quickstep and the slow waltz. I learned enough about each of them to be dangerous. She was posted to the Shetland Islands before we reached the quick waltz.

We both wore boots for the lessons. I still danced as if I was wearing them. I was taught to hold my partner well away from me, to watch where I put my feet and to keep my left arm in the air and rigidly extended. If I did that, she said, nobody could accuse me of any nonsense on the dance floor. As she knew to her cost, some of her partners became very excited and seemed more interested in her than in the dance. I still hold my partner as she said. It is ungainly but it is safe.

After one dance, during which I trod heavily on my partner, we were asked to resume our seats for the auction. As this was the principal method of raising money, the items auctioned had to be of sufficient value to attract some interest. This was not the right occasion on which to offer the cracked vase you had hoped would fall off the shelf at the expense of the insurance company, unless it was very old. The auction was conducted by an enthusiastic amateur, who intended to make the most of the event.

I had learned to stay very still during the auction. I had once scratched my nose, when the itching became intolerable, and found that I had bid fourteen thousand dollars, which I did not have, for a pink bathroom set for which I had no possible use, other than to give to someone for Christmas. Fortunately for me, someone else bought it for twenty thousand. I was congratulated for having tried to buy it. After that, I sat motionless throughout the auctions, as did many others in the room, as any movement was dangerous. One man who fainted found that he had brought an engagement ring for twenty thousand dollars. He was seventy-three and his wife wanted to know whom he had bought it for.

The auction usually finished at about a quarter to eleven, rather later than the time of ten o'clock in the schedule. The band played for about ten minutes. As the floor became crowded with dancers, everyone was told to sit again for the singer. As she had been paid a substantial fee, even if it was less than what she usually charged, she could not be kept waiting. The singer was usually fluent in both Cantonese and English and sang a selection of romantic songs in each of these. She was supposed to sing for twenty minutes and usually lasted about forty. Her act was followed by long applause, whether she had been effective or not. The expected encores lasted another ten minutes.

When the singer had gone, the dance band returned for about ten minutes before the raffle was held. Tickets for this had been sold at the tables earlier in the evening. Drums containing the stubs were dragged onto the dance floor.

The wives of the principal guests were called forward in turn to spin the drum, retrieve a ticket and hand it to the announcer, who read out its number and the prize which had been won. This was greeted with wild applause, though nobody was quite sure why they were clapping.

At one ball, the owner of a winning ticket did not come forward to claim her prize. There were cries of 'Draw it again.' The committee member who had drawn the ticket spun the drum again and pulled out another ticket. The owner of this one came forward and received his prize. As he returned to his table, the owner of the earlier ticket returned from the lavatory. She was incensed when friends at her table told her that her ticket had won. She stumped to the drum and asked for her prize, waving the winning ticket. As she was married to a wealthy man, her annoyance was understandable. She had bought three hundred dollar tickets and had been deprived of a prize worth about fifty. The chairwoman, scenting blood, agreed to send her an identical prize, properly wrapped, on the following day.

The raffle took some time, partly because of the large number of prizes, since it was thought politic to have as many of these as possible, and partly because of the substantial number of those who were asked to spin the drum, since anyone who thought they should have been asked to do so and was not was likely to phone the chairwoman next day and complain.

When the raffle ended, it was close to midnight. Most of the audience had left. There had been about three opportunities to dance, of ten minutes each; the occasion could properly be described as a ball. The charity had been supported. There was nothing more to stay for.

A few keen dancers remained, as the band played until two. On the top table, protocol reigned. If I was the senior guest, nobody would leave until I did. On one occasion I was enjoying myself, dancing with a partner who told me I was intelligent, amusing and not properly appreciated. She may well have been drinking but she was remarkably accurate. When we returned to the table, three couples on it were asleep.

Chapter 9

Repairing my shoes

At one time, there were many street cobblers operating from wooden stalls in the side street rather than from permanent premises. The rent, which the cobbler paid to the Urban Council, was low, consisting only of an annual licence fee. A receipt for this, skilfully forged, could be bought for half the proper fee at a stall in the Central Market. There was, in addition, a rather large annual charge made by one of the triad societies as protection money. Those who refused to pay it found in the morning that their stall had been wrecked. It was cheaper to be protected.

My shoes were made by hand, by Lo Kee, who visited the offices and drew an outline of my feet with a pencil, measuring the height of my toes with an old piece of string. This was, I found, a most erotic process. When I asked my wife to measure my feet, she suggested that I should visit a psychiatrist.

Lo Kee visited my office one morning to take my measurements.

'They haven't changed since last year, Mr Lo.'

'Very bad feet,' he replied, shaking his head. 'How can you walk?'

'What's wrong with them?'

'Bunion.'

'Nonsense. Women have bunions. My mother had them.'

'You have bunions. Every time I measure your left foot, it is not the same. Your left foot is growing.'

I looked at it. After a while, I thought I could see it move, though this might have been due to the holes in my sock. If Lo Kee had warned me that he was coming, I could have worn some new ones. This made me wonder how he had reached my office. I was the security officer for the department and nobody was supposed to get in without a pass.

I had recently instituted a new system, which meant that a messenger sat at a desk on each floor, asking everyone who called the name of the person he wished to see and his business. The system worked splendidly for the first week. It was especially effective in turning away those who wanted legal advice and anyone attempting to make a social visit, like the wives of Crown Counsel.

As happened with most of my excellent innovations, this remained the practice for years, the messengers quietly changing their role from obstruction to one of directing visitors where to go.

'How did you get in?' I asked Lo Kee.

'Up the stairs, as usual.'

'Isn't there a messenger, at the end of the corridor, to stop you?'

'You mean my cousin Chan?'

'If you say so.'

'He knows me well. He writes my name in the little book you gave him when I come. He charges me four dollars each time.'

'That's outrageous.'

'It's rather a lot,' Lo Kee agreed. 'I used to pay two dollars before you came. My cousin tells me that two dollars are for you.'

'He's a crook,' I yelped. 'I've never taken anything.'

'I know that,' Lo Kee replied. 'Europeans like yourself are too stupid to take money when they can.'

'Nobody can bribe me,' I replied virtuously. They never have. Perhaps I look too expensive. It cannot be because I have an honest face.

'Please do not worry about the four dollars,' Lo Kee continued. 'I just add them to the price I charge you for the shoes.'

When these needed repairing, which was often as Lo Kee must have used materials which he bought cheaply when they 'fell from a lorry', I would take them to his stall. Here he would do what he thought was necessary, rather than what I suggested.

I took a pair of my rundown brown shoes to Ho Mau, who kept another stall in a narrow lane which ran at right angles to Pedder Street. He looked severely at them.

'No good,' he replied, shaking his head.

'New heels, please.'

'You get shoes in Hong Kong?'

'Certainly. Lo Kee made them for me.'

'He does not make good shoes. I can make them much better at a cheaper price. You want new shoes?'

'No. Only new heels.'

'Sole very bad also.'

'Just new heels this time.'

'Finish tomorrow. Better to give you new soles as well. They are coming off. Look!' Ho pulled hard at the shoes, which began to come apart at the seams.

'Just glue it back where you have torn it and put on some new heels.'

'Finish tomorrow.' Ho threw my shoes to the back of his stall, where there was a heap of other shoes.

'Do you want my name?' I asked.

'You are also Lo. Lo But Si.'

'How did you know?'

'Picture in the paper.' He must have seen my photo taken outside the hospital, under the headline 'Not selected to succeed the Chief Justice'.

'Clever of you to recognize me.'

'Very good photo,' he conceded. 'Made you look old.' I was so disturbed by this that I forgot to ask him how much the repairs would be.

Next day, when I called at Ho's stall, he rummaged at the back and retrieved my brown shoes, which he polished on the seat of his trousers before he handed them to me, wrapped in a piece of newspaper.

'Forty dollars.'

'That's a lot for heels. I never pay more than fifteen for them.'

'I made new soles also.'

'I asked you to do heels only.'

'Soles very bad. You like shoes with bad soles? If you want poor job you can go to Ping Kow. I do good work. You have a good pair of shoes. You can wear them anywhere, even in the Jardine's taipan's room.'

I paid him what he asked and returned to my office, where Francis Silva, the head clerk, was waiting for me. He spent most of his time running errands for the Crown Counsel. At first, I meant to discourage this practice, which I considered to be an unjustifiable use of public money, until I discovered how useful he was to me.

'It was your wife's birthday last week,' he announced sadly.

'How did you know that? I'm afraid I forgot all about it.'

'One of the messengers told me. He saw it on a postcard which was sent to her by someone else.'

'I must give her something.'

'Leave it to me, S.G. I know where to go for a bargain. I will get you a Gucci handbag.'

'What? They are terribly expensive.'

'I mean that it looks like a Gucci handbag. Your wife will not know the difference. It is Hong Kong made,' he added proudly.

The handbag looked like an Italian one to me. I do not know how my wife knew that it was locally made, but she thanked me, saying that she had always wanted a handbag manufactured in Kowloon, instead of the Italian ones of which she already had several.

Before Mr Silva left, I complained to him about Ho, who had done more than I had asked.

'Were those the brown shoes on your side table last week? I hope you got some new soles. The old ones were in a poor state. Next time, just leave it to me. Ho is not on my list of cobblers. What did he charge you?'

'Forty dollars,' I replied indignantly.

'I can get it done for much less, though forty is the usual price for an expatriate for soles and heels.'

'I didn't ask for the soles to be done, Mr Silva.'

'I'm afraid that is not the way it works, S.G. The shoe repairers do what they think is needed. You are not the expert. You do not tell the doctor what is the matter with you. So you must expect to get your shoes back with unexpected repairs.'

Some time later, when Mr Silva was on holiday, I took a pair of my black shoes for repair. I decided to try one of the cobblers who had a stall in a steep lane which ran south up the hill from Queen's Road. The stall which I chose was next to one where they specialized in the cutting of keys. It was a favourite resort of those who stole cars and broke into premises. On the side of the shoe stall was a notice saying 'Chow Keung Kit, Shoe Repair. Ready next day. Special Price for all'. The notice was nailed to a plank which carried the words 'Tomatoes Fragile, Made in Japan, Keep this Side up'. I assumed that the reference to a special price for all meant that everybody would be overcharged, unless they made a fuss or had a special arrangement with Chow.

A short, bald man peered at me through his spectacles. They had no glass in them. Someone had told him that all good cobblers were short-sighted.

'You got shoes?' he asked.

I handed them to him, wrapped in a newspaper.

Mr Chow seemed more interested in the paper than in my shoes. He read it and shook his head.

'Very bad,' he said, shaking his head.

'My shoes, you mean?' I thought I should remind him of why I had come.

'No, no. The paper. Wife attacked her husband with a knife. She only got three years for that.'

I suppose there is no country in which the judiciary does not have a reputation for being soft and for paying more attention to the defendant's antecedents than to the effect on the victim of his crime.

This opinion is often formed from reading inaccurate summaries in the paper, but it is still widespread. Only when I joined the judiciary myself did I realize how unfair this criticism is.

'You mean that was not enough?'

'Should be ten years. All he did was to correct her for not cooking his dinner.'

'How did he hit her?'

'I think he knocked her down with a hammer. What's that got to do with it? He was provoked. On the same page, it said a man got two years for buggery.'

'What's wrong with that?'

'Very nasty. Only Europeans do it.'

'I've heard of Chinese too?'

'Only for money. They do not like it. I know Europeans do.'

I did not attempt to change his conviction, which was widely shared. So far as he was concerned, Europeans preferred any sex to no sex. The Chinese attribute this to English boarding schools.

'May I have new soles and heels?' I thought I had better talk about shoes, as I had not shown myself to know much about sentencing.

Chow pulled heartily at my shoes, breaking the stitching at the side of one of them.

'Tut tut,' he said. 'Very bad work. Very expensive to repair.'

'How much?'

'Must be eighty dollars.'

'Forty?'

'Sixty.'

'Fifty.'

Chow agreed. 'You make a poor man very sad. Do you want any balloons?' Chow showed me a packet of condoms. 'You are a strong man,' he said. 'You must need these every day.'

I declined with grateful thanks. 'Do I need a receipt for the shoes?'

'No. I know your shoes.' Chow hurled them to the back of his stall, shaking his head at my stupidity.

'Hey,' he said, as I was about to leave, 'are you law man? Same like a judge, only different?' I agreed. I could not have put it better.

Two days later, I returned to the stall. It was shut. On the nail was a notice saying 'Mr Chow away. Back plenty soon'. I asked the man who made skeleton keys for burglars where Mr Chow was. He thought he was in hospital but he often was. He did not know when Mr Chow was likely to come back. I was displeased. The least Mr Chow could have done was to leave someone in charge at the stall. He wasn't there three days later when I next called. After a week, I found him working at last.

'I'm glad that you are better, Mr Chow.'

'Better. I am best in street!'

'I mean well again.'

'Never sick. Went to China. I tell everyone I'm ill, then nobody worries about where I have gone.'

'A good visit?'

'I go to see my family there each year, to take them a lot of things which are made in Hong Kong or Taiwan. If they are made in Taiwan I have to take off the label and put on another one which shows it was made in China. There is a stall in Western Market which will put on the China label for fifty cents.'

'Have they got enough China labels?'

'Yes. They are made in Hong Kong, so we have as many as we need. Why have you come?'

'For my shoes, Mr Chow.'

'You sent someone to get them already. It was a Chinese man. He paid me fifty dollars.'

'I didn't send anyone.'

'Then I gave him the wrong pair,' Mr Chow replied, with a complacency which I though to be quite out of place.

'What about his shoes?'

'Very clever,' agreed Mr Chow. 'I will look.' He searched the pile of shoes at the back of his stall.

'Ah ha,' he shouted. 'Here is a black pair. These must be yours.'

'They are *not*, Mr Chow. They have no steel tips on the soles, like mine did.'

'Then they belong to Mr Barlow.'

'Where does he live?'

'Somewhere on the Peak. He sends somebody to fetch his shoes when I have repaired them.'

'Do you know where Mr Barlow works?'

'He is a big man in the TDC. He has a new wife, but still old shoes.' Mr Chow thought this very funny. 'You pay me and I'll give you these shoes. Then you can get yours from Mr Barlow.'

'Certainly not. I'll get Mr Barlow to collect his when I've got mine from him.'

Chow nodded. The Europeans had plenty of dollars but hung onto them. He admired that.

I traced Barlow's office in the Trade Development Council and spoke to his secretary, who had been expecting someone else to phone.

'It's Bubbles here,' she began, in the sort of voice that makes you wonder if you have overslept. 'I knew you would phone me, pussy cat.'

'I think', I replied haughtily, 'that you have made a mistake. I am not known as "pussy cat" even to my wife, who calls me "that man" when she is being friendly. I want to talk to Mr Barlow about my shoes.'

'You have no right to ring up and pretend to be my boyfriend,' she replied indignantly. 'The police know what to do about dirty phone calls.' She slammed down the receiver.

An hour later, when I phoned again, a male voice told me that Bubbles had been taken home in tears and that Barlow was out.

The next morning, I asked my secretary if she would find out whether Barlow was in and whether he had got my shoes. She entered my room a few minutes later.

'I spoke to an odd girl. She said that she had had some calls from men who pretended they were after Barlow, though she was convinced that they were perverts after her.'

'Did she say where Barlow is?'

'I think she said that he was on leave, but she was sobbing so much that it wasn't easy to be sure what she was saying.'

'What did she say about my shoes?'

'Nothing. She said Barlow followed her about in bare feet last week. She doesn't think that's anything to do with your shoes as she is sure Barlow is after her, as well as the pervert on the phone.'

'I suppose it's a long leave?'

'He won't be away for more than about six months.'

I was consoled by the thought that, if my shoes were larger than the ones Barlow had left with Mr Chow, Barlow would not enjoy wearing them, even if he packed them with newspaper.

Some months later, my secretary phoned the TDC. She was told that Barlow would not be returning to Hong Kong, as he had found another job in Britain, with a manufacturer of shoes.

The next time I passed his stall, I thought I would let Mr Chow know what had happened to Barlow. I found Chow at work, shaking his head sadly as he ripped off a heel which looked perfect and unworn.

'More shoes? Everybody come back, because I do such good work.'

I told him what had happened to Barlow.

'More dollars,' he commented.

'You'd better give me Barlow's shoes.'

'OK. You sign chit.'

I put my signature on a piece of paper in Chinese and took a pair of black shoes. I paid him fifty dollars. Chow polished them with his apron until they looked better than the pair I was wearing. I was not sure what I would do with them. I supposed that I would have to send them to Barlow. I took them home and left them in the kitchen. It's a pity they would not fit me. They looked good.

'You're not going to throw them away, surely?' asked my wife, who was always trying to persuade me to get rid of things. Only the week before, she had wanted to dispose of a shirt merely because the collar and cuffs were worn out, although there was no hole in the front of it.

'They belong to someone called Barlow, who is in England. He has my shoes.'

'Did you take two pairs to the menders at the same time? If you did, you must have been in your bedroom slippers all week.'

'I do not follow you.'

'These are yours. The cobbler lost them months ago, you told me.'

Chapter 10
The Cricket Club

The week after I first arrived in Hong Kong, Maurice Heenan asked me if I had yet joined a club.

'Not yet,' I agreed. 'I expect they all have a long waiting list.'

'There is for the Hong Kong Club and the Ladies Recreation Club. I would not advise the LRC, as you have to present yourself to a committee of women who run it. They tore me to pieces before they let me in. But there is no waiting list for the Cricket Club. It'll take anyone. It needs members badly, so you ought to get in. It's right by the Supreme Court and serves the worst lunch in town. Have you played any cricket?'

'Now and then. Though I'm not much good at it.' I was inordinately proud of the fact that I had once reached double figures for the St Albans Thursday team against the Mental Hospital at Shenley, but decided that I would try to get in without any reference to it.

Hong Kong Cricket Club (till 1975)

'I don't suppose the fact that you have actually played cricket will harm you, though it won't matter at all if you have not. There are about six hundred members. The entrance fee is a hundred dollars and, I think, the monthly subscription is about fifteen. The Club runs mainly off its bar profits. Shall I get you an application form?'

Cricket had been played on the ground since 1851, when it was next to the sea on the north side, though it was well inland now as the result of a series of reclamations. It was often described as the most valuable cricket ground in the Commonwealth. This did not take into account the fact that the Club held it on a ten year lease, which was not renewed in the 1970s.

A fortnight or so later, Maurice took me to meet the committee. I donned my best suit for the occasion. This was probably unnecessary as the secretary told me later that the Club would take anybody's money, which was the only explanation he could offer of some of the members. I was hurried round the committee at lunch time. They appeared to hold their meetings at a small table in the main bar and to be more interested in what I drank than in my suitability for membership on other grounds. It is, however, fair to record that I was asked about my prowess as a cricketer.

'I've read your form,' said George Rowe, a member of the committee.

'Good heavens, you must not do that,' said one of the other members.

'I see you have ticked the box saying you would like to play cricket.'

'That's right. I hope it won't count against me. Please erase it if you will.'

'No, no. We take all sorts,' George replied, 'even cricketers.' He laughed immoderately, and by himself. The other committeemen looked disapproving.

My form was signed. I was given a number by the secretary and told that this did not mean that I was elected, as I had not paid an entrance fee yet.

'Don't worry about that,' Maurice explained later. 'You are in all right. Some time ago a prospective member did not pay his entrance fee. He ran up a bill as a candidate. As this made him a valuable debtor, he was kept on, even though he still owed the entrance fee. He had the biggest drinks bills in the Club for years and was a popular candidate, until he drank himself to death. He never became a member. So the Club has to be careful.'

The catering, if an otherwise respectable word can be so misused, was carried out by Mr Chow, who operated in a small kitchen full of implements which had gone out of fashion a hundred years before the Japanese occupation in 1941.

Many members had joined the Club because it provided a cheap lunch in the centre of town and draft beer, which cost less than anywhere else. The lunch was largely inedible, which did not bother the young men who came for it each day from nearby offices. It compensated for its lack of quality by bulk and must have reminded many of the customers of their schooldays.

Lunch began with Brown Windsor soup, composed mainly of potatoes, gravy cubes and water. It slopped over the edge of the soup plate, except where the waiter's thumb rested. The waiters soon developed asbestos thumbs, as I saw these resting in soup which was too hot to eat. Inevitably, some of the soup was spilt, either by waiters carrying full plates or by members who were not skilful in dealing with hot soup. By the end of lunch the floor was sometimes slippery with Brown Windsor, which caused some satisfactory falls by waiters or members, the latter being greeted with loud cheers.

With the soup, which was changed to 'Thick Potato' when Mr Chow exhausted his supply of gravy cubes, came slices of toast, cut thickly and done until they were black. The butter stood in a plastic bowl in the centre of the table. It was soon covered with toast crumbs, as Mr Chow thought butter knives unnecessary. What is more, they would have been pocketed by the junior members, if he had provided them. The toast was excellent. Most of the members had their mouths full of it as they tackled the soup. This revolting practice, which I adopted swiftly, made the soup almost palatable.

After the soup came the main course. This was called, on the soiled menu which remained on the table unchanged until it fell to pieces, 'meat pie'. All main courses were so described, whether they were or not. The meat pie was submerged in a mound of vegetables, prominent among them being a pile of 'bubble and squeak'. This was an economical mixture of second hand potato and cabbage. As the kitchen never seemed to run out of it, I assume that Mr Chow had an arrangement to buy suitable leftovers from one of the nearby hotels. The mixture caused severe flatulence of a particularly unpleasant kind.

The main course was followed by 'the trolley'. There was nothing on wheels any longer. Instead a waiter walked around the tables, his chest bumping against a tray. This was suspended from his neck by a rope which became increasingly greasy and frayed until it broke, deposited the puddings on the floor and was replaced. The tray had originally been for seeds. It was converted to its present use by a coat of paint, which was worn away in several places. On the 'trolley' was a bowl of custard, another of green jelly and a heap of overripe bananas, bought cheaply by Mr Chow from a friend who could not sell them in the market. I once made the mistake of asking for jelly of another colour. This caused much confusion in the kitchen, forcing me to apologize and take a banana instead.

One of the waiters offered coffee or tea. As they tasted the same, it did not matter which you asked for. In the saucer was a mint, until the kitchen ran out of them, as it did daily. It was soft where the tea has slopped onto it. Some years before, in order to buy cheaply ten sacks of potatoes which had fallen from a lorry, Mr Chow had been obliged to purchase several boxes of mints, which had deteriorated in the sun but were still edible if you were hungry. The tradition had persisted.

Lunch was served on trestle tables, some covered with white cloths and some not. It seemed to depend on the number allowed for the day by Mr Chow. Most of the customers were in a hurry, bolting their food as if they were still in the orphanages from which some of them must have come.

At first, I imagined that the men who ate lunch had been given only an hour by ruthless employers interested only in profit and determined to exploit their junior staff. Later I discovered that many of them had spent an hour in the bar before lunch and that they were returning late to offices which would not release them until about seven o'clock.

The Club was administered by a committee which was appointed each year after an election in which those who were unwise enough to stand were returned unopposed. It was, therefore, fatal to allow your name to be put forward. About 1965, George Rowe spoke to me. I hoped it was because he had forgiven me for running him out the previous season.

'How long have you been a member, Denys?' he asked. That should have made me suspicious. Everyone called me 'Roberts' in those days, unless they wanted something.

'Nearly three years,' I conceded.

'You've played for several of its teams?' This was a polite way of saying that I had been rejected by most of them as below even their low standards.

'Not with much success.'

'You were unlucky, Denys. Everyone says so. You often come for lunch, don't you?'

I agreed. The sudden switch in subjects confused me.

'You will agree that we serve the best bubble and squeak in town.'

'It is the only bubble and squeak in the Far East.'

'So isn't it about time you put back something into the Club in which you have had so much pleasure?'

This was an odd way of describing the depression which descended on me when I was given out leg before wicket playing for one of the Club's teams. I had hit the ball firmly to square leg and was on my third run when I saw the umpire's finger in the air.

'No,' I replied. I had no intention of making a donation to a Club which had misused me so cruelly.

'Good! I thought you would see it my way.'

'See what?'

'That you are an obvious chap for the committee. I'll put your name on the board.'

I thought of a number of compelling reasons why I should not join the committee. It was too late. For the next twenty years, I continued to be a member of it, since I was unable to persuade anyone else to take my place. A majority of members continued to oppose any kind of reform.

The ground, which was smaller than the average for a cricket ground, was surrounded by buildings. On the north stood the old Hong Kong Club, Sutherland House and a hole in the ground which later became the Furama Hotel. On the east was the Cheerio Club, replaced by a multi-storey car park. On the south were the Rating and Valuation Department, the Hilton Hotel and the Bank of China. To the west was the Supreme Court, with balconies which overlooked the ground and were well used when Sir Ivo Rigby, an enthusiastic watcher and indifferent player, was Chief Justice.

The playing area was further restricted by a large square in one corner which served as a bowling green. It was the flattest and most verdant part of the ground. The ball travelled faster over it because it was rolled. Fielders were told to be careful not to damage it.

Next to the bowling green was the children's playground, which had been built and equipped at the expense of a Club member who was a bachelor. As he had no children himself, he believed that the provision of a sandpit, swings, slide and climbing frame in the playground would prevent them causing trouble in the main pavilion. It was no surprise to anyone but himself when this did not happen.

For several years, a Club team called the Wanderers played frequent non-league cricket on the ground on Sundays. The batting was opened, if the Wanderers chose to be first, by Stuart Barnes and myself. Indeed, it is said that one Club member, on hearing that we were still at the wicket, asked the secretary to phone him when we were out so that he could come to the ground. It has been a constant source of sadness to me that I have never been more than an adequate batsman. Barnes was worse. He was left handed and held the bat as if it were a spade and his right arm was broken. Week after week, he prodded and glanced, hardly scoring in front of the wicket. He was also difficult to get out.

Barnes was eager for the short single, provided that this would increase his score. He was reluctant to run for anyone else, if you can properly describe his sideways lurch, like that of a badly wounded dog, as a run.

'Come on,' he shouted at me, having prodded a ball between his legs and been unable to locate it. He charged down the wicket towards me. The fieldsman at short square leg juggled with the ball and I managed to make my ground.

I glared at Barnes, who replied with a grin and pulled at the stained cap which he always wore. This did not belong to any cricket club of which anyone knew. It was believed that it had been given to him for bowls. Barnes had nearly run me out three times that morning. I decided that I had been patient beyond measure but that I should now run him out. Among other factors, it would be an easy road to popularity.

In the next over, I steered the ball at chest height between two slips, each of whom shouted 'Yours' and made no effort to catch it. The ball rolled towards third man at a fast speed.

'Come on,' I shouted, reasonably confident that Barnes would be run out if third man was awake. I was half way down the wicket and going well when I saw that Barnes had not moved.

'No,' he said when I was only a few yards away. I turned and ran back and was run out by yards.

'Bad luck, old boy,' he said as I passed him. 'It was my call anyway.'

My recollection of the old ground is obscured by the remembrance of the many occasions on which I was run out by Barnes. I thought that my memory had been distorted by a measure of bitterness. When I consulted Ted Wilson, an experienced player from Africa who specialized in the lofted cow shot, described by him as 'the controlled pull-drive', he assured me that he had suffered in a similar way.

In 1975, the Cricket Club was removed by the Government to a new site on the way to Repulse Bay, about three miles from the centre of town, on top of a reclaimed area in a valley near Wong Nai Chung Gap. By this time I had become President of the Club, presumably in the belief that, when the lease of the ground was discussed, I would be able to ensure its renewal. This gravely overestimated my influence and overlooked the fact that I should have to leave Ex. Co.

whenever the Club's affairs were discussed. I was asked to withdraw when the lease was debated. The Club members did not believe this and were convinced that I had let them down. I tried to derive some credit from the offer of a new ground, well out of town, to replace the one, in the centre, where we had been since 1851.

About 1974, the Government gave a twenty year lease to the Club of a levelled site which was somewhat larger than that of the old ground. The Club raised a substantial sum of money in debentures and built a new clubhouse on the site.

In order to ensure that the ground should be in good condition in time for the season in 1975, the Club employed a grass expert, at considerable expense, to advise it as to what to plant and how. In accordance with his advice, the Club imported bags of peat, most suitable for the production of a bog, and grass which would have grown like wildfire in Sussex but did not flourish at the Gap, as the new ground came to be called. Three months before the new ground was due to be used, the rough turf which had served the old one was transplanted to the Gap and relaid. It did not look attractive but enabled play to begin at the proper time. As the years passed, it became better, until it provided a flat and hard wearing surface.

The new Club provided a swimming pool, squash courts, a manager's flat, a tennis court, a bowling green and an excellent restaurant. Those who actually played cricket became an even smaller minority. Later on, car parking, staff quarters and another tennis court were provided. A library full of stained paperbacks was provided for the Club's intellectuals. For the first time that anyone could remember, there was a waiting list.

In spite of the improved facilities, which inevitably brought with them greater expense, it was fashionable for many years to regret the blessings of the old clubhouse, which had not been so obvious during its existence. Bubble and squeak was brought to the Gap, though it was asked for less often as the endless pleasures of chips became known more widely.

The opening of the new clubhouse at the Gap was marked by a cricket match. The captain of my side, a man of relentless and misguided humour whose name I have happily forgotten, insisted that I should open the innings with Barnes.

Barnes was determined that he should score the first run at the Gap. He therefore trotted ahead of me onto the field and took guard. Only when he had made his usual mark, a trench outside the leg stump which he never appeared to use again, did he realize that the bowling was from his end. This did not weaken his desire. During the first over, the edge of my bat induced two balls to fly between the slips to third man. Even Barnes could have walked a single each time. He sent me back. At the start of the second over, Barnes again asked for his guard. Once more he dug his hole outside his leg stump.

'I'd like the screens moved,' he said to the umpire.

'Nonsense,' the umpire replied. 'You can't see that far.' The umpire knew enough about Barnes' batting to realize that moving the screen would make little difference.

'I insist,' replied Barnes. 'And what is more, I can see perfectly well that there is a woman in a bathing dress sitting on one of the struts.' Four members of the fielding side hurried over to persuade her to move. It took a long time.

Barnes squared up as soon as the screen had been moved to his satisfaction, though it appeared to me to be exactly where it started. Barnes missed the first two balls, which were outside his off stump. He pushed the third toward gully and called for a suicidal run. It gave me pleasure to send him back. He missed the next two balls. The last delivery of the over struck him on the pad and ran to the boundary.

The umpire signalled four leg byes. Barnes insisted that he hit it. In the next over, I scored a single from a cover drive which found its way to fine leg. Barnes has no doubt that the scorebook is wrong and that he scored the first run at the Gap.

Chapter 11

Armistice Day

For several years there had been disagreement as to whcther or not the unofficial members of Ex. Co. and Leg. Co., collectively known as 'the unofficials', should wear morning coats on Armistice Day. C. Y. Kwan, the senior unofficial member of Ex. Co., opposed the dress as being un-Chinese. Sir David Trench, the then Governor, favoured its adoption, partly because he had to wear a uniform on that day and partly because, with a fine war record of his own, he took Armistice Day seriously.

'Why do you say it is un-Chinese, C.Y.?' he asked.

'Because you never see a proper Chinese in a morning coat,' he replied.

'You don't see proper Chinese in suits either, C.Y., only in a cheongsam.'

'We have been wearing suits for fifty years, not morning coats. Besides, I do not have one.'

'That is a strong argument,' the Governor agreed. He knew that C.Y. invariably gave him excellent advice, so long as he was not allowed to think about it too much. His reactions were excellent, so long as they were not confused by thought.

'I will give you a firm lead,' said Sir David. 'I leave it to the unofficial members to do what they think is right.'

'That's not fair,' C.Y. protested. 'Nobody will know what to do.'

'Let them follow their consciences.'

C.Y. thought it unwise to say that some of his colleagues did not seem to have such things. 'What about the officials then?'

'They will wear morning coats then. The judges have to wear long wigs, don't they?'

'They look terrible,' said C.Y., who was greatly cheered by the thought of the judges.

While Sir David was Governor, some unofficials wore morning coats and some did not. C. Y. Kwan borrowed one from a tall European and looked bizarre. He was a short, squat man whose coat tails reached nearly to the ground.

He was succeeded by Sir Y. K. Kan, a tough, clear thinking man who enjoyed giving unpalatable advice. He had bought a morning coat. As he explained, it was not because he wanted to get one, but he thought it was necessary in order to give face to C. Y. Kwan.

Y.K. had been wearing his coat for some years when Sir Murray Maclehose became Governor. M.M. also had a white Colonial Service uniform which he had been told he must have as a colonial Governor. He had previously been a member of the Foreign Service, which regarded members of the Colonial Service as of a lesser standard than themselves. Members of the Foreign Service, at least in the senior branches, took a written examination. This established that all of them were literate. The members of the Colonial Service, by contrast, were appointed after an interview, because they were good chaps and held the necessary qualification, which was kept low. In the case of some unpopular posts, the interviewing board was prepared to dispense with the first requirement. It held fast to the second, so that it could continue to claim that it did not lower its standards just because one of the minor colonies was desperate.

M.M. had worn his colonial uniform on arrival. He knew from experience that, five minutes after he put it on, however carefully it had been ironed and hung, deep creases would appear in his coat and trousers and that the ostrich feathers in his hat would collapse and lie limply on his spike. Nor had he yet mastered the sword, which kept getting between his long legs.

'I wanted to discuss what we should all wear at the Armistice Day parade,' he began.

'We discussed that at length under Sir David,' replied Y.K. 'He was very firm about it and said he would make no decision.'

'I wonder what you and your colleagues would think about a more informal occasion,' suggested M.M.

'What would the judges wear?'

'I thought perhaps suits?'

'Not them, Governor. They've paid about £200 each for their periwigs. They are bound to insist on wearing them.'

'Couldn't I just tell them what to do?'

'I don't think that is a good idea. They are an awkward lot. As soon as you make the most innocent suggestion, they go red in the face and talk about the independence of the judiciary.'

'This is only about morning coats.'

'Don't touch it, sir. They'll petition the Secretary of State, saying that such a change threatens their right to make up their own minds.' Y.K. shuddered. He did not want to become involved in another fight with the Chief Justice, who had appealed to London when the Colonial Secretary had secured a slightly larger car.

'All right, we'll leave them alone with their periwigs.'

'I'm afraid that you will have to wear a uniform. It's expected.'

'Why is that?'

'Because the Japanese were here and killed a lot of Hong Kong people.' Y.K. did not explain how the two were connected.

'What are you going to wear?' asked M.M. 'There's no need for you to dress up.'

'I have a morning coat,' said Y.K. 'I shall wear it, even though it makes me look dreadful. My colleagues will do the same.'

Only after Y.K. retired from Ex. Co., some years later, did a lack of uniformity among unofficials creep back.

M.M., however, found another way of not appearing in his white uniform. After 1972, he look his leave in November each year, leaving his Chief Secretary, who was acting in his absence in his place, to attend in a morning coat.

Armistice Day began with a ceremony at the Chinese War Memorial. This was a granite gateway, situated in the Botanical Gardens, close to Government House. On the gateway were Chinese characters. I did not ask what they meant, assuming that the words referred, like the memorials in England, to the glorious dead, as if a young man should be pleased to have been killed at twenty-two. The Governor, wearing his uniform, if he was not abroad, squeaked his way to the memorial and laid his wreath, bowing three times as he did so. The unofficials also laid wreaths and bowed. It was a quick, quiet ceremony, without prayers or music, unlike that which took place in Statue Square.

In the middle of the Square was the Cenotaph. This was said to be modelled on the one in Whitehall, though it was somewhat smaller. It was inscribed to those who had fallen in 1914 to 1919, and enlarged to include 1939 to 1945. This was not tactful, as the Chinese had been fighting the Japanese for some years before that. M.M. decided that the ceremony needed to be revised. Nobody could remember when this had last happened. He called a meeting of his senior officials.

'Where does the vicar stand?' he asked, to start the discussion.

'If you mean the priests, they are on the grass next to the microphones, which did not work last year so that nobody heard the prayers,' said the Secretary for Chinese Affairs.

'We have to have an Anglican, a Catholic and a Nonconformist, or it means trouble,' Y.K. added. 'The atheists are not represented.'

'Why do they stand on the grass?'

'They always have, sir.'

'That doesn't seem to be a compelling reason.'

'It's a very good one,' explained the Secretary for Defence. He attended the meeting because the soldiers who provided the guard of honour fainted every year during the two minutes' silence. This was usually broken by a heavy fall of rain and an unpleasant oath from the sergeant major, who was part of the detachment.

'If you change anything, sir,' he went on, 'you get trouble. If you leave things as they are, nobody will grumble, even if they don't like it.'

'Let us hope', the Commissioner of Police commented in a cold voice, 'that the microphones work better this year.'

'They did not work because one of your men tripped over the wires,' retorted the Secretary of Defence, who did not like the police habit of scattering plain clothes men about in the crowd.

'I know what he is getting at, sir,' exclaimed the Commissioner of Police. 'He's upset because we didn't manage to stop all the traffic during the silence last year. What can you do with a bus which drives at full speed the wrong way through town?'

'Try arresting the driver,' M.M. suggested.

'We did, but the A.G. said we ought not to prosecute.' He glared at me.

'Public interest,' I said.

'I'll remember that phrase, A.G. It's very useful.' M.M. smiled to himself. He reminded me of it, whenever he wished to do something improper.

'The Anglican bishop says that he would rather stand on the other side this year,' said the Secretary for Chinese Affairs. 'It's shadier there.'

'I expect this is a silly question,' interposed M.M., who often used this phrase when he knew it was not, 'but who is in charge of the ceremony?'

'Well,' the Colonial Secretary smiled, 'we don't actually have anyone in charge of the whole thing. We've got different people who look after parts of it.'

'No wonder it's a dreadful muddle.'

'I think you're exaggerating a little, sir. We have been doing it this way for years.'

'I have what I think is the solution,' said M.M. 'We'll give it to the Director of Protocol. He hasn't got enough to do.'

'He's a Foreign Office man,' protested the Secretary for Chinese Affairs. 'He doesn't know what to do at all.'

Old Supreme Court from New Supreme Court

'Then he is admirably equipped to tidy up, isn't he? Thank you all for your help. It was most useful.'

Some years afterwards, I went to the judiciary. From there it seemed quite different, since it was organized by the administration. It was therefore much easier to be forthright about the mistakes in organization which occurred. It was no longer my fault if anything went wrong.

The Supreme Court building had been opened about 1912. It had been designed by a prominent English architect of the time, but had been put up the wrong way round, presumably by a Chinese foreman who read everything from left to right.

Originally it was designed to hold two courts, but had been patched and adapted until there were ten, some of them wholly suitable for a dog in season, but not for much else. About 1976, however, a large piece of plaster fell dangerously close to one of the judges, who happened to be an Irishman. Thinking that the IRA had caught up with him, he hurried from the court, shouting 'Save the women and children.' The Chief Justice of the time, remembered for the terseness of his judgments and the breadth of his collection of frogs, discovered that it was not, unfortunately, an attack on the

Irish judge, whom he did not much like, but a general assault on the building by those who were constructing an underground railway.

'It's all to do with the moisture,' explained the Director of Public Works.

'Are you suggesting that the judge concerned is a wet?' I asked.

'No, no. You've missed the point, sir. It's the Mass Transit Railway. It's sucking up all the moisture from under this building.'

'Why not put some back? The rains start next month.'

'It's even worse, sir. The building is breaking its back. We've found a fault in it.'

'Congratulations, Director. I might have known I could rely on you.'

'Part of the building is on soft soil and part of it is on rock. As soon as the water left the soil, the building on the soil started to settle. As the other part couldn't, the building started to break. That's why the plaster fell.'

'Will there be any other falls?'

'Rather!' The D.P.W. seemed to relish the idea. He had never really trusted judges.

'In that case, they had better go somewhere else.'

For several years, while the Mass Transit workers shored up the Supreme Court and extended their tunnels, the judges operated in another building, which had originally been built for a sect of French monks. It was empty. As nobody could think of any other use for it, the Supreme Court sat there for some years.

In 1982, however, the judges moved back into the old building, remaining there until they occupied a new Supreme Court in 1984. This was too far away from the Cenotaph to be a convenient assembly point for the judges, who therefore changed and assembled in the old Supreme Court for the Armistice Day ceremonies. It was something of a gamble as to how many would turn up and, if so, how they should be dressed.

'Where on earth is Barker?' I asked the Registrar. I had counted the judges three times and come to a different total on each occasion.

'Don't worry, C.J.,' he replied soothingly. 'They're all here. All twenty-nine of them.'

'You see,' I yelped. There should be thirty-two.'

'Including yourself?'

'Of course. I always come, don't I?' I was no longer sure of anything.

'There's a vacancy, you know. And one's on leave. So there shouldn't be more than thirty.'

'That's what I mean. We're short of Barker.'

New Supreme Court, 1986

'Has anyone seen Barker?' shouted the Registrar, who did not mind if anyone had but thought it right to keep me happy.

'I saw him changing in his office,' replied one of the judges. 'So I knew he is coming. He was using some shocking language about his buckle shoes.'

'I can hardly walk when I've got mine on,' I replied. 'But that doesn't make me late.'

Three other judges told me what trouble they had walking in buckle shoes. This explained why the line of judges was known as the 'Limping Chorus' by outsiders. I had imagined the term was solely abusive.

At this moment Barker appeared, grinning cheerfully.

'Sorry I'm late,' he said. 'My car broke down.'

'As well as your shoes?' I enquired.

'You should have gone without me.'

'Better to be late than not have you at all.' I walked to the front of the line where the bailiff, carrying the mace, was looking at his watch and fidgeting.

The judges were dressed in an assortment of colours, varying from deep red to near pink. Most of them were wearing periwigs, some white and new, others old and made for someone else. One wig had been made locally for a play; its wearer looked like a pantomime dame. The appellate judges wore their black and gold robes, designed by the wife of one of them. Some of them looked as if fancy dress did not suit them. The gowns had been fashioned by prisoners who had been promised extra remission if they made no mistakes. It had thus been possible to devise a gown within the Government allowance for it.

Judges are by nature an ill disciplined, individual and bloody minded lot. They dislike standing in line, though sometimes sufficiently unaware of protocol to insist on standing upwind of Bloggs J. who could not control his wind. It was necessary for the Registrar to march up and down the line, shouting at the judges to stand in the correct order.

Some were wearing their red cross sashes; some were not. Some had medals pinned to their hoods, making them look lopsided. Some had mislaid their medals; others had not earned any. One judge was later found to have been wearing some medals to which his entitlement was, to put it kindly, not fully established. The lace ruffles ranged from the one given to a judge by his grandmother, which was a pale yellow, to the white nylon one which had been made for another judge locally and was washable. Several of the neck ruffles bulged uneasily from the collars, as they came loose from the front stud which was meant to hold them.

I was supposed to lead the judges out at 10.42. I found myself alone at 10.43. The others had not followed me, as one of the line was having trouble with his black nylons. These kept falling round his ankles, because the garters which held them up had perished. He limped onto the parade with one hand in his pocket, trying to hold up his stockings. To any interested spectator, it looked as if he was playing with himself. This is how it looked from the Supreme Court balcony, which was occupied by senior officials and judges' wives.

'I see', muttered Mrs Bates to the judge's wife standing next to her, 'that Philip is playing with himself again.'

'Nonsense,' replied Mrs Turner. 'He must be holding up his trousers.'

'Doesn't get enough at home, perhaps?' Mrs Bates shook her head sadly.

'That's not true,' replied Mrs Turner indignantly. 'Why, he – oh.' She stopped, with a red face. Mrs Bates was a beast.

I led the judges past the group of ex-servicemen which stood on one side of the square. Some of them looked as if their names ought to have been on a war memorial long ago. Others looked so young and fit that I preferred to think they were cheating, rather than that I was ageing faster.

I cheered myself up, as I walked by, by recalling the demise of Lance Bombardier Evans, who expired when a shell landed beside him as he sat on a makeshift lavatory, looking at the nudes in the latest edition of a magazine. Evans had, in his last words, expressed uncharitable thoughts about the Germans who fired it, the pioneers who had located the WC in the open and the cook for preparing food which was responsible for him being there. Only by straining at the meaning of words could Evans be described as one of our glorious dead who had given his life in the cause of freedom.

We were supposed to arrive after the unofficial members, who stood next to us; the Almighty would have been most impressed by the protocol. This year, some of the unofficials were late. They climbed over the crash barriers and made their way to their places within the next quarter of an hour. The last of them arrived in the middle of the two minutes' silence to which he lent colour with a loud cry of 'Shit' when he caught his coat tails in the barrier.

Some of the judges found it difficult to stand for two minutes without moving or fainting. Somebody told Turner J. that he would not faint, if he moved his body. He did so whenever he felt that he was about to pass out. This happened frequently, so that for most of the silence he jerked like a puppet, until Bates J., on his left, stamped on his foot. This was so painful that Turner had no difficulty in avoiding the faint, doing no more than mutter at the pain in his foot. Crown J., however, had been kept up most of the night by his Chinese mistress, on whom he had tried his judgments. She always nodded her approval, which is what he needed. He saw no reason not to faint, as it might get him off the parade next year. He had reckoned without the judges on either side of him. As he began to sway, they closed in on him and held him upright.

I had a wreath to lay, on behalf of the judiciary. It was made of poppies and was slightly smaller than the one laid by the Governor and slightly larger than that produced by the unofficial members. I stood waiting while the Governor laid his wreath, wondering if, in his tight trousers, there was any chance that he might fall. Unfortunately, this never happened, in spite of my hopes. I was supposed to lay a wreath after the Governor. It did not always work like that. On one occasion, no wreath was put into my hand, as it usually was, by one of the Supreme Court clerks. By mistake he handed it to the judge standing next to me, who at first did not know what to do with it. By the time he passed it to me, the unofficial member who was to follow me was well in front. We raced for the Cenotaph. I won because he tripped on the first step and released an oath in Cantonese.

At the end of the service, the judges returned to the Supreme Court, where I thanked them all for coming. It was a vain attempt to ensure that they would all attend the following year.

Chapter 12
Solicitor-General

When the Colonial Office had offered me this vacancy, it had contrived to make it sound interesting. In particular, I was to assist the Attorney-General, whose wide range of responsibilities was listed. I was not told, as I soon discovered, that he was either capable of discharging these various duties himself or had already delegated them to experienced men, who would not welcome my interference.

I was, like any good public servant, prepared to grumble on my arrival about the way in which I had been misled. The salary was generous, my quarters were spacious and well furnished, the school for my daughter was excellent and close nearby. None of this, of course, prevented me from complaining. I found a ready audience for this, though everyone melted away when I said something laudatory.

'The Colonial Office is out of touch. I don't suppose anyone from the office has been out here for years.' I said this with the sort of sneer which my mother had used when looking at one of the girls I had taken home.

Everyone who heard me nodded. My strictures would have been correct thirty years before, when the only way to Hong Kong was by steamer which took a month. It was true no longer, as a member of the Hong Kong department of the Colonial Office had visited the Colony shortly before and had developed an unmistakable dose of clap while carrying out a personal research of the social conditions in Wanchai, the home of the bars and brothels at the time. As he told his colleagues, on his release from hospital, it was the cracked cups which were responsible.

I was, in spite of my feeling of annoyance that I was unable to complain that I had been misled, full of enthusiasm when I walked from my hotel to the Central Government Offices, in Lower Albert Road, in which the Attorney-General had his offices on the second floor.

In the main hall, on the ground floor, I was stopped by a messenger, dressed in a dark blue uniform, which closely resembled that worn by prison warders.

'Do you want to speak to someone, sir?' he asked. He was most courteous, but I was on the defensive. That is the effect which any uniform has had on me since 1942, when I first met and loathed one of those non-commissioned officers in the army who make your life a misery.

'No, well, not really.'

'This is the Central Government Office, Lower Albert Road. The tram to the Peak is over there, underneath St John's Building.'

'Yes, but –'

'This building was opened by His Excellency in 1954. But it is not open to the public, because it has a number of Government departments.'

'Is the Legal Department here?'

'Have you an appointment?'

'No, but I hope they are expecting me. I'm supposed to have an office there.'

'Then you have an identity card?'

'Not yet, I'm afraid. I only arrived here yesterday.'

'Ah, so,' he replied in a suspicious voice.

'It was the *Cathay*,' I explained, thinking that he might be persuaded to let me in, if he knew rather more about my voyage. 'I had an outside cabin, which gave me an excellent view, except at night or when it was misty.'

'No card, no office,' he said firmly. 'If you give me your name, I will call the information officer.' I nodded. The attendant was only doing his job, I reminded myself, fighting back the urge to batter him to death in as painful a manner as possible.

I was waiting for the information officer when Morley-John arrived, sweating gently, as he seemed to do whatever the climate was.

'Hallo, S.G.,' he said. 'I do hope you were not waiting for me.'

'I thought it better,' I replied.

'Let's go and find your office. Did you have any trouble getting in?'

'Yes. You will be pleased to know that the attendant would not let me past. He is fetching someone he called the information officer.'

'That's the security chap. He vets anyone who asks for the Legal Department. Last year someone forced his way in there and demanded to see the Deputy Public Prosecutor. He was shouting that he was being victimized.'

'Was he?'

'Well, actually, yes. But this alerted us to how easy it is to get into the department.'

A year or so later, after a sharp struggle with the Financial Secretary, who was convinced that this was a device for establishing new and unnecessary posts, I managed to station two of the office attendants on the floor of the Attorney-General's chambers, as I insisted that the department should be called. This change of name was one of my few achievements during four years of office as Solicitor-General.

It would be pleasant to be able to claim that the office attendants were effective. No doubt they were, when present. As they spent much of the day making tea, which was later sold at fifty cents a cup, their effectiveness as a barrier against unwelcome visitors was intermittent.

Morley-John looked untidy as he led me to the second floor. This cheered me. I only discovered later that he always looked as if he had just soiled his shirt, even if there was no reason for it. He led me along a passageway, on the walls of which was a line of photographs of past Attorney-Generals. At the end, on the left, was a door which carried a tack, attached to which was a notice reading 'Acting Solicitor-General'.

'You won't need that,' said Morley-John, putting the notice in his pocket. 'Everyone will know who you are. They learn fast in Hong Kong.'

'I am sure that mothers will soon be telling their children that, if they don't behave themselves, Roberts will come for them.'

Morley-John laughed briefly and pointed to the desk. It was empty, except for a blotter, which was spattered with drops of ink.

'Are you a smoker?' he asked. I thought the question unnecessary as I was holding a half smoked cigarette in my hand. This was before the days when smokers became defensive when asked about the habit.

'Intermittently,' I replied. 'I happen to be smoking at the moment.' It would only have complicated matters to have told him of the eleven occasions when I had given up.

'Good.' Then you won't mind about the burns. I did try to get the desk top repaired, but all they did was to send me forms to fill in. It's been like that for months, ever since Maurice Heenan went next door. He is not very reliable with a pipe.'

'It's a relief to see there is no backlog.' I gestured at the empty desk. 'I'm sure that is entirely due to your efforts. I expect you've been working late every night to make certain I didn't have too much to do.'

Morley-John had a red face at all times. It went somewhat redder.

'The desk is a little misleading, I'm afraid. I had to leave a few things for you. Your secretary has got them. There is a bell under your desk. Press that and she will come. At least, she will if she has nothing better to do, like going to the lavatory or making up her face. She also does work for the A.G., so she may say she is too busy to attend to you. Most of the time, she knits. Her shorthand is excellent and her knitting is even better. Her name is Mrs Wilson, but she answers to Margaret as well.'

'Where is the A.G.'s office?'

'Across the passage. He won't be in yet. He keeps odd hours. Probably because he is a New Zealander.' Morley-John never explained what this meant. 'Comes in about ten and stays until seven. Please excuse me as I have to go to court.'

'An awkward case?'

'It would have been, but it won't be now. I'm going to tell the judge that we do not intend to prosecute. I just hope that he will agree quietly.'

'Surely he has no choice?'

'I know that. So does everyone else. He doesn't. I'll have to persuade him that it's for the prosecutor to decide whether to go on or not. I will pretend it's a new point. That seems to reassure him. We call him "Daddy". He's really very nice. It's just that he can't make up his mind about anything.'

I rang for Margaret, who appeared after an interval, which made it clear that she would come when it suited her to do so. She was a dark, handsome Eurasian girl. She wore glasses with black rims which made her look studious and a tight fitting cheongsam which did not. She walked into the office, partly concealed behind a large pile of files, which she placed on my desk with a sigh of relief.

'I'm Margaret,' she said. 'I'm your secretary. Just press the buzzer if you need me and I'll come if I'm not busy. Please have a look at the files. Mr Morley-John says he has been too busy to deal with any of them. So I expect they are all urgent!' Margaret was right.

Others in the chambers were almost as important as Margaret. Mr Choi, who was in charge of drinks, was essential. It is not possible for a civil servant to manage without tea, especially if you do not have enough to do. There was another buzzer for Mr Choi, which I rang twice a day. He entered without knocking, as usual. If I had been carrying on an intrigue from the office, I would not have got away with it.

'More tea?' he would ask, having looked pointedly at my empty out-tray.

'Coffee,' I replied, more to assert myself than because I wanted it. Mr Choi made me feel insecure.

'No coffee. Only tea. Mr Molo-Jo had the tea.'

'I would prefer coffee.'

'I try to find some, just for you.' Mr Choi brought me tea. The profit on it was larger than on coffee.

The chief clerk was a small, dapper Eurasian named Francis Silva. He was in charge of the registry which served the chambers. He spent most of his time making life agreeable for the twenty or so counsel who then composed the chambers, filling in forms for them, posting their letters, buying their presents and taking their messages. He was indispensable.

'Mr Silva,' I said one morning. 'I have done a dreadful thing.'

'Oh dear. I expect you have filled in your application for a driving licence wrongly. Never mind, I have another form in my office.'

'Worse than that. Tomorrow is Mother's Day. My daughter has forgotten to get anything. She has done a picture of a mother dragon with its babies, but I doubt if this is enough.'

'I have already got two Mother's Day presents, one for Mrs Carter and one for Mrs Tibbets.'

'What were they?'

'A fluffy kiwi and a fluffy kangaroo called Joey. The kiwi has no name, I'm afraid.'

'What would Mrs Carter and Mrs Tibbets do with fluffy toys, even if they do come from New Zealand and Australia?'

'I got the same for them last year, Mr Roberts. They were a great success. Mother gives the toy back to the child to look after for her and everyone is happy.'

'I don't think fluffy toys are a good idea, Mr Silva. What about some chocolate? I know my wife eats it.'

'What is your favourite brand?' asked Silva, who suspected where the chocolate would make its way to.

'Chocolate toffees would be best, I think, though I couldn't get any of them last week.'

'Leave it to me, Mr Roberts. I will find something suitable.'

Later that morning he laid on my desk a tin of chocolate caramels. These were well received by my daughter, who thought them most suitable for my wife, whom she knew did not like them.

The following night, my daughter found the tin and was violently ill from an overdose of caramel. I was up for most of the night looking after her as my wife said that, as I had been unwise enough to bring home the caramel, I could look after my daughter. The next year, I took home a fluffy toy.

Mr Silva played the violin. I do not think he had practised for the past twenty years. His music, if you could distinguish it, consisted mainly of tunes from the classics. He took his violin to every chambers party and hid it modestly behind his chair.

At the end of dinner, he would be asked to play. I had been told that this was one of the S.G.'s tasks and probably my most important one.

'I don't think I should,' he replied, showing a reluctance which he did not feel. He had a burning desire to perform.

'What about Handel's "Largo"?'

'I haven't brought the music for it.'

'I'm sure you can manage without that. You must remember it well.' The first comment was correct, as he never brought any music. The second was not.

'I just happen to have brought my violin with me. So, I will do the best I can without music or practice.'

Mr Silva played Handel's 'Largo' with great feeling. He tried, and failed, to hold back his tears as he murdered the 'Largo' and Brahms' 'Lullaby', which was his usual encore. He was never asked for a third piece. I doubt if he had one in reserve.

The files which Margaret had brought me were examples of the sort of work which was sent to me during the next four years. Several of them dealt with personnel matters, which absorbed much of my time, mainly because nobody else would deal with them. There was, for example, a Treasury circular about the hours of work and the leave entitlements of office attendants, with frequent references to the 'exigencies of the service', a phrase which appeared to be used whenever 'no' was intended.

There was a Colonial Office report on a Mr Johnson, serving in Uganda, who was interested in a transfer to Hong Kong. He was described by his superiors as disinclined to work, resistant to instructions and fonder of alcohol than of his wife. I decided that a bloody minded, lazy alcoholic would be perfect for Hong Kong. We were very short at the time. If he became intolerable, we could transfer him to the judiciary or the Registrar General's Department.

The next bundle of files contained a number of requests for my consent to prosecutions. Some of these were months old. As I later discovered, these took place anyway, as it had been shown to be unwise to wait for the S.G. to reply.

There were two thick files, on which my advice was sought, on a criminal matter. In Gibraltar, if the case was difficult, I would send it outside to the member of the local Bar who was to prosecute. This was not yet the Hong Kong method. I read both files with care. Each involved the minute examination of accounts. My predecessor had already advised twice. As I did not understand the figures, I passed the file back to the D.P.P., suggesting that it was essentially a matter for him to decide. I think he was trying me out.

Several files dealt with drafting matters. I was experienced in this, as I had used scissors and paste to incorporate a number of UK Acts into the law of Gibraltar. With the exception of the law draftsman himself, and his senior assistants, the bulk of the draftsmen were in his section, either because nobody else could think what to do with them or because they were too pleasant to get rid of or were nearing the end of a contract which would not be renewed. Some of the drafts submitted to me for clearance were not comprehensible. I therefore spent some of my time redrafting them. Some years later, from the bench, having failed to make any sense of a section, I enquired bitterly who had drafted such a dreadful provision, to be told that it was one of my drafts.

I was asked for advice in other matters by Government departments which usually wanted to do something illegal or impracticable or both. A short, succinct opinion was not well regarded, since this showed that a proper importance had not been given to the problem posed. It was not sufficient merely to tell the department what it could do. This had to be included in a long opinion which should show that the question was a difficult one. The counsel who had answered 'no' when asked if the Marine Department could seize the *Queen Mary* for going too fast in the harbour was transferred to drafting, where he could do less damage.

Another responsibility was the library, a room much used by Crown Counsel as a place in which to sleep without disturbance after a rough night or a busy morning. There were books, but these were seldom used. I was able to improve it considerably, by importing chairs so that counsel could sleep better, instead of the straight backed ones with which they had been obliged to manage before. I also managed to persuade the Treasury that a library should contain books, which was not easy. It was therefore filled with reports and text books, which were used by counsel from time to time to confuse the judges.

Before long, I had worked out a pattern for the day, one which would, I hoped, give me a reputation for energy without too much effort on my part to earn it. I arrived at half past eight, well before anyone else except for the office attendants and the odd Crown

Counsel who was appearing in court at ten and had left his papers behind.

For a few months, I lived in a flat near the top of the Peak tram and took two hours for lunch, as nobody was then in his office to answer my calls if I was unwise enough to make any then. When I moved from there to Middle Gap Road, I stayed in the office and munched an apple. This helped to foster the mistaken belief that I remained at my desk to keep up with my work. It was not known that I slept on most days. I locked the door, so that I was not disturbed, and the office attendants would assume I was working on confidential matters.

The official day ended at five o'clock. At five minutes to five Stewart Collier, who took me home to Middle Gap Road in his car, knocked on the door and asked if I was ready to go. Collier was a gifted prosecutor, and a man of many skills outside his work. After a couple of clashes with judges whom he regarded as slow and obstructive without making much effort to conceal his view, he had been transferred to the drafting section. He did not welcome this. He was not a good draftsman. He was, however, an excellent driver. He drove a maroon sports car, which he maintained himself, and donned his driving gloves to drive. Some years later, he became so disillusioned with drafting that he arranged a transfer to the District Court.

I soon discovered that there was hardly enough work to keep me busy, unless I went looking for it. Maurice Heenan seldom bothered me, except on formal matters which he was too busy to deal with himself. The three main sections, prosecutions, law drafting and civil cases, were run by counsel who needed no help, though they gave me insoluble matters from time to time, rather as a bone is thrown to a dog. I was sometimes asked to go to court, or to give advice when a law officer was expected to reply.

As the department expanded, I became more of a personnel officer involved with matters which I had not handled before. Sometimes, this work was of interest. Margaret Wilson came into my office one morning. I had not pressed the buzzer for her. She closed the door behind her and spoke out of the corner of her mouth.

'It's Miss Collins,' she said.

'What is?'

'She's in trouble.'

'Look, Mrs Wilson. I know that I deal with personnel matters. But I can hardly ring up the hospital and arrange an abortion appointment.'

'It's not that kind of trouble. She phoned me up and asked me if I had the file she gave me.'

'Well, have you?'

'Of course not. It's a code. It means she is in trouble. When I went to her office, the door was locked and a man's voice told me to... to...'

'Go on, you can say it to me.'

'Bugger off,' she said, blushing prettily. 'So, would you please go along and get her out?'

'Perhaps she wants the man to stay?'

'Certainly not. She would not have phoned me if she did.'

I knocked at Miss Collins' door twice without response, except for being given the same instructions as Mrs Wilson. The third time, I said who I was and that I had sent for the police. The door was opened by a man who was naked above the waist. He was wearing tattered shorts and soiled gym shoes. He glared at me aggressively.

'You must be cold in the air conditioning,' I suggested. I could think of nothing else to say.

'What if I am?' The man was taller than me and had well developed biceps.

'I thought you'd like to go somewhere else where it is warmer.'

'Yeah. Like Darwin. She's frigid.' He pointed angrily at Miss Collins, who was holding on to the filing cabinet as if it comforted her in some way.

'Is that correct?' I asked her. She nodded vigorously. 'There you are,' I added, 'you're wasting your time with her.'

'You're right, mate. The sooner I find a hot sheila the better.' He grasped my hand, shook it violently and left, smelling strongly of sweat.

'I don't think he'll come back,' I said, rather pleased with myself.

'I don't suppose he will now.' Nor did he. She did not seem to be at all grateful.

One morning I came in early to find a woman asleep on the floor behind my desk. She was wearing blood stained bandages round her wrists. She had cut them with a razor but, fortunately, not deeply. I had met her once or twice at the home of the Crown Counsel, who had employed her to look after his children when his wife had left. She was Swedish and had fallen in love with her employer. He had told her that she was engaged to look after the children and not to become his wife. She had chosen this way of making him feel sorry for her. I hurried her to a doctor, who cleaned her wrists, replaced her bandages and told her not to do it again. It was not, he said, a serious attempt.

'Birgitte,' I said, 'why did you do this?' I found out later that her name was Vela, though this did not seem to matter.

'To make him love me,' she replied, bursting into tears.

'That's not much use if you are dead, is it?'

'I did not mean to kill myself, only to frighten him. Now I shall have to do it all again.'

I saw Lionel Brent, her employer, later in the day and told him what had happened.

'So that's where she got to last night,' he commented. 'I had to get a neighbour to look after the children this morning.'

'She says she is in love with you, Lionel, unlikely though this may seem.'

'I've told her that she is supposed to look after the children, not me.'

'She doesn't believe you. Don't you think she'd better go home to Sweden? She seems to be rather unstable.'

'I suppose you mean that anyone who tried to kill themselves for me must be round the bend, do you?'

I returned to Birgitte, who had been put in the YWCA, at my request.

'I've spoken to Lionel,' I began.

'He hates me,' she interrupted, bursting into tears again.

'He does not. He has given me your ticket back to Sweden.' I handed it to her. 'He told me how flattered he was that you should think he is good enough to die for, but he is not worthy of you and thinks you ought to go home.'

This pompous nonsense seemed to satisfy her. She left for Sweden the next day. Two years later she sent me a Christmas card saying 'Married last month, very happy. Vela (Birgitte)'. The card arrived in June.

Chapter 13

Opening of the legal year

It was the custom to celebrate the opening of the legal year in January. This was known as the Irish solution, as the legal year had already started in September, when some judges and counsel were still on holiday. The ceremonies began with two church services, in the middle of the morning, one for the Catholics and one for the Protestants. This was followed by a parade of troops, inspected outside the Supreme Court by the C.J.

Afterwards, there was an address by the C.J. followed by others from the A.G., the Bar and the Law Society. This took place in the main court in the Supreme Court building. The acoustics were so unsatisfactory that little of what was said was heard. This part of the ceremonies was attended by members of the judiciary, the A.G.'s chambers, the consular corps and the legal profession, in conditions of which the commandant of a concentration camp would have been proud.

Each year, Sir Michael Hogan, the C.J., delivered a stream of figures of cases. He was much admired for his memory, as he never seemed to have to refer to a note. He probably did not need one, as his recall was total. Each year, after reciting these figures, he held the Attorney-General responsible for the various matters which the C.J. hoped would be put right in the coming year.

After the other speeches, which consisted mainly of telling the C.J. how effective the judiciary had been in the previous year, which nobody believed, a reception was given by the C.J., using his chambers, those of his secretary and those of the senior puisne judge.

In 1967, when I first attended as A.G., I did little but smile happily and thank the C.J. for his gracious speech. In January 1968, however, I used the opening of the legal year as an opportunity to announce an amnesty, lasting a month, for anyone who surrendered arms, ammunition or explosives, possession of which would normally attract a heavy prison sentence. Not surprisingly, my speech had, for once, driven Sir Michael Hogan from the front page. His remarks were as persuasive as ever, if you could decide what he meant to say.

Some days later, he called me to his chambers to discuss, as he put it, a 'number of matters which are still outstanding between us'. I had attended these meetings before. He did not start with what was really troubling him, but with another matter of lesser significance. This time, he opened with the transfer of Pike.

'I am rather short of magistrates. Do you have trouble in finding sufficient Crown Counsel?'

'We've started to recruit in Australia and New Zealand, C.J.'

Although he used the oblique reply himself, he was not keen on others employing the same device.

'Dangerous,' he said. 'I expect I shall have to do it myself, sooner or later, but not yet. I would rather keep to the traditional sources.'

'Like Ireland? I know there's a lot of unemployment there.'

'We must not', Hogan corrected, 'assume that people enter the Colonial Service only because they cannot make a living any other way.'

'I'm sorry, C.J. It's certainly why I joined, but I'm sure that others, like yourself, are different.'

'Maybe,' he conceded. 'I wish I could say the same about Pike.'

'Yes. I've heard complaints about him from counsel. He's rather a poor magistrate, they say, but not much worse than the others.'

'In what way do they say he is unsatisfactory?'

'It's the sort of thing counsel usually says when he has just lost a case.'

'Do go on, Denys,' said the C.J. 'It's sometimes useful to have an outside view of the judiciary.'

'Pike is said to be unpunctual, to make up his mind too early, to be brusque with counsel and to acquit a lot of villains. So he seems to have the usual judicial characteristics.'

'No rumours of drink or women?'

'I haven't heard that. He's a bachelor, so I expect he has too much of both.'

'I have been told that he is too fond of women.'

'Perhaps that's why he is unpunctual.'

'Do you know,' Hogan sounded indignant, 'he actually chases women.'

'I suppose we should be thankful that it's not boys, C.J.'

'I don't think you are taking me seriously enough, Denys. This fellow Pike went so far as to follow a woman onto a bus, outside his magistracy.'

'Good gracious, how terrible!' These comments seemed to be expected of me.

'Unfortunately for Pike, it was the wife of a new magistrate. She's only been married a year and was most upset.'

'I expect it's just an isolated event, C.J. He'll settle down and become a normal incompetent lecher, like the rest of us.'

'That's not all,' he went on, ignoring me. 'At Christmas we had our usual reception for the staff. I found Pike and one of the stenographers kissing in the garden.'

'Perhaps it was the mistletoe.'

'There was none in the garden. If there had been, it would not have explained why the girl's knickers were round her ankles.'

'It's the sort of thing that happens at our office parties too, C.J.'

'But we can't have this in the judiciary, can we?' I agreed. 'We must try to maintain a good reputation.' I nodded. 'So far, we have been fortunate. Next time, Pike may involve himself with a member of the public and there will be a scandal. So what would you do?'

'Call him in and shout at him?'

'I've tried that. He says he'll do his best but the girls pursue him. I don't believe him.'

'End his contract?'

'I don't like to do that. He will make a fuss. He'll probably go to the papers. One of the women he has – um – pursued is a reporter on the *South China Morning Post*. I thought you might be able to help me.'

'If I can, of course.'

'I knew you would see it my way, my dear fellow. You can hide counsel in the advisory or drafting sections. I can't hide a magistrate anywhere. He's always in the public eye. Everyone gets to know him. So can I tell Pike that we have discussed him and that you have agreed to accede to his wish for a transfer to the Legal Department?'

'Has he asked for this?'

'Not yet,' Hogan agreed, 'but he will.'

Pike did. For the next two years he drafted, and pursued a variety of women. At the end of his contract, he did not renew. He told me that there must be easier ways of earning a living, like collecting garbage or being a lavatory attendant.

'Sometimes', Hogan went on, steepling his hands, 'I feel quite remote from the real issues.'

'I am sure that you are not.'

'No doubt that is why I give the opening of the legal year rather more importance that it really warrants. How do you think it went this year?'

'As well as it always does, C.J.' I guessed he would soon be coming to the real point of the meeting.

'Your speech was most compelling, of course, and so well put. I hope the amnesty has been a success?'

'A lot of arms have been surrendered.'

'Did you happen to notice radio and press coverage of the legal year this time?'

'I rather think I did.'

'What you said was well reported. Naturally, it was of some general interest. So I am not criticizing the press when I say that I received a somewhat smaller coverage than usual myself.'

'I'm sure that isn't really so, C.J., though the press are very unreliable. What you said was beautifully put, if I may say so.'

'I fear that the competition was too much for me this year. I just wonder, and it is entirely a matter for you, of course, if you would consider whether, in future, the Attorney ought to discuss matters of general importance on a day reserved for the law?'

In his usual courteous, firm and circuitous manner, the C.J. was telling me to speak shortly at the opening of the legal year and leave the press to him. I did not try to compete again with him or with his successors. When eventually I succeeded him, I realized how right he had been.

Opening of the legal year (from *South China Morning Post*)

Sir Geoffrey Briggs, my predecessor as C.J., retained the church services, at the insistence of the Registrar. The latter argued that it would be bad for the public image of judges, who were thought to be practising Christians, as well as wise, patient, courteous and learned. It is as well that he did not know what people really believed. In the past, two separate annual services had been held. It was decided to hold only one a year, alternately in the Catholic cathedral and in the Anglican cathedral; this arrangement seems to have been fair and reasonable as it upset members of both sects.

The first year, to prove that I had an open mind, so far as religion is concerned that is, the service was held in the Catholic cathedral. I had been there once before, to attend the funeral mass given for a bishop whom I knew and respected. I was suffering from a heavy cold and blew my nose several times. As I was doing this, my picture was taken by one of the photographers who were allowed to operate during a service. The photo appeared in one of the papers the next morning with the caption 'Roberts overcome with grief at funeral'. It brought me much credit with those who thought I was not capable of emotion.

I was therefore well prepared to have my picture taken in the cathedral. This happened whenever the service was held. Each time, my periwig looked more ragged and ill fitting, as it was. I had bought it from Maurice Heenan, who got it from his predecessor, who picked it up from a deceased judge in Nigeria. It looked as if it had been buried with him. According to the discoloured label on the periwig, it had been made for Nathaniel Potts Esq. The steel box in which it came bore the name E. E. Dalrymple Q.C. Nobody knew anything of either of them or whom the wig had been made for. It is therefore not surprising that it did not fit me.

As it was a non-denominational service, the preacher came from the other faith. Whoever he was, he always reminded the judges, probably taking as his text the phrase 'Judge not, that you be not judged', that they would have to answer for their own misdeeds, in due course, when they came themselves before the great judge. By the time the preacher had finished his address, it was clear that the judges were sinful, weak, merciless and wholly unsuitable and that the maxim 'Do unto others as you would have others do to you' was not being observed by them. I left the service feeling humble and inadequate. This did not last long. Within a few minutes, I was in a sullen humour again.

This began with the car parking. Neither cathedral was built when cars had been invented, though efforts were made to ensure that the judicial procession should be able to leave in an orderly way. No doubt this would have worked at the end of the first service at the Catholic cathedral if the exit had not been blocked by a car which had broken down and belonged to a reporter who had arrived late. It took several minutes to move the car, which was damaged in a most satisfactory way before it came to rest in a drain at the bottom of the hill which led to the cathedral.

The police force was most helpful, whatever they may have thought of a judiciary which seemed to have an unpleasant habit of disbelieving many of its members. It therefore stopped all traffic some minutes before the judicial procession was due, on its way from the religious service to Edinburgh Place, where a guard of honour was to be inspected by the C.J.

The public, which knew nothing of legal years, had no idea why cars were not allowed to drive along some of the principal routes during the afternoon. They responded in their usual restrained way, by leaning on their horns, if these were still working, and shaking their fists at the traffic constable who was preventing them from going any further.

We therefore drove to City Hall through a mob of angry motorists at each cross-roads. At least this inconvenience informed some members of the public that it was a day of celebration, as well as giving pleasure to the judges. I was hot in my periwig; my buckle shoes hurt; my tights were twisted. If someone else suffered as well, I felt slightly better.

At the City Hall, the judges were ushered to a screened-off area at the back where tea was served while we waited for the rest of the judges to arrive. Some people never seem to learn from experience. I do not. Year after year, I drank two or three cups of tea while I was waiting, knowing that half way through the speeches I should need to get rid of the liquid. The speeches themselves were seldom of sufficient interest to divert my attention from my bladder, so that I twisted and wriggled in acute discomfort, until my own speech at the end, when it disappeared.

The judges left the tea area and assembled in Edinburgh Place for the inspection of the guard. This was provided by members of the local military service corps, who had been issued with new uniforms and especially polished boots for the occasion.

The inspection of a guard of honour presents the inspector with a problem. Should he actually inspect its members, which means saying 'Polish those boots', 'Get that rifle sling tightened', 'Stomach in, lad' and 'What a shower'. Or would it be wiser to walk round the guard slowly, pausing in front of selected soldiers and appearing to look closely at them before passing on? I adopted this method for the first couple of years, until the man I was scrutinizing carefully fainted. After that I kept moving.

At the end of the inspection, I thanked the guard commander for a fine parade, a phrase which I used every year irrespective of the state of the guard. It was always well received.

I returned to the rooms behind the tea area, where the judges waited until those who attended the inspection of the guard, and their guests who had been invited to the concert hall, had taken their places.

The numbers for each part of the ceremonies were different. About 800 were asked to the cathedral, experience having shown that 600 would accept and 200 or so would arrive. Some 1,500 were asked to the concert hall and to the reception. About 800 went to the concert hall, knowing that they would have to listen to several speeches, and over 1,000 attended the reception, which was held upstairs.

The procession of judges wandered through a multi-storey car park to the back of the stage. Those who were to sit on the platform with them were taken on first. The curtains were open throughout. The committee planning the event rejected my suggestion that everyone should be seated on stage before the curtains were raised and that a suitable fanfare should be provided, preferably as I entered, followed by a male voice choir singing something suitable in the background. The committee was influenced by the fall of a silk, who tripped over the wires backstage and commented on this in foul language.

In the early years of its use, most of the seats in the gallery were unoccupied, except by those who had arrived late and were not allowed to enter the downstairs part of the hall. It was therefore decided that schools should be invited to fill these seats, in the belief that this would impress upon them the importance of the courts in their society.

Soon after they had first attended, a hundred or so of them were asked to comment on what they had learned. A majority had no idea of why they had been invited, though they were in favour of coming, as it was during school hours and saved them from having to study maths instead. Several said that those on the platform looked odd in their unusual dress, which must be uncomfortable, as they had to wear it every day. Others said that they now knew that Europeans could make long speeches. They had no idea of what had been said, but the speeches seemed to be full of long words which they had not come across before. They had greatly enjoyed the reception. The fact that they had not been invited to this did not prevent them from coming in as nobody stopped them. The food was good.

Every year, there was a stream of guests arriving during the first speech, made by the President of the Law Society. Some of the members of the audience were being trampled on by the newcomers, so that his remarks were punctuated by cries of pain as the latter trod on the feet of the earlier arrivals. Many of the audience turned to see who had come in late and what hats the latecomers, if female, were wearing.

In later years, nobody was supposed to be admitted during his speech, and ushers were stationed at the back to refuse entry to anyone who was late. It was like seeing a dam burst. A wall of people, up to a hundred strong, surged into the concert hall as the Law Society representative sat down. Thus the audience for the next speaker, the Bar representative, was much larger. The Law Society speaker was unhappy. The previous system of an uncontrolled shambles at the back was reinstituted. As few people listened to what he had to say, little was lost. He received applause each year thereafter, much of it in sympathy for the fact that he had been interrupted so often.

The next speech was made by the Chairman of the Bar Association. This usually consisted of a list of matters which either the C.J. or the Government, or preferably both, should put right during the coming year. It was a disgrace that nothing had been done before.

The Attorney-General followed him, not necessarily because he had anything of importance to say but because he was senior to the others, a factor of some importance. He had seen a draft of all the speeches before they were delivered. He was therefore able to give a series of undertakings, on behalf of the Government, that the various matters raised by the profession would be carefully considered and the appropriate action would be taken. What he really meant, and this was well understood, was that nothing at all would be done about the complaints which had been aired. The A.G. was expected to finish, as indeed he did with his tongue in his cheek, with a rousing tribute to the judiciary, to its eminent service to the community, to the prevalence in a multi-racial society of the rule of law, and to its independence.

Initially, each of the first three speakers was asked to limit himself to five minutes, so allowing half an hour to the C.J., since three-quarters of an hour of listening was more than enough for an audience which was looking at its watches and wondering when the reception would start, as most of them could do with a drink. Each year, the three preceding speeches became longer.

The days when Sir Michael Hogan spoke for over an hour were gone. The C.J. limited himself to less than thirty minutes, though he found it difficult to speak for a shorter time as there were many to thank and a series of statistics to deliver, showing how busy the judiciary had been in the past year.

As few people were listening to the last half of his speech, he used this to mention anything which was unpopular, so that he could later protest that he had raised the subject during the course of his annual speech. He concluded with a graceful tribute to his colleagues, thanking them warmly for all they had done in the past year.

The C.J. was clapped at the end of his speech. On the first occasion, warmed by the reception given to him, he mentioned this to the Registrar, who assured him that part of it was due, of course, to the wit and content of his admirable speech, but the Registrar felt obliged to say that most of the applause was due to the relief that there were no more speeches to come and keen anticipation of the reception.

The procession from the stage made its way to the reception hall upstairs. Here the Chief Justice was supposed to greet his guests, before they swooped on the trays of drink which were held by the waitresses. First, the guests, waiting with dry mouths, were stacked up on the stairs leading to the reception, while the C.J. greeted other guests, who had elbowed their way to the front. Each of them, as he entered the room, felt obliged to congratulate the C.J. on the success of the day and for his fine speech, which had addressed the main problems which faced the judiciary with such aplomb. The C.J. rather liked this and made no effort to hurry, until the Registrar reminded him that a lot of people were waiting to get in.

The C.J. found that, by the time he had greeted all the guests and a number of uninvited people, some were leaving. They talked with him on the way out, so that he was not able to move from the door. The second year, the C.J. shook each guest's hand, said that he must not keep him as he realized how thirsty he must be and waved him toward the drinks. This seemed to work better.

The C.J. therefore abandoned his position at the door and stationed himself in the centre of the reception hall. At first, few people came to speak to him, so that he was left to wander round the hall on his own, talking to various groups, thanking them for coming and saying what a splendid day it had been.

As the evening progressed and the time for the end of the reception had passed, the C.J. found himself among the last hundred, who were more interested in food and drink than in the ceremonies. At this point, everyone spoke to him, telling him what a shambles it had been but that this did not matter so long as the reception was good.

Chapter 14
Looking for Dave

One of the odd duties undertaken by the S.G., as personnel officer, was to retrieve counsel from the restaurants or bars if they were needed urgently elsewhere.

Probably the most able prosecutor in the chambers was an Australian named David Earl. He was a man of mordant humour, who had formerly been Registrar of the High Court of Uganda. Dar Lyon was one of the judges of that court and was sitting in a small, remote town. He was accompanied by his second wife.

Lyon J. had been a fine batsman in his youth and still played the piano with much skill. He had been married twice to women who soon realized that these other accomplishments were more important to him than his marriages. Dave arranged for the first wife, who was visiting Uganda, to spend a night in the town where the judge was sitting, without informing her that the second wife was there as well. After the initial shock, the two women became firm friends, united by mutual suspicion of the judge, who was more effective as a pianist than as a husband. They left Uganda together. Dave was blamed for the collapse of Lyon's second marriage and was transferred to Hong Kong.

Dave had been prosecuting a member of one of the triad societies for theft and blackmail in one of the District Courts. It was unusual for Crown Counsel to appear there, as the bulk of cases was handled by two chief inspectors of police, Hidden and Smith, both much liked, greatly respected and highly competent. Although neither was legally qualified, they seemed to have little difficulty in arguing points of law. When they retired, they were replaced by Crown Counsel, who were far more expensive and probably less effective.

In theory, Dave was subject to the control of Dermot Rea, the D.P.P., a cheerful Irishman with mild haemophilia. He was prematurely bald and bled generously whenever he scratched his head. He knew Dave could safely be left to conduct a case, though Dave sometimes had to be reminded of when and where he was supposed to be.

'I'm sorry to trouble you,' said Dermot, coming to my office one afternoon. 'We can't find Dave.'

'Has he just finished a difficult case?' I asked. I knew something of Dave's habits.

Dermot nodded. He visited me sometimes to get me to agree with some decision which he had already made. He did this to give me face, not because he wanted to know what I thought. He had been in the East for a long time.

'It was, but it finished yesterday. He is supposed to be doing another case this morning, but he hasn't been seen in chambers all day.'

'He usually comes in the day after he's finished a case, doesn't he? Even if it's only for a few minutes to collect his letters?'

'He does. But we can't find him in any of his usual places. We tried them when his wife rang up to ask us if we knew where he was, because Dave did not go home last night.'

'If an Australian girl is worried, there must be good reason for it. Can we get any of his mates to go out and look for him?'

'It's after four, so there isn't anyone left in the prosecution section, except me. I even looked in the library. There had been a couple there but the librarian told me he was supposed to wake them up at three, which he did.'

'I suppose I'd better come with you,' I said reluctantly. 'I don't seem to be too busy.' I gestured at my empty desk. There were some files in the drawers because they were too difficult. Apart from them, I liked to have nothing left at the end of the day, even if this meant passing on a file to someone who did not know what to do with it.

'Before we go, Dermot, I'd better tell Maurice.'

'He knows all about Dave.'

'He does?'

'The last time that I told him that I couldn't find Dave, Maurice laughed and said he'd been with the Australians in North Africa and that they were impossible to control but managed very well if they were left alone.'

'Should we leave Dave alone, do you think?'

'We'd better find him now that his wife has phoned,' Dermot commented.

We left chambers in a taxi. Dermot explained that, if we went in his car and parked it outside a bar, most of the police force would know that he had been to Wanchai, and that he would be subjected to suggestive remarks.

For the next two hours or so we searched the area asking for Dave, starting at the 'Ocean Bar. Topless Girls Inside'. Inside the lights were dim, the drinks were watered and the girls expensive. I approached the bar, behind which were a plump woman in a bright red dress and a man with steel teeth.

'I am looking for Mr Dave Earl. I need to find him in a hurry.'

'You are police,' said the woman indignantly. 'Why do you come here and threaten us. We paid you last week.'

'Did you hear that, Dermot? They are making corrupt payments.'

'Of course they are. How else do you suppose they stay in business?'

'We must report this.'

'Not now, S.G., please. Let's try to find Dave first.'

'We are not police,' I said. 'We come from the Legal Department. We only want to help him.'

Steel teeth sniffed. He did not believe that anyone would do such an unusual thing unless he was well paid for it.

'Does he know you are looking for him?' he asked.

'Not yet. I haven't found him to tell him.'

'Mr Dave comes very often,' the woman explained. 'He drinks beer; he talks to the girls; he falls asleep. He will not go upstairs and have jig-a-jig with anyone.'

'I'm glad to hear it, of course. But has he been here today?'

'He was here yesterday, but he left when the tourists came.'

'The prices go up when that happens,' said Dermot.

We next visited the 'Happy Bar. Tourists Welcome. Bottomless Girls', which was twenty yards along the street from the Ocean Bar. In between were two shops, one selling shoes and the other sanitary fittings. The former had a notice saying 'No shoes sold without fits'. The latter had a pink bidet in the centre of the display window with a sign saying 'You can't be without one'. It did not explain what it was to be used for. I supposed it must have been for feet which were painful after the shoes bought next door had been worn.

As we entered the Happy Bar, I was seized by the arms and pulled towards a table. The bar was in almost total darkness. As I became accustomed to the gloom, I could see that some of the girls were past their prime, if they had ever had one. The girls at my table were young and eager for custom.

'I've only come for a drink,' I protested.

'Everybody say that,' replied the girl. 'Me Angela.' The girl on the other side, who looked heavily made up in the gloom and reminded me of Fagin, answered, 'Me Melanie.'

'Me give you a good time,' said Angela. 'Me give you better one,' replied Melanie.

'I am only here', I explained, 'to look for Dave Earl. Do sit down, Dermot, and stop laughing, You are not being any help to me at all.'

'It's only wind, S.G.,' he explained. 'That's why I'm standing.'

'Me thirsty,' Melanie said. 'First drink, then jig-a-jig.'

'I came here to look for someone.'

'Like me?' Melanie giggled.

'No. We want Mr David Earl.'

'Drink first.' I bought a round of drinks which cost rather more than a bottle of champagne in an expensive hotel. Both of the girls insisted on ordering whisky. I expect they got cold tea, but there was no reduction in price.

'Do you know Mr Earl?' I asked after the girls had sipped their drinks.

'You pay me for jig-a-jig first,' Angela suggested.

'No. I don't want to do anything but find Mr Earl.'

Dermot handed her a note. 'All right,' she said. 'I'll find out.'

She returned to the table with a short, tough looking man.

'Who you want?' he demanded.

'Mr David Earl.'

'You from the Urban Council?'

'Certainly not.'

'I have licence.' He put a crumpled paper on the table. This permitted the person named, which was indecipherable, to conduct a bar at another address three years before. Under the licence was a $100 note.

'I'm not interested in that.'

'OK. You're from the police. Your friend wants another hundred?'

'Rather,' said Dermot.

'Take the money back,' I shouted. 'It is wrong to offer a bribe to a public officer.'

'You do not mean that,' he replied. 'Ah, I've got it. You are Social Welfare.'

'I am not.'

'You want to know the age of Angela. I have her birth certificate.' He laid it on the table. I examined it out of curiosity. It referred to Mei Law as twenty-five. Angela looked fifteen.

'Her Chinese age is a year older.'

'The pregnancy is included,' Dermot whispered.

'Ah, now I see. You want Angela's green card.'

'That's what the services give girls, to show they haven't got the pox. They go to an army clinic each month and the doctor stamps the card. If the girl hasn't got it, that is. If she has, he gives her some pills instead.'

'Do you mean that these girls are whores, Dermot?'

'Never touch a girl unless she has an up-to-date card, S.G. Mind you, that isn't much of a protection, as there is a man at North Point who produces green cards that look exactly like the original. The army has changed the cards several times. That works for a bit but he soon catches up.'

'Who is the squat man who keeps offering us money, Dermot?'

'He's the ponce, I expect. I'll ask him. Are you the pimp?'

'What you call me?'

'Are you the man who tells Angela when she can take a man upstairs for an hour?'

'Of course. You want? Angela is very clean girl. For policemen I make no charge.'

'Look at our trousers,' Dermot suggested. We were both wearing the dark grey pinstriped trousers which we affected for the office, partly because they were cheap and partly because they were supposed to show that we belonged to the legal profession.

The short man looked at them 'You want the girls to dress up?'

'When did you last see a police officer wearing trousers like this?' I enquired.

'Special branch wear funny clothes, so nobody knows who they are.'

'We'd better move on,' Dermot suggested. 'I'm afraid they don't know Dave here. Or if they do, they won't tell us.'

'Hey,' said the short man. 'Are you looking for Uncle Dave?'

'Am I, Dermot?'

'Probably.' I nodded.

'Why you not say so?'

'He was here yesterday,' said Angela.

'Why didn't you tell me that before?'

'You did not ask for Uncle Dave. Only for some Mr Earl.'

'Where is Uncle Dave now?'

'He leave yesterday. Very happy. He had plenty beers. I promise him free jig-a-jig but he left.'

'Where did he go?'

'I think Pussy Cat Bar. Very kind man, Uncle Dave. Never wants a girl. Only lots of beer.'

'That's him,' said Dermot. 'We've got the right man. Most Crown Counsel have it the other way around.'

I put $20 on the table. 'That's for your next round of cold tea,' I said to Angela.

'For you, no charge,' said the pimp, smiling broadly at me in a way which disclosed that he was badly short of teeth. He must have decided that I could make trouble for him. I'm sure it was the striped trousers. It was good to feel that, after all, they were justified.

I picked up the $20 before he changed his mind. Dermot, who seemed to know exactly where to go, led me to the Pussy Cat Bar. The bar was empty, save for a woman in a short skirt who was picking out her ear alongside a silent jukebox.

'No girls,' she announced after looking at Dermot and myself.

'We don't want girls,' I replied.

'No men either. The police take all my girls for inspection. Except those working upstairs, if you would like to wait.'

'I only want to ask –'

'Hey. Are you from Double X?'

'That's one of the smaller triad societies,' said Dermot. 'It controls most of the bars.'

'I paid last week. Now you want more money. And you let the police take all my girls. What do I pay you for? Nothing.'

'I'm dreadfully sorry that you've been let down so badly,' I replied. 'It really wasn't our fault. All we are doing is looking for Uncle Dave.'

'Uncle Dave? Why you not tell me? He is a lovely fellow. No girls, only beer.'

'Is he here, madam?'

'You can see he is not. He was here yesterday.'

'Did the police take him away, as well as your girls?'

'Of course not. The police like Uncle Dave. He went to the Long Legs. Bye-bye. You make them send back my girls.'

'I should have thought of that before,' said Dermot as we left. 'You take the second left, first right and it's the second bar you come to, just past the Topless World. It's where the members of the chambers usually go.'

'That's useful to know,' I commented sarcastically.

'You're not meant to know,' said Dermot. 'So please don't tell anyone. If you do, they'll all go somewhere else and I shan't know where to look for them.'

'All right. I'll keep quiet. But surely it's too expensive for them?' I remembered how much I'd had to pay in the Ocean Bar.

'They get a special price because everyone thinks that they are senior policemen, so the girls are respectful and the beer is cheap.'

Inside the 'Long Legs Bar – Very Cheap Drinks', the light was rather better. I could see across the tiny dance floor, on which two girls were locked together.

'Have you seen Uncle Dave?' I enquired of the girl who greeted us when we entered.

'Call me Lauren,' she said. 'You want a drink?'

'No, thanks, we –'

'No drink, no girl,' she replied archly.

'We want Uncle Dave.'

'You from the police?'

'No, no. Legal Department.'

'That's what they all say.' There was no point in trying to explain the distinction to her. I was becoming less sure that there was any.

'Uncle Dave is very nice. He does not jig-a-jig. He drinks beer. Sometimes he goes home and sometimes he sleeps here.'

'We only want to find him, I assure you.'

'You look like kind man, for a policeman,' said Lauren, 'so I will take you to see Uncle Dave.'

We followed her up a flight of stairs. She put her finger to her lips as she opened a door. Inside was Uncle Dave, sleeping deeply and noisily in bed. His jacket and shoes were on a chair beside it.

'As we have found him, Dermot, we'd better wake him up and tell him he's in court tomorrow.' Dermot shook Dave by the shoulder. He opened his eyes and looked at me.

'Have you come for a drink or a girl?' Dave asked.

Dermot intervened hastily. 'It's my fault, really. We got worried because nobody knew where you were. What is more, your wife phoned up.'

'What did she ring up for? She doesn't care what happens to me.'

'I expect she wants you to sign a cheque,' I suggested.

'Oh. Then I'd better go home, I suppose.'

'You promised me last year that you wouldn't bring the S.G. in again, after poor Hooton had to fight off the girls in the Pussy Cat Bar,' said Dave accusingly at Dermot.

'It wasn't my fault, Dave.'

'I expect that Hooton had some sort of animal magnetism.'

'Not him. Hey, what day is it?'

'Wednesday. You have a case in the District Court in the morning,' Dermot said. 'I hope you will be fit enough for that?'

'I always am, aren't I?'

'Well, yes,' Dermot admitted. 'But if we hadn't found you, you might have slept on and missed it.'

'You say my wife phoned. Did she say where you should look for me?'

'She said she didn't know.'

'Loyal old bat. She knows where I come after a case. But she doesn't like to tell anyone else.'

As we left, he pressed a note into Lauren's hand and made a sign at the man at the head of the stairs, who grinned at him and made no attempt to stop us.

'I gave him the triad sign,' Dave said, as we boarded a taxi. 'I keep in with the triads. They give us somebody to prosecute from time to time. This satisfies the cops who aren't getting a bit of squeeze themselves.'

'You mean that an innocent man may be convicted?' I asked. In spite of all the evidence to the contrary, I still believed there was a difference.

'No, no. He's not innocent. He belongs to another triad society. So if he goes to prison, the society looks after his family until he gets out.'

The taxi took us back to chambers. It was nearly seven when we arrived.

'I'll go and get my papers for the morning,' said Dave.

'I'll be in tomorrow morning early, just in case you need my help,' Dermot promised.

Dave turned and smiled at us. I realized why the bar girls loved him and why nobody bothered if he took time off after a case. It was one of the most charming smiles I have seen.

'I don't think I have thanked either of you for coming to look for me. I really do appreciate it.' He left us with a cheerful wave.

I went down the next morning to court and sat unobtrusively at the back. I wanted to see if Uncle Dave had recovered. He had. The way he conducted his case was impressive.

A couple of years later he retired on what he called medical grounds. In spite of my protests that he was more capable drunk than most counsel were when sober, he insisted on me certifying him as suffering from ill health from his addiction to drink. He soon built up a highly successful practice in Australia. When last I heard of him, he was a teetotaller.

Chapter 15

Going to court

I suppose that advocacy is similar to playing an instrument. If you do not practise regularly, you will not be much good! I tried the violin at fourteen; the piano at sixteen and fifty; the guitar at forty. A series of teachers, already expecting little of their pupils and seldom being disappointed, told me that whatever talents I had must lie elsewhere. My predecessor as S.G. often appeared in court. Some of my colleagues, whom I did not like better as a result, told me how effective he was.

I had not been in Hong Kong long when Dermot Rea came to see me.

'So, what has gone wrong this time?' I asked. Dermot seldom consulted me unless something had gone amiss and he wanted me to take the blame.

'It's not that at all, S.G. It's just that I thought that you would like to go to court again.'

'You know that I would like nothing less.'

'I will sit with you and pull your gown, if you look like going wrong.'

'My gown will soon be in tatters,' I replied. 'What sort of case is it?'

'It's all about the Habeas Corpus Act of 1679. One of the judges seems to think that it might apply here.'

'Who is it this time?' I had quickly absorbed the disenchantment of the chambers with most judges, whom we thought were old, not too bright and let a lot of villains go free. I later discovered, when I sat on the bench myself, that this was a narrow and unjustified opinion.

'It's Mills-Owens. When I did the pleas this morning, counsel for Tang Kei Lum argued that Tang should be released as Tang was not tried at the last sessions.'

'Who is Tang's counsel?'

'Colonel Terence Shurlock, I'm afraid. He can't have thought up that argument by himself. He must have been talking to George.'

The latter was a member of the Bar who was famous for his specious arguments. 'The Colonel must be sure that Tang is guilty or he would not have tried this one.'

'Sounds just your sort of case, Dermot.'

'I got it postponed until tomorrow, in case you wanted to address the judge.' He did not add that I was at my most persuasive on points which were irrelevant.

'I will let you know in half an hour if I can change my diary.' He grinned and left. He guessed that there was nothing in my diary.

I hurried to the library. For the next two hours, I examined the ancient law reports. These used some peculiar Latin phrases, which may still be in use in Scotland. As the cases were mainly in my favour, I told Dermot that I had been able, at great inconvenience, to rearrange my diary and that I would be in court the next day. I spent much of the evening in the library, searching for further authorities which were in my favour. I phoned my wife to let her know.

'And who is the woman this time?' she asked, somewhat unfairly I thought.

'It's not a woman. I'm in court in the morning.'

'Don't forget that we are expected at the Clintons' for drinks this evening, just because you are involved in a respectable activity for once.'

'Tell them I'll come if I can.'

'Is it a difficult case? If so, you'd better get someone to help you. Remember what a mess you made of your last case in Gibraltar.'

I left the library about nine o'clock. Books lay in heaps all over it. I took about twenty volumes home with me and read them avidly until the early hours of the morning. I woke several times during the night rehearsing the arguments which ought to baffle Colonel Shurlock. On each occasion, I got up and made a note of the point in case I forgot it in court. It was a pity that I was unable to read these notes in the morning.

On my way to chambers, I recalled the reference to Gibraltar. Even if I dried up there, in front of a jury, this wasn't a jury case. Besides, Tang was charged with the respectable crime of smuggling, whereas the man in Gibraltar had made off with charity funds. And the judge's name in Gibraltar began with 'F' and not with an 'M'. In spite of these obvious differences, I was still worrying, but decided not to use severe illness or sudden bereavement as reasons for not appearing, as I might need them another time.

Colonel Shurlock had no authorities on his desk in court.

'Hallo, old boy,' he said. 'A pleasant surprise to see you here for your debut. It is your debut, I expect?'

'Only here, Colonel. I have been in court before.' I did my best to sound confident. 'Did you get my list of authorities?'

'Yes, thank you. I put it somewhere but I lost it. I shan't be using any myself. It's a matter of common sense really.'

I hoped that he was wrong. If the Colonel was right, the common law had developed over the centuries without any regard for realities.

The judge listened to both of us with barely concealed impatience. The Colonel reminded him that the Act of 1679 applied and that Tang must be released as he had not been tried at the last session.

'Where is Tang now?' the judge asked.

'Rotting in gaol, my lord. Bail was refused, with no justification. He is only charged with smuggling.'

'He has previous convictions for robbery, grievous hurt and blackmail,' I replied.

'May I remind Your Lordship of the golden thread?'

'Which one?' asked the judge, who was well aware of what the Colonel meant.

'It says that a defendant is innocent until he is proved to be guilty.' Defence counsel often referred to this useful phrase when they could not think of anything else.

'A fine principle, Mr Shurlock. Have you anything else to say to me?'

The Colonel had. He argued that a defendant must be tried at the High Court session in which he was charged or be released and that the Habeas Corpus Act said so. He spoke for an hour without any reference to a case.

I replied, with frequent reference to my notes. I was obliged to omit several of my submissions, as they were not legible in my notes. For over an hour, I read to the judge passages from old cases which showed that Tang should not be returned to his mother.

The judge decided that Tang should be tried, because Tang should have objected at the beginning of the session and not half way through it. The Colonel protested that it was unfair to penalize his client because he had only just thought of the argument. The judge consoled him by remarking that he was clever to think of it at all, even if it was a technical argument without any merit.

As I left court, I was greeted by Morley-John, who was accompanied by two Crown Counsel. They had all come to see me fall on my face.

'It's the first time that I've heard Mills-Owens say that a point was technical,' he commented.

'I expect that he had made up his mind before he heard me,' I replied modestly.

'Never mind. You won. Difficult to see how you could have lost, mind you.' He had not heard me on other occasions or he would not have said that. 'It's a great relief to know you can appear in court if necessary,' he added.

Fortunately, it did not happen often. On the next occasion, I argued at some length that the singular included the plural, and vice versa. Mr Justice Blair-Kerr was appointed as sole commissioner to enquire into the conduct of Chan Kin Kin, who had told one of the local newspapers how the special branch of the police force operated. Blair-Kerr acted under an ordinance in which the plural was used. Half way though the enquiry, the newspaper decided to challenge the validity of his appointment, no doubt realizing that he was likely to be critical of it.

I appeared on his behalf, as it seemed to be generally accepted that I was something of an expert in arguing points of little merit. I assembled, for the Full Court, authorities to show that the plural included the singular. I did not think that the judges would be satisfied with a Hong Kong ordinance which said so.

The court decided that Blair-Kerr was correct, in spite of the fact that the newspaper was represented by Leo D'Almada, of Portuguese origin, who was the most effective advocate in Hong Kong.

'It was a pleasure to see you here,' he said, with a charming smile, when the case was finished.

'As soon as I saw you,' I replied, 'I knew that the paper had a poor case, even though you made it sound convincing.'

'The Crown must have thought it mattered, or you would not have come yourself.' I did not believe him, but we both purred.

'I expect it was a matter of principle,' I replied. I could not think of one, except the distaste of losing a case against a paper.

Some months after, there was an appeal to the Privy Council in London. The Full Court was upheld. The enquiry was finished and its report published long before the appeal was heard in London.

'I know what an experienced prosecutor you are,' Shurlock began in another case. It is only when I am to be asked to do something that people are laudatory about my advocacy. 'I expect that you prosecuted a lot of people in Africa, before the Habeas Corpus case,' he continued.

'Yes, in front of assessors who did not know what was happening.'

'And you appeared often in Gibraltar, with great success, I'm sure.' I nodded modestly.

'What have you to say to that, Mr Shurlock, as if it matters?' asked the trial judge, who was Judge MacFee.

'It's monstrous,' shouted the Colonel, who was representing the defendant. 'My poor client does not even know what is alleged against him.'

'The ten charges cover the same period as the one, your honour. The total is the same. It is broken up, so that the defence can see more clearly what is alleged,' I replied.

'I ask that no plea be taken to these outrageous charges, until I have had a chance to consult with my client,' the Colonel complained. 'For all I know, the Crown will change its mind again and allege theft at the next hearing.'

Judge MacFee adjourned the case for two weeks, commenting that this interval should be sufficient for the Crown to decide what charges to bring. I held several conferences with accountants, police and Crown Counsel. They all gave me conflicting advice. I decided to ignore them all.

'I would like to hand in some new charges,' I told Judge McFee. He compared them with the previous ones.

'They are different again,' he commented.

'Yes and no,' I replied. 'The total is now larger. That explains the extra charges. Except that the last one is new and alleges a conspiracy with his partners to defraud his clients.'

The Colonel sprang to his feet, protesting that it was outrageous that his client should be treated like this.

The judge asked me if I really wanted to add the new charges. When I nodded, he fixed a date for trial, saying that he hoped that the Crown had authorities to support the addition of the conspiracy charge.

He obviously had not heard of my last appearance in Gibraltar against a defendant who had helped himself to the funds of the charitable trust for which he was working. The jury acquitted him on the ground that a confession had been extracted from him. They must have had doubts about the cuts over his eye, the broken nose and the bruises, all of which, I was assured, were sustained when he fell down the steps to his cell.

'I have not had great experience with juries,' I said to Heenan. I did not mention my unfortunate experience in England, when I dried up while addressing one.

'It won't matter, as this case is in front of a judge sitting alone in the District Court,' said Heenan.

'Then it does not sound like an important case, Maurice. Surely a Crown Counsel could manage it?'

'It's embezzlement by a solicitor. People must realize that we take this very seriously. He took about $100,000. He's been at it for two years. It came to light when one of his clients had trouble getting his money back. So I'm sure you would like to do it?'

'Ah, well, I –'

'Good. I knew how keen you would be.'

The following day, I appeared before Judge MacFee in the District Court. Someone else had been appointed to the High Court vacancy which he thought he should have been given. Prosecutors were an obvious target of his uncertain temper.

'I appear for the Crown,' I began.

'So I should hope,' he replied, 'as you can't appear for anyone else. Do you want me to take a plea to this charge of embezzlement?'

'I want to replace it with ten other charges of conspiracy to take part in fraudulent conversion in the same period.'

I spent much of the next weeks in the library, reading the cases about conspiracy, many of which seemed to contradict one another. The more I read, the more convinced I became that I should have charged him with embezzlement, as the first version had alleged, and that there was little evidence of conspiracy.

Two nights before the date fixed for the trial, I fell ill. This had nothing to do with the case, of course, even if I had not slept for four nights thinking about it. Dermot Rea told me not to worry, as he would have the trial postponed. On the day before that fixed for trial, he came to see me in my office.

'It's all been dealt with,' he announced. 'The solicitor pleaded guilty to six charges of embezzlement. I had a lot of trouble getting McFee to change the charges yet again. The Colonel shouting that this was a disgraceful way to treat his client did not help. I told the judge that I would not proceed on the other charges. I did not think you would mind.'

'What a pity, Dermot. I had been looking forward to appearing in court again.'

Maurice Heenan knocked on my door, before entering with a smile. It was a genuine one, as if he was really amused.

'What have you done to Sir Michael Hogan?' he asked with a laugh.

'Me? I always do whatever he wants, whether or not I agree with it. That's called power.'

'Surely it's only normal ambition? Whatever you call it, you seem to have impressed him.'

'Why are you telling me that unlikely tale, Maurice?'

'He's been asking for you.'

'I like it better here, Maurice. There isn't enough to do and if something is awkward Dermot or Graham Sneath do it.'

Maurice giggled and continued, 'I take it that you have heard of the Star Ferry Riots?'

'Certainly. Somebody is making a lot of fuss about a rise of ten cents in the first class fares on the cross-harbour ferries.'

'The C.J. and three others have been appointed to hold a Commission of Enquiry into the application for the extra fares.'

'Why does he want me? The answer must be very clear, even to an Irishman.'

'He seems to think you are a specialist in Commissions of Enquiry.'

'I've only been on one, which went all wrong, when my main witness decided to remain silent.'

'According to him, you were very impressive. Shall I tell Sir Michael that you have volunteered for this very important assignment and are flattered that he should have thought of you?'

I nodded with reluctance. Nobody had asked me to do anything for years, except my barber who asked me to keep still while he shaved my neck.

In April 1966, there were disturbances in Kowloon, in protest at the proposed rise in fares which the operating company attributed to increased operating costs, faster depreciation of the ferries and the building of the cross-harbour tunnel.

The company had applied in October 1965 for an increase in fares. Mrs Elliot, an elected member of the Urban District Council, launched a petition, for presentation to the Governor, to which members of the public were asked to append their signatures. This petition, signed by 23,000 persons, opposed any increase in fares in public transport services. A second petition, signed by 155,000, was presented to the Governor by Mrs Elliot in January 1966.

Before the Commission, Lo Kei, a leading demonstrator, alleged that Mrs Elliot had paid individuals to take part in the riots. She replied that some police officer, whom she was unwilling to name, because he would be victimized, had warned her that she would be blamed. Although pressed to do so, she still refused to give his name. For this refusal, she was severely censured by the Commission. The latter concluded that she had made a significant contribution to the riots, however good her intentions had been.

During the years when I was in Hong Kong, Mrs Elliot made many approaches to various Government officials to ensure that the person who had complained to her was fairly treated. In the absence of an elected legislature, a crusader like Mrs Elliot was necessary and in some cases very helpful. Many of the grievances made to her were later directed to Umelco, when it opened an office to deal with complaints. Perhaps her activities were partly responsible for this?

Mrs Elliot came to see me on a number of occasions, usually with a complaint about the way in which the police had dealt with the matter concerned. She tended to accept as truth the allegations which had been made to her. If she did not believe them, she would have done nothing. She did not ask me, at a later stage, what had been done. Sometimes the grievance was put right, though in most cases it was not. She was unlikely to accept this, as her mind was made up that a member of the public had been ill treated, neglected or unable to secure any answer.

I have no doubt that, for all her faults, Mrs Elliot was an essential voice in a colonial society. She was brave, resourceful and vigorous. Sometimes she was persuaded to join in bad causes; she made many enemies, especially in the public sector. She may have been gullible and inclined to make up her mind when she had heard only one side of a problem. For all her faults, she was an essential brake on an otherwise monolithic machine, which did its best but was not harried as often as it should have been.

Chapter 16
The courts in 1967

The courts continued to operate throughout the disturbances for most of the time as if nothing unusual was happening, though they were sometimes obliged to take special measures. During many of the turbulent days of the summer of 1967, the Government imposed curfews, obliging everyone to stay indoors in certain urban areas at night. This did not last long, since it elicited a hail of protests from restaurants, night clubs, bars and brothels, whose business was adversely affected.

Naturally, left wing supporters refused to obey a British regulation 'designed to keep the masses subservient'. A number of them were arrested for breach of curfew, or for taking part in illegal assemblies, as all gatherings in the urban areas of more than six people were prohibited without a licence.

When a magistrate entered his court in the morning, he often found himself facing defendants who refused to plead to the charges against them, and their supporters at the back, who waved the red book at him and chanted.

'Try and ask them if they plead guilty or not guilty,' the magistrate said to his clerk, when there was a temporary silence.

'The defendants say you are a British lackey and they refuse to say anything, as this is a British court and it has no right to try them as they are comrades.'

'The usual reply,' sighed the magistrate. 'I will record a plea of not guilty.'

The chanting began again in the public gallery. This time it was accompanied by a banner.

'Usual stuff?' asked the magistrate.

'It says "Down with the running dog judge. Out with the Fascists". Nothing new, sir.'

'I like that bit about the judge. Perhaps we ought to have a left wing administration after all.'

'Shall I tell them to keep quiet or we'll clear the building.'

'Please do. Though you'll have to wait for a lull, as they seem to be chanting in unison from the red book. What are they saying?'

'Roughly, sir, that the days of the capitalist are numbered and that if a capitalist tries to lift a rock it will fall on his own feet.'

The crowd at the back did not respond to the warning. Instead, they shouted abuse at the magistrate, who asked for this to be translated.

'I want to record what they said, just before I close the building, S.K.,' he said to his clerk. 'You know how particular the C.J. is about what he calls open justice.'

'They say you are the son of a whore, sir, and should do unpleasant things to your mother. You are a Fascist murderer, a despoiler of young girls and an oppressor of the people.'

'What a busy fellow I am, S.K. Is that all today?'

'I'm afraid so, sir. Nothing about your sister this morning.'

'Please tell them that I shall now close the building. The defendants, of course, will remain in custody downstairs.'

The magistrate remained in his chambers, until the mob of red book holders had been excluded from the building. He knew this had happened when there was chanting from outside. He was joined by another magistrate, who had also been described as a running dog.

'Anything new this morning?' asked the visitor.

'Usual stuff. I've had to clear the building again.'

'I was just about to do so, when I heard the noise outside. My crowd left to join in. You'll never guess what I've been doing to my sister.'

'Probably the same as I was doing to my granny yesterday. I suppose we'd better go and try these chaps. What are you fining for breach of curfew?'

'I started at $20. As there has been rather a lot of it, I've increased the fine to fifty. As nobody ever pays, I gave them a month in lieu.'

When the magistrate returned, the four defendants still refused to plead, demanding that their friends be allowed in the court to see that justice was not being done to a compatriot.

'If you don't keep quiet and say whether you are guilty or not, I shall record a plea of not guilty and have you removed to the cells, so that I can try you in your absence.'

The defendants replied that he was a Fascist beast and that he was oppressing the people. The magistrate ordered them to be taken away. When they had left the court, he heard the evidence and called them up, one at a time.

'Anything to say, apart from "Imperialist lackey"?' he asked the first defendant, who declined to answer.

'Very well. I convict you as charged. Fine of $50 or one month in lieu. Can you pay?'

He received a string of abuse in reply.

'Anything relevant, S.K.?' he asked. 'Apart from the fact that my parentage is in doubt.' S.K. shook his head.

'I will record that he refuses to pay. Please remove him to prison and send up the next defendant. I wonder how they manage in prison, S.K. It must be very overcrowded in there.'

'They manage, sir. I have a cousin in the Prisons Department.'

'What will happen to this man?'

'I expect he will be sent to the place which has been kept for demonstrators on the leper island. It's wired off and well guarded. They're kept by themselves, so they soon get tired of waving their red books, which they're allowed to keep.'

'I hear the food in prison is good.'

'They only get that if they leave their red books outside the dining room.'

'Like leaving you gun in the cloakroom in Manila?'

'The newcomers will start chanting at first. The others tell them they won't get fed properly, unless they keep quiet. So most of them do.'

'Have there been any escapes?'

'Not since a couple of them disappeared and everyone else was told the island was surrounded by man eating sharks. Those who did escape were caught by patrol boats and taken to another prison under different names.'

At the height of the disturbances, a Communist was arrested for taking part in an illegal procession. He was taken to one of the police stations, where he abused the sergeant in charge and was forcibly subdued. During the struggle which took place, he received a severe kick in the spleen, from which he later died. The Solicitor-General, a capable and intelligent man named Sneath, insisted that the two police officers responsible for the death should be prosecuted for manslaughter. He listened courteously to warnings that this would be bad for the police morale and would encourage the Communists. Sneath explained, when he decided to prosecute, that it was important to show that nobody could act outside the law, whether they were Communists or not. It was a brave gesture. Whether he was believed was a matter of doubt.

Because it was a delicate and unpleasant job, Sneath undertook it himself. The evidence against the police officers concerned was strong. The judge summed up to the jury in favour of a conviction. The jury acquitted. Sneath was soon reconciled. He had maintained his principles. The jury had ignored what had really happened.

I only heard of one attempt to cause harm to a member of the judiciary, apart from the usual threats which were made against them in court but fortunately were not carried out. Tony Leathlean, who spoke in a nervous manner punctuated with snorts, had been dealing with many Communists in his court. Like other magistrates he had been vilified but had not taken this seriously. He lived in a rented house in a remote area of the New Territories. On his return one evening, a home made bomb exploded behind his car in the drive leading to his house. The explosion was badly timed and did not injure him. There was some damage to his car, though bloodstains near the gate suggested that the bomb had done some damage to the person who set it off.

Leathlean reported the incident to the police, saying that he had heard the noise at the time but had not taken it seriously, as he assumed his cook had eaten something which had disagreed with him. The police never discovered who was responsible for planting the bomb. Leathlean was moved to a safer quarter where, within a month, he hurt his leg badly by falling down the stairs outside it.

The Chief Justice, a clever Irishman who never let his left hand know what his right hand was doing if he could help it, had much experience of troubled colonies, having served in Palestine, Aden and Malaya before he came to Hong Kong. Although intensely practical about the extent to which his courts should remain open to the public, he was much less so in relation to his bailiffs. He considered that any restraint placed on their activities amounted to an interference with the judiciary's independence.

A police officer, Inspector Jones, had been libelled in one of the left wing papers, which asserted that he had entered the premises of a printing press, run by one of the comrades, without a warrant and had smashed the machinery because it had been used to print material which was critical of the Hong Kong Government and wholly accurate at that. Inspector Jones replied, in a public statement, that he had not smashed the presses, because he had no authority to do so. The next day, the presses were repaired sufficiently to print another critical article.

With some hesitation, the Governor had given permission to the Inspector to sue the newspaper. The Government would pay his costs. A writ was issued and served on the premises of the paper, by pushing it under the door. The next day it was returned containing the Chinese characters for 'Foreign documents not accepted. No translation attached'. It was laboriously translated and again left on the premises. It was returned the next day with the words 'Not accepted. Hong Kong courts have no jurisdiction over comrades'.

The defendants were deemed to have entered an appearance. The Inspector duly sought judgment in default of defence in the High Court. He had claimed $HK 80,000 in damages, rather than a sum at large. The editor of the paper did not reply to letters sent by the Inspector's solicitors demanding payment. The solicitors therefore asked the High Court bailiff to enforce their client's award. The bailiffs went with reluctance to the address of the newspaper. They were refused entrance, as no capitalist lackeys or imperialist running dogs were permitted. If they were unwise enough to force their way in, the newspaper would defend its premises. The bailiffs noticed that the men in the background were holding meat hooks. They returned to the court, their writ of seizure and sale not served.

The Chief Justice waited a few days, in the hope that the difficulty might be solved in some other way. He knew from past experience that problems were often solved by doing nothing. This one was not. He therefore wrote to me, asking if I could arrange for a force of police officers to accompany the bailiffs, since the Commissioner of Police had told him that he did not feel that it was part of his duty to provide escorts for bailiffs. Of course, if any of them was killed or suffered serious injury, he would take the appropriate action.

As I was in no hurry to do anything about bailiffs, I replied a month or so later, after two reminders, asking if it was correct for bailiffs to be supported by the police whenever they were serving a court order.

The Chief Justice insisted that all court orders must be enforced. In support, he quoted a passage from a speech delivered by the judge at the opening of Sligo Assizes a hundred years before. The latter had stressed the importance of giving strong support to the bailiffs in their difficult task. In Ireland, they could not have operated without it. I decided to take the matter to the Security Committee.

'Who on earth let Jones sue?' growled the Governor.

'You did, sir. You said it was time the newspaper was taught a lesson.'

'Did I? I must have been in a bad mood. Does the C.J. know the background, Roberts?' I nodded. 'What do you suggest?'

'I could try telling him that the police are very busy dealing with riots, explosives and violent crime, so that they won't be able to give the bailiffs the support they would like.'

'I haven't got enough men as it is.' The Commissioner of Police glowered at the Financial Secretary, who smiled back at him confidently. It was quite simple for him. More police meant less of something else. He had to maintain a surplus, as a sign of confidence. Some heads of department seemed to want him to spend his way out of trouble.

'There seems to be a principle involved, sir,' I answered.

'Oh, God!' exclaimed the Governor, who did not like the word, which I often used when advising caution. 'What is it?'

'Shall he support the bailiffs, as the Chief Baron urged at Sligo Assizes in 1870?'

'Sod Sligo,' muttered the General. 'And the Irish as well, while we're at it.'

'Why should we help them?' The Governor looked over the top of his glasses whenever he disagreed with anyone. He looked over the top of them more often as his tenure of the post lengthened. 'Before we know where we are, we shall have the police storming the Bank of China to enforce some private debt of $20.'

'The C.J. seems to think it's an important principle,' I insisted.

'That's what judges are for,' he replied. 'They find principles everywhere, lying about waiting for someone to trip over them.'

'Sligo Assizes reminds me of the Irish racing driver,' said the General. 'He stopped at the pits four times, once for petrol and three times to ask the way.'

'Very amusing,' agreed the Governor, glaring at the General. 'What about Jones? Can't we pay him out of the special fund?'

'It will set an unfortunate precedent,' said the F.S. 'No control by the auditor.' I knew the special fund was a mistake.

'Please tell Jones, Commissioner, that when he gets his damages he is to keep quiet about where they came from. Otherwise, his future with the force is in doubt. I will record your dissent, F.S.'

The F.S. nodded. He did not expect to be able to stop another unjustified item of expenditure. It would be a blessing if this emergency would cease, so that the Government could return to a proper system of accounting. Already there was an item in the accounts for $40 million for educational books which had been spent on water cannon and tear gas for the police.

The Chief Justice sat behind a high table, in a panelled office with a tall ceiling. The fan had been replaced by an air conditioner. This was so noisy that anyone who wished to be heard in his room was obliged to shout. This gave the impression to an outsider that the discussion had moved into the realms of ill humour. A long table was covered with books, files, judgments and papers. Many of these had been dealt with already. Like many men with tidy minds, Sir Michael preferred to sit in the middle of chaos. To him, an empty desk meant that its owner did not have enough to do. He gave the impression of someone who was overworked. He probably was, as he was reluctant to delegate. He was at his best when thinking politically, or in giving ground, when he had decided that this was inevitable.

I waited in the office occupied by his secretary, Mayreen Fook. She had been with him for some years. Although Chinese, she had been reared in South Wales and spoke admirable English with a strong Welsh accent. Twelve years later, when I became a judge, she was still there, with much experience of what my predecessors had done. I tried to follow her advice. When I did not, I was usually wrong.

Sir Michael greeted me warmly and waved to a chair, having removed from it a pile of dog eared papers.

'I expect you want to ask me about poor Charles,' he said. I did not, but the chance of talking about something other than the bailiffs was too much for me. I nodded.

'Poor Charles Denman is not very well.'

'I'm sorry to hear that, C.J. It must be a great worry to you.' The C.J. looked at me sharply, to make sure that I was not being light hearted about one of his magistrates. I kept a straight face, as I had learned to try to do when dealing with them.

'It's his head this time.'

'Has he had a fall?' Everyone knew that Denman was a very odd man. Perfect for the bench, it was said.

'I'm very much afraid that he does not have the right temperament for the bench. He's had a serious breakdown.'

The phrase 'temperament' covered anyone from an incurable alcoholic to someone who was mildly eccentric.

'I expect', I ventured, 'that you were going to say that he might be quite a good Crown Counsel?'

'Well now, Denys, what a good idea. You are full of them. I would never have suggested such a thing. Now that you've done so, I expect you are right as usual. I was going to ask you how I should get him boarded out. His contract has another two years to run.'

'I suppose the Colonial Office sent him?'

'I can't blame them this time, as I interviewed him myself. I was so short at the time that I even went to London to see applicants.' He shuddered at the memory of it. 'The trouble with Denman is that he can't make up his mind about anything. Do you know, the last time he came to see me he was without socks. Mayreen told me it was because he couldn't decide which to put on first.'

'I don't suppose that would matter if he was a Crown Counsel,' I agreed. 'If he was a legal draftsman, nobody would even notice. You could just sack him.'

'That would be most unkind. Far better to let him finish his contract.'

'And much less trouble?'

'Certainly, though of course I was not worried about that.' Sir Michael was a master of the answer which was partly candid and partly misleading.

I nodded in agreement. I should have to pay a price for Jones' bailiffs. A couple of years of Denman's drafting was not too much.

'That's excellent, Denys,' said Sir Michael warmly. 'I will write to you, saying that, as a result of our discussions, I felt able to accede to Denman's request for a transfer to the A.G.'s chambers.'

'Has he asked to be sent across?'

'Not yet. But he will, I'm sure. The alternative is even less attractive.'

'Please say that Denman is an able man who does not happen to have the proper judicial temperament.'

'Of course, my dear fellow. Was there anything else you wanted to mention, while you were here?'

'I'm afraid so. We're having a lot of trouble getting the Commissioner of Police to promise to escort the bailiffs into left wing premises.'

'Did I write to you about that? Do remind me.' A file entitled 'Inspector Jones' Claim' lay on his desk. I reminded him. 'I know', I said, 'how strongly you feel about this.'

Sir Michael nodded gravely.

'There don't seem to be enough police to go round. I can't manage to persuade the Commissioner of the importance of upholding the rule of law.'

'Fiat justitia ruat coelum,' Sir Michael quoted with a sniff.

'It's a fine principle, but –'

'You were going to tell me that it is uncomfortable when the roof caves in? But it is unfair on Jones. He has been awarded a large sum in damages but won't get his money unless we send in the bailiffs to seize whatever they find on the newspaper's premises.'

'I think you ought to know that Jones expects to get paid tomorrow, so he won't need to enforce his judgment.'

'Who is proposing to pay him?'

'A well-wisher, he said.'

'Oh, really? In Malaya, where we did this, it was the Government which paid up. Anyhow, even if the Jones problem is solved, it does not settle the real issue. What will happen the next time we need to enter left wing premises?'

'Inspector Jones will be the last public servant to get permission to sue until the present disturbances are over.'

'What about a private citizen who wants to sue?'

'It won't happen very often. If you want to do business with them, you can't very well sue them. If you insist, of course, it may take some time for the courts to deal with a claim against a Communist. Don't you agree that the courts are very busy?'

'I expect you warned the Commissioner that he may be in contempt if he won't let his officers obey a court order.'

'Several times, C.J. He insists that he would like to help, if only this was possible.'

'The authorities are very clear. There was a strong case decided at Cork Assizes in 1878, as well as the one from Sligo.'

'May I have the reference?'

'Yes. It's in the Irish Law Reports. You won't be able to distinguish it.' He gave the reference, which was in a book I did not have in my library.

'While you are here,' he added, 'I wonder if I could just mention another matter. I've had a bit of trouble explaining this to the Governor.'

'How can I help you?' I asked. Provided that this involved spending someone else's money, I was glad to do so.

'I've been trying to get my assistant registrars' posts upgraded for a long time.'

'I received a firm negative on two occasions. Fortunately, I have been able, each time, to raise new matters with the Governor. Not that it is him, of course. He only signs what is put in front of him.'

It was better not to let Sir Michael know that, before he signed a letter to the C.J., the Governor, having asked 'What the hell is the C.J. asking for this time?', insisted on being carefully informed of the details of his reply. 'If I am not briefed,' the Governor said gloomily, 'the C.J. will sidle up to me at a drinks party and I shan't be able to refuse him.'

'Your support would be a great help,' said Sir Michael. 'It would ease the annoyance I would otherwise feel at the refusal of the police to support the bailiffs when necessary.'

The registrars were not upgraded, as I continued to oppose this proposal.

Chapter 17
Ex. Co.

The Hong Kong Annual Reports are a beautifully produced record of the Government's successes, though its failures are not specified, unless they have already received such publicity that a mention of them is unavoidable. In these reports, a paragraph describes the Executive Council as the Governor's principal adviser, as indeed it often is, although most Governors do what is necessary and report to 'Ex. Co.', as it is generally known, afterwards, if they remember or consider it politic to do so.

It was usual for Ex. Co., during my years of membership of it, to complete its listed business by about eleven o'clock, having started at half past nine. It often lingered after this to discuss 'other business'. This consisted mainly of matters raised by an unofficial, or non-Government, member, and varied from the trivial, which often lasted some time and aroused deep emotions, to matters of importance, which were not recorded.

On two occasions, Ex. Co. sat later than half past twelve, until each time hunger forced it to a decision by one o'clock. After I left Ex. Co. in 1978, somebody decided that coffee ought to be served in the middle of the morning. Afternoon meetings have become common since then.

I first sat in Ex. Co. in 1963, when Maurice Heenan took a long leave. He could not have gone at all if he had not assured the Governor that I would be able to take his place. As he explained to me, he was desperate to go.

'The A.G. does not have much to say in Ex. Co.,' Maurice went on, 'so you should have an easy time.'

'Speak only when you're spoken to?' I asked. I should have been able to manage that. It's what my father always said when I contradicted him. Especially if I happened to be correct.

'That's about right. The present Governor is a charming man, very urbane, so that you've no idea what he is thinking. He used to be an administrative officer here. So he sees the A.G. as obstructive, who will tell him what he can't do. This is a nuisance, especially if he has done already what the A.G. says he can't. So he seldom asks my advice, except when he does not want to do anything. Then he accepts what I say.'

'Does he get annoyed with you?'

'I don't suppose he expects much else from a New Zealander.' Maurice chuckled and failed to light his pipe.

'We don't seem to be very helpful.'

'I don't think we are supposed to be. All we can do is to try to steer Ex. Co. in the general direction of the law. Sometimes the Governor may conveniently forget that he asked you. It's useful to him to know what he should not be doing. If you want to protect yourself, you can write a note to him afterwards, confirming the verbal advice that you gave. You will find a folder of notes in my safe.'

'Does it work?'

'Certainly. He can pretend that he never heard the verbal advice, but he can't ignore what he gets in writing. Just don't write too often.'

'Does the A.G. speak if a bill comes to Ex. Co.?'

'The draftsman of the bill sits at the end of the table to explain it. Some of them', he added with a shake of his hand, 'are only drafting because I can't think of what else to do with them. So you may have to speak about a bill, if the draftsman can't.'

'Who takes part in a discussion?'

'It's a hierarchical system. The senior unofficial speaks first. He repeats himself until he is sure everyone has grasped his point. The other unofficials either support him or say very little. This probably means that he has already discussed it with them at length outside Ex. Co. If they don't agree with him, they keep quiet. So you usually get a united opinion.'

'How do you alter that?'

'It's difficult. If the Governor finds himself with conflicting advice, he usually adjourns for what he calls further consideration. He then tries to lobby unofficial members separately.'

'Does that work?'

'Quite often. A Governor still enjoys considerable authority, partly because of his office, which means that people don't like to disagree with him, and partly because he knows more about public administration than they do. He is, however, a bit weak on public opinion, which used to be ignored much more in Hong Kong. The unofficials are very good at that. They know how people are going to react. I hope your right arm is in good shape?'

'Not if I am expected to join in a punch-up, Maurice.'

'It's only for voting. If you support something, you raise your hand. Sometimes, when I come out of Ex. Co., I've done little else for the past couple of hours.'

'What do you do if you want to disagree?'

'If you read an Ex. Co. paper and don't like it, just let the Colonial Secretary know. Otherwise he will assume that you support it. I am sure that you will manage splendidly. Just keep quiet until you have found your feet.' I wish I could have followed his advice.

The Governor, Sir Robert Black, had been in office for five years. He was therefore, like most long serving Governors, inclined to brush aside opposition, believing that he knew best, as he usually did. He remained a courteous man, whether he intended to follow your advice or not.

Before my first Ex. Co. meeting, I was sworn in. This required me to take a number of Victorian oaths, which were read out wrongly by the clerk. He was corrected by the Governor, who continued to smile as my induction was ruined.

The next item was a set of building regulations, which were not expected to cause any trouble, as they had already been before Ex. Co. on another occasion and been altered to accord with the views of unofficials. They regarded controls over buildings as unnecessary, though prepared to agree to anything which would stop structures from falling down.

At the bottom of the table was Gilchrist, a cheerful Irishman who had copied the legislation on the subject already in force in Ireland. He regarded this as suitable, as nobody paid much attention to it there either. It was the usual practice to copy the laws in some other territory if the legislation concerned was thought to be necessary, even though nobody wanted it. Gilchrist, as usual, was having difficulty in keeping awake. I did not think that I could rely on him. He was only drafting because he had fallen asleep twice in court in the middle of a case which he was supposed to be prosecuting with vigour.

'I would like to know why we have to have Regulation 16,' demanded C. Y. Kwan, the senior unofficial member. He was a competent local solicitor who enjoyed picking holes in a draft, even if he agreed with its principles.

The Governor turned to me. 'Well, A.G., what do you say to that?' He smiled as if he was amused. No doubt he was.

As this was my first Ex. Co., I had read every word of every paper and made notes. I had no idea why Regulation 16 was there.

'I think the draftsman should know that better than me,' I replied. I thought that this answer showed me at my most persuasive.

Gilchrist looked surprised. 'I only put it there because somebody told me. I can't remember who it was. And they have it in Dublin.'

'The regulation says that you can't build without a permit if the structure is worth over a million dollars,' I explained.

'It comes from the Irish regulations,' Gilchrist added proudly.

'Has it been altered, Director?' the Governor asked Michael Wright, the Director of Public Works, who was sitting next to Gilchrist.

'It used to be a hundred thousand dollars. It was increased to a million because Mr Kwan and his colleagues wanted less control by my office.'

C. Y. Kwan nodded. 'So long as that is made clear in the press release, we will support it. I have some other comments of substance. There is a comma in Regulation 7 and a capital letter in the next one. Both must come out.'

I agreed. Gilchrist nodded, though whether in agreement or because he had not heard I was not sure.

'There is a "not" left out of Regulation 11,' said C. Y. Kwan.

'That's right,' said Gilchrist. 'A double negative would put you back to where you were before. Unless you wish to be there, of course.'

'Good,' said the Governor. 'We are all agreed with Mr Kwan?'

'That's all I have,' said C. Y. Kwan. 'Though I believe Mr Gordon has something.'

Sidney Gordon, an unofficial European member, was an accountant. He was a believer in more off-street car parks. They were his passion.

'I want to ask what is being done under these regulations to make building owners provide spaces for cars?'

'There's a regulation about that,' replied Wright.

'Regulation 12 only requires one car space per unit in a new building.'

'The regulations only deal with large buildings,' Wright replied.

'I've been trying to persuade the Director for years that he should insist on two spaces for each flat. If he doesn't, the traffic flow will dry up.'

Wright turned to me. 'Perhaps the A.G. would find it difficult to change the regulations.'

'Oh, no,' I replied helpfully. Wright glared at me. I soon learned that, if the head of a department expected me to find something difficult in Ex. Co., I did.

'I have, of course, considered what Mr Gordon said,' Wright continued. It was well known that Gordon would always ask for more parking spaces. 'Maybe we should require developers to provide one and a half per flat.'

'Two would be better,' Gordon insisted.

'Good,' said the Governor. 'We are all agreed? One and a half spaces as an interim measure. Mr Gracegirdle – the draftsman, I mean – will make the amendment. Any other comments?'

'There's an appeal tribunal, with a chairman to be appointed by the Chief Justice,' said Dr Rodrigues, an unofficial member. 'What does he say?'

'He hasn't been asked,' replied the Colonial Secretary.

'Would that not be politic?'

'He's never objected yet. If we do have to appoint anyone, we will send him a list to choose from, as usual.'

'We need that regulation,' Wright said. 'I've been discussing it for weeks with unofficials.'

'Any objection, A.G.?' the Governor asked.

I agreed with the Director, having no idea what to say. I happened to have given the same advice to Maurice Heenan, though for different reasons. He had served in Palestine with the C.J. and, whenever the latter complained about the insensitivity of the Government in not asking him if he objected to making an appointment, Maurice mollified him by talking about Jerusalem.

The next item was the deportation to Macao of a Chinese man who had been convicted of housebreaking and theft. The magistrate who tried him had recommended that he should be deported.

'Will they take him?' asked C. Y. Kwan, who was annoyed with the Chinese People's Government, who had refused to accept criminals for several years.

'Yes,' replied the Colonial Secretary. 'We will put him in a cabin with a warder and lock the door.'

'It's a scandal', Gordon said, 'that public money should be used to pay for the private accommodation of a felon. Honest citizens have to pay for their own cabins!'

'The ferry company does not charge for this. It's a public service.'

'That's my money,' C. Y. Kwan protested. 'I am a shareholder.'

'While we're talking about free rides on the ferry to Macao,' said Gordon, 'what about the Frenchwoman who kept taking off her clothes. Did she pay?'

'If she'd been younger, we might have paid her,' muttered the General, who had said nothing so far.

'It wasn't just us,' replied the C.S. 'It was the Portuguese in Macao. They didn't let her land. Whenever she was refused permission, she took off all her clothes. She went back and forth and stripped for weeks. In the end the French consul sent her back to France as a distressed subject. The ferry company kindly paid for her cabin.'

'It's no wonder the ferry company pays such a poor dividend,' C. Y. Kwan complained. 'If it gives away all these cabins it's surprising that it makes any profit at all. I would like to know what the A.G. did about her.'

'I am sure he handled it himself,' Sir Robert replied. I thought he was being serious. The General, who sniggered, evidently did not.

'If she had not been returned to France, we would have prosecuted her for indecent exposure, sir, if she had ever been allowed to land, which seems doubtful.'

'When did we last try to deport a criminal to China?' asked C. Y. Kwan.

'The last time we tried, we got the man back in twenty minutes,' said the C.S., 'as soon as the frontier guards got orders from Canton.'

'We will try again,' the Governor agreed, 'though I expect we shall get nowhere.'

'We might offer them some unconvicted chaps as well,' Gordon suggested. 'I have a list of several people I would like to get rid of.'

Several ordinances gave a right of appeal to the Governor in Council. A few years later, this was dealt with by a sub-committee of Ex. Co. In 1963, the full Council heard it. On this occasion, a wealthy developer was represented by counsel. Two stall holders appeared in person. All were objecting to the widening of a road. Their advocate addressed us at length, repeating himself to make sure that we had followed his argument. He complained that his clients had purchased a site without any knowledge of the proposed road and that they would lose a lot of money if the land was resumed. The stall holders had been running an illegal food stall for a long time. They did not mind the road being widened, but asked for space nearby and suitable compensation for having to move. After they had withdrawn, the Governor asked if anyone wished to comment.

'I declare an interest,' said one unofficial. 'The developer is my cousin, though I must say I found his arguments not at all compelling.'

'Perhaps you should have withdrawn before the appeal,' the Governor suggested. He looked at me. I had an uneasy look. He mistook this as an indication of principle. In fact I had mislaid my packet of cigarettes, as I was giving them up again and kept hiding the packets from myself.

'Maybe,' the member continued. 'But I expect Council would like to know that my cousin is a crook. He swindled me out of a lot of money last year. He knew all about the road when he bought the wasteland. He's sold half of it already for more than he paid for the lot.'

'We agree,' added C. Y. Kwan. 'A lot of people have been swindled by that man. He's a member of one of the triads as well. His objection should be rejected.'

'What about the stall holders?' the Governor asked.

'We should pay them nothing,' said the F.S. 'The stalls are illegal.'

'They have been there for years,' Dr Rodrigues said. 'It's a bit late to say the stalls are illegal.'

'They have been paying protection money to the hawker force which is supposed to control them,' said Y. K. Kan.

'If we move them,' the C.S. said, 'the Urban Council will give them a licence and a proper site round the corner. We will only have to pay removal expenses and a few hundred dollars' compensation.'

'The F.S. dissents,' announced the Governor. 'Otherwise we dismiss the appeal. What is next? Ah yes, the bill about oysters.'

Gilchrist was at the end of the table again, though he had, so far as I knew, had nothing to do with the bill.

'I'm here in place of O'Malley,' he explained. 'He drafted the bill but we can't find him anywhere.'

'I expect he's taken the day off,' the General said. 'It was Irish National Day two or three weeks ago.'

C. Y. Kwan reminded the Governor that he had spoken to Maurice Heenan about Clause 11 of the bill, but that it had not been altered as they had agreed. Heenan had promised to replace the words 'notwithstanding the provisions of subsection (4) of this section' with the words 'subsection (4) not withstanding', which C. Y. Kwan believed to be a great improvement.

I agreed hastily, just in case Gilchrist objected on behalf of O'Malley. A rambling discussion ensued as to whether the bill was needed. Some unofficial thought the oyster farmers could manage without one. Others said they needed more protection if they were to make a profit.

'I declare an interest,' said an unofficial. 'I shall withdraw from this discussion as I own one of the pearl fisheries. Before I go, I would like members to know that, if I were allowed to stay, I would strongly support the bill.' He then withdrew.

The Governor, having given the impression that he agreed with everyone, closed the discussion by announcing that the bill, as amended in the way proposed by Mr Kwan, should go to the Legislative Council.

'Has any member anything to raise under any other business?' he asked.

'I want to talk about my land in central,' said Weng, another unofficial.

'Do you have an interest in this?' the Governor asked.

'Of course,' replied Weng in a puzzled voice. 'Who else could tell members what has happened?'

'Perhaps we ought to hear him,' the C.S. suggested. 'We can make a note that Mr Weng has an interest in the matter.'

'Any objection, A.G.?'

'Well, sir, I –'

'Heenan accepted this as a practice, though he was opposed to it in principle,' the Governor explained.

'Like a lot of other things,' the General added.

'If it was all right with Heenan, I would not like to disagree,' I replied. At least this would prevent me from worrying about things I did not agree with.

'I can't develop my land,' said Weng. 'It's not a question of the merits, of course. I just can't get an answer from the Director of Public Works.'

'No reply at all?' asked the C.S., pretending to be horrified. 'How long has this been going on?'

'I don't mean that he did not send any answer at all,' Weng went on. 'He did not give me a proper one.'

'You mean he said "no"?' asked the Governor.

'All he will say is that I can't do it, because my land is part of a bigger scheme, which is not ready. The delay is costing me a lot of money.'

'I expect he's tried bribery and had found it doesn't work,' the General said to me in a whisper. The Governor heard it and glared at him.

'The scheme has not come to me,' said the C.S. 'I will discuss it with the Director, if that is what the Council wants.' Council did.

'I want to raise the question of the clocks,' said C. Y. Kwan. 'Are we going to change them, or are we not?'

'What do they do in China?' asked Gordon, who knew perfectly well.

'They don't change them at all.'

'That is why the harvest is late,' proclaimed Weng.

'I thought we appointed a working party to look at this last year,' the C.S. suggested.

'It cost a lot of money,' the F.S. observed. 'We sent people all over the Far East to find out what they did and why.'

'The group suggested that we should not change the clocks at all,' C. Y. Kwan agreed. 'I think they were wrong and that we should have another group.'

'It might come to the same conclusion, Mr Kwan.'

'We don't have to accept what it says. Let us be bold!' said Weng, who had shares in one of the electricity companies, which would benefit if the clocks were put forward an hour.

'I will ask the C.S. to consider if we should have yet another working group to look at the clocks again. It would not surprise me if he decided against it. If nobody has anything else to raise, that concludes our business.' The Governor looked swiftly round the room and left before anyone could mention something else.

'Come and see the Governor before he goes,' the C.S. said, leading me to a small room nearby, where the Governor was sitting behind a desk, signing bits of paper.

'I wanted to congratulate you on having come relatively unharmed through your first Ex. Co. in Hong Kong,' the Governor said.

'That's kind of you, sir.' I was relieved, as I was suffering pangs of doubt about the many errors which I thought I had made.

'You only intervened when you had to do so. Then you were vague and seemed to agree with everyone. Exactly what we need from a law officer.'

Chapter 18

1967

Early in 1967, the Cultural Revolution in China becamc more ominous and it was widely expected that Hong Kong would be affected, directly or indirectly.

In the early months of 1966, the Political Adviser, seconded from the Foreign Office, told me that Mao Tse Tung, Chairman of the Communist Party which ruled China, believed that his revolution could only succeed if the bureaucrats and rulers of China were replaced and re-educated.

The turbulence reached Macao in 1967, when mobs forced the Portuguese Government of that Colony to consult the Chinese in future before any decision was taken. The British Consul-General was made to stand in the sun outside his office; this was occupied by crowds which chanted loudly, demanding freedom and brandishing red books, in which the sayings of Chairman Mao were recorded. The Consul-General, a brave man, refused to recognize his errors and apologize for them, as he was told to do. After some hours, he was allowed to enter his consulate, which had been ransacked. He was soon withdrawn, and British affairs in Macao were dealt with by Hong Kong. His treatment was a warning of what might well happen in Hong Kong as well.

The Government of Hong Kong was pragmatic in its approach. It did not permit itself to be inhibited by principles, in dealing with an opponent that had none. It reacted as best it could to a determined body of Chinese Communists who were receiving some support from Peking, though how much was uncertain. It was only later that it became apparent that the local supporters of the left wing had acted on their own initiative on many occasions, and that this often forced Peking to back a course of action which it would have preferred not to take.

The principal body that dealt with the emergency which was declared was the Governor's Security Committee. This was originally formed so that the Governor should be kept in touch with the activities of the police, the military and the special branch. It was expanded by the inclusion of a number of officials, among them the Attorney-General, who proved more useful than anyone, except the A.G. himself, had expected.

Sir David Trench, the Governor, had long administrative experience, a fine military record and not so much imagination that it prevented him from acting ruthlessly where necessary. He was a heavy smoker. The only sign that he was under pressure was a large number of half finished cigarettes in his ashtray. He handled the emergency with much skill and did not allow his failures to affect his future action.

Sir David was reluctant to seek advice from the A.G. or from the Commander of the British Forces, as each was likely to refer to the difficulties involved, rather than to whatever advantages there might be. From time to time, however, he felt obliged to do so.

'You've heard the police, A.G. They want to force their way into a left wing school. Do you see any objection to this? I imagine not?'

'Well, sir, it all depends.'

'That's the perfect answer,' said Sir David sourly. 'It tells me nothing and it does not commit you.' The noise suggested that most of the other members present found this amusing.

'I get stuff like that from the army legal chap,' complained the General, a large man who had a preference for acting first, as he thought necessary, and asking if it was in order later. It usually was, as the emergency regulations were widely drafted, so as to give legality to various actions which would not have been permitted in normal times.

'I expect he was right, General,' I interjected.

'If there were no lawyers, I'd march on Canton,' he added. 'You fellows have got no red blood.'

'There's an emergency regulation, Governor, which says you can authorize anyone to enter any place, which would include a school. If you would sign a piece of paper, authorizing all police officers to enter this school, you would be acting within the law.'

'Very important,' said Sir David. 'Please make sure the law is wide enough.' He signed a blank sheet of paper and passed it to me. 'Just type in what has to go above it,' he added.

'Can I rely on the regulation which says that a police officer can enter any premises if he thinks an offence is taking place there?' asked the Commissioner of Police.

'Do you think there is?' I asked.

'Certainly. The little buggers are making bombs in the school.'

'Then you can enter and seize the apparatus.'

'What about the subversive literature which the pupils get to read, and the unpleasant references on the blackboard?'

'Am I on the blackboard?' the Governor asked.

'Rather! I mean, yes, unfortunately,' the Commissioner of Police replied.

'You can seize that as well,' I agreed, 'so long as you reasonably suspect it is subversive.'

'They will do when they've read the stuff,' the General commented, 'even if they don't now.'

'Just make sure that those concerned have a reasonable suspicion before they enter.'

'How shall we do that?'

'Information received from a delicate source that cannot be disclosed,' I suggested.

Not long afterwards, the police broke down the door of the school and arrested the teacher, who was instructing his fourteen year old pupils in how to make bombs. The pupils made the mistake of yelling 'Yellow running dogs and capitalist lackeys' at the police. The latter, when the pupils resisted arrest, handcuffed them, took them ten miles out of town and left them to find their own way home. The school was closed.

Shortly after this, the Governor told the Committee that he was supposed to go on leave, though he thought it better to remain.

'I have asked the Colonial Office for advice. We leave it to you, as the man on the spot, they said.'

'I think you should go,' said Cater, the Defence Secretary, a shrewd ambitious man who pared his nails unceasingly when he was thinking. 'If you don't, people will say you were frightened to go because things are getting out of hand.'

'If I do go, they'll say that I'm only interested in my own affairs and don't give a damn about Hong Kong.'

'What do you think, A.G.?' I did not imagine that my reply would have any effect. He just wanted time to think.

'I've got the same problem. I'm due to go on leave in April and not return till September. I don't think I ought to go.'

'So long as the Solicitor-General is here, I'm sure it won't matter.'

I didn't think it would either, though I would have preferred him to be rather more hesitant about it.

'It will be a sign of confidence if you go, A.G. And on balance, I think I had better go myself. It will only be for a month and I can come back if necessary.'

I was away for more than four months. I went to the Colonial Office on two occasions to offer to return, as news of mounting troubles came from Hong Kong. Each time I was told that the Colony was managing well without me.

Indeed, nobody seemed to notice that I was not there, especially the Communists. To my satisfaction, however, they included me on their list of those who were enemies of the people. My name was among those who were identified as running dogs on the railway trucks which came in daily from China, bringing fruit, vegetables, rice and pigs, as the emergency was not permitted to interfere with trade. I felt that I had been accepted.

Shortly before I left on leave, the Security Committee considered the case of the vanishing policemen.

'We have lost a twenty stone European police inspector called Knight,' said Cater. 'He is too large for it to have been an accident.'

'Was he on his own?' asked Sir David.

'He insisted on talking to a mob of women who come through the gates each day to cultivate the land on our side. They were carrying banners saying "Down with the imperialists. Give us back our land".'

'Have we taken any?'

'Certainly not.'

'What happened to the inspector?'

'He was taken over the bridge by the women,' the Commissioner of Police explained. 'He's not the only one. We've also lost two constables named Wong. One went the wrong way on his motorbike. The other walked across the street in Shau Tau Kok, where the frontier runs down the middle of the road, and was grabbed.'

'I thought people had been crossing that street for years,' the Governor said.

'That's correct, but not in uniform. I think he was going to see his girlfriend, so he didn't have time to change.'

'Or even to get his uniform off,' the General commented.

'More likely he was visiting a brothel. It used to be cheaper over the border,' Cater suggested.

'Been shut down by the Communists,' said the General. 'I've had complaints about this from some of my troops.'

'What are the Chinese going to do with three of our police officers?' the Governor enquired. 'They must be a nuisance.'

'They are holding them while they decide what to do. I expect they will conclude that two Wongs don't make a Knight,' commented Cater.

'Very funny, Cater,' the Governor agreed, laughing through his cigarette smoke. 'Have we sent a protest?'

'No, sir, but we've sent a message to say we will take Knight back without making a fuss, if they will push him over. He was handed over by the women to some soldiers who were sitting in a sentry box near the bridge.'

'Picking their noses and wondering why they were there,' muttered the General. 'Like most soldiers.'

'A truck came and took Knight away. He was protesting, in Cantonese, that they had no right to do this. As it's a Shanghai battalion, I don't suppose anyone understood him.'

'That sounds like Knight,' said the Commissioner of Police. 'He's very good at speaking up, even where there is nothing to say.'

'Very well,' the Governor agreed. 'We'll do nothing for a week and hope the problem will go away. Is there anything else which calls for another wise and decisive directive?'

A week later, the Wongs returned, one on a motorbike and one on foot. Neither knew why he had been arrested or released. They had often crossed the border without trouble before. This time, they were told by the Chinese not to come back again.

The Chinese decided that the best thing to do with Knight, since they could hardly be seen to allow a European to return to duty, was to encourage his escape. He was moved to a police station close to the frontier.

The first time his door was left unlocked, Knight did not move. He wanted to be sure that he would not be shot escaping. The second time he heard two Chinese police officers talking.

'Where are you going?' asked the first in a loud voice outside his cell.

'Lin Ma Hang in Hong Kong. I have a girlfriend,' the second replied with a snigger. 'A friend will leave the door unlocked for me in the fence.'

'It is moonlight tonight,' said the first. 'And the gate is only a few yards away from here by the path.'

Knight decided that he was meant to escape and that it was safe. He followed the first speaker to the wire and passed through it safely.

The Governor agreed that the papers could be told that all three had escaped, after many dangers, which they could not describe in public.

There were other occasions when truth was used sparingly. The Defence Secretary was an inventive man and devised schemes which embarrassed the Communists in different ways.

The Bank of China made loud propaganda announcements from the roof of its premises and played Chiu Chow operas. A ring of vans was stationed round the bank, each equipped with a loudspeaker and a record of a Chiu Chow opera. Not all the vans carried the same opera. They played continuously. It is said that even a Chinese ear, accustomed as it is to sounds that are weird to a Westerner, finds Chiu Chow opera disagreeable. A few hours later, officials of the Bank of China removed the loudspeakers from the roof.

Several local shops were owned and operated by the mainland Government. The profits from them were remitted to Peking. In each shop there appeared a prominent notice calling on customers to contribute to a 'patriotic fund for the assistance of oppressed comrades in Hong Kong'. A grim faced woman stood by each notice and reminded every customer, as he left, of his duty. Before long, it was widely rumoured that anyone who entered a left wing shop was expected to contribute 20 per cent to this fund. The number of customers dropped. The notices were removed, but business did not pick up for two or three years.

The main left wing daily was widely read, not only by the faithful, but by many others, because its racing correspondent gave better tips than those which appeared in any other paper. His column was removed when the Defence Secretary planted letters in other papers that the tipster was a 'capitalist roader'. The circulation of the paper dropped by two-thirds.

Known left wing businesses, in which wage rates were low, were picketed by police officers masquerading as unemployed men and women, carrying banners with the usual rates of pay displayed.

The parents of children at left wing schools were told, in a whispering campaign, that their children would be taught how to make explosives and that this was dangerous as several pupils had already been maimed. Spurious statistics were published, showing that pupils from these schools achieved poor results, because much time was wasted on indoctrination, instead of being spent on education. Many pupils were removed and sent to Government schools.

Britain maintained an embassy in Peking. This was headed by a chargé d'affaires, who worked with his staff in the centre of the city in difficult conditions. The editors of several left wing papers, which had accused the Hong Kong Government of genocide, suppression of freedom and Fascism, urging their readers to take to the streets in protest, were convicted of sedition by a District Court and sentenced to imprisonment. A few days later, a large chanting mob appeared outside the British compound in Peking, carrying banners denouncing exploitation, British colonialism and, of course, Fascism. The British compound was ransacked and some of its buildings were set on fire. The chargé and his staff, who had been forced to watch the destruction, were allowed to go.

From time to time, they were threatened but not again subjected to physical violence. They were protected henceforth by members of the People's Liberation Army, who surrounded the compound with barbed wire, 'to protect the British from the righteous anger of the people'.

For some years, the British presented an annual bill to the Chinese. This included the expense of rebuilding the damaged parts of the mission and of repairing the wagons, with slogans painted on them, which were sent to Hong Kong from China. The bills were not paid. During the disturbances, however, the wagons continued to cross the border from China to Hong Kong. The Chinese authorities, if asked why they permitted trains to cross, answered that the goods and livestock were to help the people starving under the Fascist rule of the British. It was far too profitable a trade to dispense with.

Some of the Hong Kong owned wagons carried painted slogans demanding the immediate removal and painful death of the Governor and a number of named senior officials. It was a boost to my sense of my own importance when the first wagon was seen with the message 'Death to the Fascist Roberts'. It was like being a 'prison graduate' in Africa; unless you had been imprisoned by the British, you were not taken seriously in the 1950s and 1960s.

In 1963 and 1964, there had been a serious drought. During this, the Government had hired tankers to bring water from the Pearl River, near Macao. Even so, households were limited to a four hours' supply of water every fourth day. The Government, determined not to be caught again, opened negotiations with the Chinese in 1964. Within a year, the latter had built a large reservoir at Shum Chun, near the border, for the collection of water from the East River. An agreement was reached for the supply to Hong Kong of a stated number of gallons each year, between 1st October one year and 30th June the next. In the other three months, more water could be supplied if both parties agreed.

By 30th June 1967, the C.P.G. supplied all the water which it was obliged to send under the agreement. The Hong Kong Government asked for more in July and received no answer. On 1st October, the C.P.G. switched on their taps and the water flowed across the border again. In July 1968, extra water was sent as soon as it was asked for.

The Communists had tried to concentrate their strength on those activities which they considered to be vital to the life of a community. If these could be disrupted, it would control society. So a general strike was called for a day in May 1967. Sympathizers were found mainly in the transport, wharf and water services.

During the week before the appointed day, the stevedores armed themselves with cargo hooks and demanded to see Forsgate, the wharf company manager, an ex-Merchant Navy officer who had been dealing with difficult men for most of his career. He was a tough man, but never lost his sense of humour. The stevedores were unlucky to have to deal with him. A dozen of them, brandishing their hooks, marched into his office, led by Fung, who was a senior union official, demanding a big increase in wages.

'Capitalist swine!' he said, raising his fist to Forsgate.

'And Fascist,' Forsgate added, more cheerfully than he felt, as he did not like the appearance of the cargo hooks.

'Exploiter of the masses. Cruel landlord. And pig,' added Fung.

'You have been talking to my wife!'

'We shall make you pay for what the English have done, Mr Forsgate.'

'A good idea, Fung. I am Scottish. The English have been exploiting us and the Welsh for ages. It is time we all united.'

'We will make the English apologize for the indignities they have inflicted on us.'

'The English are a bit stupid. They may not realize that you mean what you say.'

'It's the workers,' shouted Fung. 'They always mean what they say.'

'Besides, the English will think I've agreed with you because of your cargo hooks. They won't think I'm really repentant. Shall I phone them and tell them?'

'Phone your employer and tell him we are going to close his warehouse.'

'I'll try. He may not believe me.' Forsgate phoned his managing director and explained what was happening. The sound of the stevedores could be heard over the phone.

'They sound quite unpleasant, Gerry.'

'I think they are. They've locked my door and demanded an apology. It's like a board meeting.'

'Can you get out, Gerry?'

'Not in one piece.'

'Have a haggle, while I organize some police.'

'I am authorized to offer a raise in wages to anyone who is still working for the wharf company next week,' Forsgate announced.

'Promise what you like. We shall close the warehouse. It will be a blow for freedom. Please go home, Mr Forsgate, and let us get on with what we have to do.' Fung led his men from the room. Forsgate could hear them shouting outside.

The police, summoned by the managing director, arrived at Forsgate's office soon afterwards.

'Where were you when I needed you, Inspector?' Forsgate asked.

'In the background, sir, just in case. It's been a rather busy morning. Do you want to charge anyone with anything?'

'I don't think I'd better. Poor old Fung was only doing what he was told. Let's see who turns up for work next week. I've promised them extra wages.'

The day before the strike, the New China News Agency, which represented C.P.G. in Hong Kong, announced that loyal workers would not attend the next day. 'There will be a strike of all workers against the Capitalists and Fascists who are reducing our compatriots to slavery.' The Hong Kong Government replied that, so far as public servants were concerned, those civil servants who did not turn up for work would be sacked.

About sixty thousand workers stayed away, a third of them genuine supporters, a third sympathizers and a third because they were intimidated. Among them were several hundred Government employees, mainly in the post office, the public works, and the water department.

In an uncharacteristic moment of firmness, the Government announced that anyone who was not back at work within two days would be sacked at once. The private companies, which had borne the brunt of the strike, namely the bus, ferry, electricity and wharf companies, issued similar warnings.

The next day, few workers reported for duty. They did not take the employers seriously. The comrades had been victorious in Macao. It would be the same in Hong Kong. The next day they were sacked. They did not mind this, as the New China News Agency had promised to pay the wages of any strikers who stopped work at their behest. Some had inflated their wages and claimed this larger sum. Other workers were paid both by their employers and by NCNA for some weeks, before the latter became aware of this.

Within a month, two-thirds of the strikers had apologized for taking part in the strike and had returned to work. The wages of the rest were paid by NCNA. After three months or so, the NCNA told them that these would no longer be paid, so they had better find some work.

The bus and train services, mainly manned by left wing supporters, were badly affected by the strike, leaving a serious gap. This was filled by the 'mini bus', which had not previously been operated in Hong Kong, except when privately owned. It carried twelve to fourteen passengers and appeared on the main roads, to replace the buses and trams which no longer plied these routes.

Fung, who had led the strikers to Forsgate's office, remained loyal to Peking and drew his wages from the NCNA, until the Agency told him that the motherland was no longer prepared to subsidize a lot of layabouts and he'd better find a job. By using a false name, and with the help of another wharf worker who operated a taxi to augment his wages, Fung obtained a licence to run one. By the end of the year, he was earning more than he had been paid as a stevedore. By the middle of the 1970s he owned several taxis and had become a rich man. In spite of this he continued to drive a taxi himself from time to time. About 1976, he took Gerry Forsgate, who had not recognized him, from a restaurant in Central to the wharf.

'How much?' asked Gerry at the end of the journey.

'It's free, Mr Forsgate.' Fung turned. 'Do you remember me, without my cargo hook?'

Chapter 19
Attorney-General

In 1966, Maurice Heenan accepted the offer of a job at the United Nations, which meant that he retired a year early from Hong Kong. Shortly before he left for New York, he said goodbye to me in his office.

'I have recommended that you succeed me as A.G. I could not think of a better man for the job.'

I hoped that he did not mean what he said.

I was sorry to see him go. He was patient, good humoured and wise. Whenever the going was rough, I could shelter behind him and leave him to take a difficult decision. In future, I should take it myself and find someone else I could blame. Happily, I was able to do so, when necessary.

About three months after Maurice had gone, I had received no confirmation that I was to be his successor. I spoke to George Rowe, who was the Establishment Officer, though he did not allow this to interfere with his cricket. I waited until George had made a respectable score for the Wanderers, a team for which we both played on Sundays. It had been a long wait, as George was having a run of low scores. As he explained to me, they were largely due to the stupidity, incompetence and lack of knowledge of the laws of cricket of the umpires.

'Well done, George! What a pleasure it is to see you on top again.' I gave him a slap on the shoulders and a broad smile. This revealed the unsatisfactory bridge work from which I was suffering at the time.

'It was nothing really,' he replied with a large smile. 'I could not have done it if you and Barnes had not softened up the bowling for me.' Happily, George seemed to have forgotten that I was dismissed for five, even though it was true that Barnes had stayed for an hour for his twelve.

'I've just had a letter from Maurice.'

'Really? Good. That's fine. Maurice who?' George beamed at me. He was in an excellent mood, even if he was not thinking about anything else but his own score.

'Maurice Heenan. He went to the United Nations about three months ago. He says he is very happy there.'

'So he should be. New York is lovely in the autumn.' I did not remind him that it was winter there and that it would be covered in snow.

'I know what you are going to ask,' George said . 'Who is going to keep wicket?' I nodded. 'Do you feel like it?'

'Whatever you say, George.'

'There isn't anyone else, as Townsend and Hughes are not playing today.'

'It'll be a pleasure, George.'

He looked at me with suspicion. 'You're being very accommodating. Are you sure you're all right?' George was used to civil servants collapsing, in order to secure early retirements on medical grounds. 'You don't look quite yourself. I expect you've been at the bottle again, like most lawyers.'

'Certainly not. I hardly drink at all. I had jaundice in 1956.'

'So you do not want to leave for medical reasons?'

'It's not that. It's just that I've been acting as A.G. for over three months and have not heard anything about Maurice's successor.'

'I can't talk about that,' said George righteously. 'You'd better pad up. And try to remember to put on a box this time. I don't want to have to carry you off half way through the innings, like we had to last month.'

'Three months is nothing for the Colonial Office,' he added as we walked out together. 'It takes them as long as that to decide that they've got to reach a decision. I'll have a look at the file. We ought to have had some reaction from them, even it it's only a lot of questions to which they already have the answers.'

I kept wicket with great enthusiasm. It would do no harm for the Establishment Officer to see that I was keen, active and fit. The catches and the stumping chances which I dropped or missed were all difficult, as I explained to George in the changing room afterwards.

'Especially', he agreed, 'when the batsman rushed down the wicket and fell over. What a pity you dropped the ball.' George laughed, which he would not usually have done. He must still have been happy about his own half-century, a rare event as he could not see more than a few feet through his thick reading glasses.

The following morning, George telephoned as I was drinking my third cup of lukewarm tea.

'I expect you want me to play on Sunday? I will be happy to keep wicket again if you are short.' My secretary had just replaced the bandage on my thumb which I had hurt the day before.

'I thought I asked you in the changing room yesterday?'

'You did. And I still can. If you want me, that is.'

'I didn't ring about that. We must try to separate work and recreation. You mentioned Heenan's successor yesterday?'

'Oh, did I?'

'I've just had a look through my cupboard. Some of the files have been there for months. Left by my predecessor. A lot of them. You'll never guess what I found?'

'I give up.'

'The file about a new A.G. It was at the bottom. I can't think how it got there. There doesn't seem to be any difficulty this end.'

'What does that mean?'

'Hong Kong will support you. We badly need you as opening bat for the Wanderers. If we don't watch them, the Colonial Office might bring in an A.G. who only played tennis. We can't have that.'

'The Colonial Office may have someone they want to shift in a hurry – like a chronic alcoholic or someone who has been interfering with small boys.'

'I suppose that is how you got here from Gibraltar?' George laughed. I did not join in. 'Anyhow, nothing seems to have been done to fill the post. I will send off a savingram today, putting your name forward.'

'I'm sure it's not your fault, George.'

'Somebody should have enquired about the vacancy,' he agreed. 'I shall have a sharp word with my staff.'

George phoned me again on Saturday morning.

'You won't believe this, but I've had a reply about the A.G.'s post.'

'Already? Then there must be some difficulty.'

The Colonial Office legal division was under the control of a clever Scotsman whom I did not know well. Those who had interviewed me had left; one was growing roses in Devon, one was sitting in chambers in the Temple and one had gone aloft. I could therefore rely on nepotism no longer, except that overseas appointments were supervised by Grattan-Bellew. He owed me a favour, because I had lent him ten shillings in 1956. I hoped he would remember that and not worry about merits.

'Can you bowl medium pace?' George asked.

'Certainly. Just let me know what you need.'

'Not long hops, which is what you usually deliver, at any pace. I've got Townsend to keep wicket, but I may need you to bowl. See you next Sunday.'

'George, before you go. And I'm sure someone is waiting for you in the nets. Can you tell me if the office has decided whom to send us as A.G.?'

'Didn't I tell you? I'm getting quite forgetful. The Colonial Office has approved your appointment. They say they have nobody else to offer us.'

'I shall try to justify your confidence, George.'

'I really do think', George went on, 'that you ought to practise in the nets this afternoon, just in case I have to put you on to bowl tomorrow.'

I spent all afternoon in the nets, bowling at one stump in preparation for the following day. I hit it twice in three hours, and was well satisfied. The next morning, Townsend did not appear, so I had to keep wicket again.

Soon afterwards, I decided that it would be a good idea for me to move into Maurice Heenan's house, if I could persuade the Government to allow me to do so. It had been built as a single house before the war, converted into two flats in the 1940s and changed back into a single house for the Heenans, not much more than a year before he left.

D.R. as Attorney-General, Hong Kong

What I did not realize was that he had undertaken that it should be changed back into two dwellings when he left the house. The Government housing manager, Prosser, told me this with some pleasure, when I asked him if I could move. He enjoyed refusals, especially if they were delivered to a more senior colleague.

'I'm very much afraid', Prosser said, shaking his head in simulated regret, 'that Mr Heenan's house is not available as a single unit.'

'Why is that?' I smiled unconvincingly. I was determined to maintain a good relationship with him. I might need him again, especially if I did not succeed this time. My wife described this as my two-faced expression. I preferred to think that I would be remembered as courteous in all circumstances.

'We made him promise that, when he retired, his house would be split into two again.'

'How can he make a promise which will be binding when he's gone?'

'Of course, he can't. But he has. I am afraid we have to live with it.' Prosser shook his head sadly. 'Naturally, you can appeal if you like.'

'That would hardly be worthwhile, in view of what you say. Do you think that, instead of moving, I could have another shaving point put into my present house?'

'I can't answer that, until I have looked at the regulations,' he answered. 'I am sure it will be difficult.' Prosser shook his head, as if he regretted what he had just said.

A few days later, Prosser wrote to me, referring to our conversation and saying that he was sorry to have to inform me that the regulations permitted one shaving point for every two bedrooms. As there were three bedrooms in my house, the shaving point which I already had was the extent of my allowance. He ended by suggesting that I might think of moving into a larger house, where there were four bedrooms, which would allow me to have two points.

The cost of an additional point would have been $100. I offered to pay it and was told that this was not provided for.

A year or so later, I asked the Public Works Department if an additional bedroom could be built over the garage next to the house. The department replied, some weeks later, that it would consider my request. I was relieved that they had not heard that it was an unlucky garage. If they had done so, no permission would have been given. It was unlucky because my car had expired in it.

One night I was awakened, about 3 a.m., by the sound of a horn. As I listened, this died away, until it sounded like a plaintive cry in the distance. In the morning, when the garage was opened, the car

I had parked there was found dead. Outside, there seemed to be nothing wrong. Inside, it was burnt out. Every combustible part of the engine and the upholstery lay in a charred heap. The insurance assessor, before he wrote off the car, said that he had never seen anything like it before and that there must be a singularly evil spirit in the garage.

It was over a year later that I received a letter from the Public Works Department, saying that my proposal for a fourth bedroom had been approved at a cost of $120,000. I did not tell them that my daughter, who would have occupied the room, had just left for a boarding school in England.

It took about two years to build. The department refused, however, to install in the extra room a shaving point, without authority from the housing manager. I wrote to Prosser, with some pleasure, reminding him that a second point was available to anyone with four bedrooms, and referring to our conversation of three years before.

I received a reply within the week, signed by someone I did not know. He told me that Prosser had had to retire early on medical grounds, but that he was happy to give his permission.

It was a somewhat limited victory. The regulations were altered the following year, so as to allow for an electric shaving point to be put in every bedroom.

It is often assumed that any Attorney-General, since he is in charge of prosecutions, will be subjected to pressures not to take action in many cases. I can only recall two instances in which this happened to me.

Weng Mui Lam, one of the unofficial members of Ex. Co., caught me one morning as I left the Council Chamber.

'Can I speak to you, A.G.?' he said in a whisper. 'Alone if possible.'

I took him to my office. He shut the door behind him.

'It's about K.J.,' he explained.

'K. J. who?' I asked, being deliberately obtuse, as I had clashed only the week before in Leg. Co. with K. J. Yeo, who thought I had made a grave error in imposing an enhanced figure on his house for rating purposes. He refused to believe that it had nothing to do with me, simply because that was what I usually said when I could not think of an answer.

'K. J. Yeo,' he explained. 'He won't come and see you himself, so I thought that I ought to do this, as it would not look good, from the public point of view, if you were to prosecute a fellow member of Leg. Co.'

'What has he done, Mr Weng?'

'You mean you don't know? You control prosecutions! You keep saying so.'

'I do. But that does not mean I know the details of every one.'

'You must know this! It's most important. K.J. is a member of Leg. Co.'

'Yes, but what did he do?'

'He was parked in the wrong place.'

'That is very serious,' I agreed. 'Where did he commit this terrible offence?'

'That's the point. He left his car outside a funeral parlour.'

'The one at North Point?'

'So you know it?'

'I seem to spend most of my time there.'

'But you don't get towed away.'

'I don't park it in the wrong place.'

'You have a driver.'

'You win, Mr Weng. Just tell me what happened.'

'When he came out of the parlour, he was already upset.'

'The tears were running down his cheeks, I expect.' K.J. had been seen laughing at the funeral of his second wife and had acquired a considerable reputation for enjoying innocent fun as a result.

'They were. Imagine what he felt when he came out and found that his car had gone. He thought it had been stolen. As it had. The police had dragged it away from the front entrance of the parlour and it was round the corner. In a narrow alley full of dustbins,' he added.

'Leave it with me,' I replied. 'I will see what I can do to help.'

'I'll tell him that you'll stop the prosecution, shall I? He will be pleased.'

'You must do nothing of the kind, Mr Weng. You've done your best for him, even if you should not have spoken to me at all.'

'Really?' asked Mr Weng. 'Then who should I talk to?'

I asked Dermot Rae to make some enquiries about what the police meant to do. He returned the next day, smiling happily and scratching his head until it bled.

'Stop giggling, Dermot, and tell me what the police intend to do about this very serious infringement. If this sort of thing is allowed to go on, we shall no longer be safe in our beds.'

'I'm told that seven cars were towed away from the front of the funeral parlour and that four of them belonged to members of Leg. Co. They've all had notices saying that their prosecution is being considered. That's the last they'll hear of it.'

'Has the decision been taken already?' Dermot nodded. 'Then we'll leave it at that. It's not important enough to make the police do something, even if Weng will be convinced that it was only because he spoke to me that K. J. Yeo was not pursued to the grave.'

On the other occasion, I had already taken a decision not to prosecute a clutch of students who had held an illegal meeting in Victoria Park, to protest against the imprisonment of one of their members. The Director of Information Services, an astute man who understood public opinion much better than I did, came to see me the day I had announced to Ex. Co. that I did not propose to do anything more about the students.

'Don't you think', he said, knocking his pipe, which appeared to be full of liquid, on the edge of my desk, 'that you ought to say something about the students?'

'I've already told Ex. Co.,' I protested.

'Do we think it is enough?' By using the plural he wished me to know that other people were involved as well as me.

'Why not?'

'They have broken the law, which forbids any public meeting unless you have a licence.'

'If they hadn't broken the law, I would not have had to tell Ex. Co. that I was going to ignore it,' I replied testily. I was beginning to feel defensive. Only the day before, it had seemed a courageous and forward looking act. I was starting to wonder whether I was merely trying to avoid trouble.

'Everyone is expecting you to do something,' he continued.

'So you think I'm wrong?'

'No, no. I didn't say that. I think you were right not to make martyrs of the little sods.'

'I thought a gesture of this kind would be well received,' I said gloomily. 'It's the only time this year I have done something charitable.'

'Never mind, A.G. Everyone makes mistakes. I suggest, however, that you should do a short television clip, explaining why you have decided not to prosecute. I'll write it for you. You won't even have to learn it. We will put it on a screen for you to read. Then you will sound spontaneous. Do you wear glasses?'

'Only for reading. Not for long distances.'

'Good. We won't have to make any special arrangements, as you'll look more impressive without your glasses.'

'Do I need to look impressive?'

'Not so much impressive as wise. Do you think you can do that?'

It was evident the next morning that I had not managed it.

'I saw your performance last night,' said Sneath. 'Very interesting is was.'

'You advised me not to prosecute the little swine,' I protested. 'If it hadn't been for you, I'd have brought the charges.'

'I didn't coach you to twitch all over the screen. You looked as if you had just had convulsive therapy.'

I found this very hurtful.

'Never mind,' he said, in an effort to cheer me up. 'I don't suppose that anyone is likely to have remembered the smile.'

'Did it not come across well?'

'It seemed more like a rictus to me, but then I know you don't find students amusing.'

It was my own fault for allowing the Director to tell me what to say. He hedged my remarks with so many provisos that at the end of the programme I did not know what I had said. I was obliged to issue a short press statement to make it clear what I had intended to say.

It should not be thought that the seven years which I spent as A.G. were without incident. In a number of respects, I left a firm mark.

I can, for example, look back with pleasure, indeed with awe, at the flood of almost useless legislation which was inflicted on the Colony during my time in that office. I received much misguided praise, for modernizing the law, from those who were sensible enough not to have read it. I took pride in the growth in the revised edition of the laws from twelve to eighteen volumes in seven years.

I resisted a periodic request for Crown Counsel to be stationed in departments to advise on civil matters, on the unconvincing ground that this would be uneconomic and not make the best use of their invaluable services.

I was not, however, able to stave off those who insisted that more should be done to centralize prosecutions. I arranged for the admirable work which was done in the District Courts by two gifted chief inspectors, Hidden and Smith, to be carried out by Crown Counsel, who, before long, had grown in number to ten.

I stationed counsel in the newly established Independent Commission against Corruption, insisting that they should not stay there for more than a year. My successors had to deal with those who commented that this showed a lack of confidence in the incumbent. I was, I suppose, vindicated some years later when the senior counsel, seconded to the Commission for several years, pleaded guilty to a number of charges of corruption.

During these years, I gave frequent advice to the Government. This consisted largely of reminding it of what it could not properly do.

I noticed that the number of requests for my advice became less every year.

There can, of course, be little argument over the dramatic improvement in the standard of my performances of music. At the age of thirteen, I had taken to the violin. I had played in the school orchestra when it was short in number, being instructed firmly to make motions with the bow but on no account to play anything. I abandoned the instrument soon after and took to the piano, at which I attained Grade 2, to the delight of my father, who liked any kind of music, and the dismay of my mother, whose housekeeping money was reduced by the fees for my lessons.

In Hong Kong, I renewed my piano lessons, with a long-tempered girl named Margaret, who kept telling me that I would never get anywhere if I did not practise. I protested that I was too busy to do so. She continued to teach me for several years, at the end of which I could play anything in Grade 1. I felt that her faith in me had been vindicated.

Chapter 20
Legislative Council

The Legislative Council Chamber, as it was grandiloquently called, was built a few years after the War, at a time when air conditioning was not widespread. The plant later installed in the chamber, however it was regulated, maintained a temperature which soon lulled a member of Leg. Co. into sleep, disturbed though this might be by an occasional 'Aye' as his colleagues assented to a bill or motion.

The windows of the chamber were high in the walls, so that there was no view. Those who were able to see the seats at the back, which were called the public gallery, could extract interest by seeing who had attended. Unhappily, most of the seats in which members sat faced the Governor, who could see, from his raised platform, who was awake. He made no effort to wake unofficial members up. Nor did he interfere with official members when he realized that the Colonial Secretary was a devoted sleeper.

Official members were well disciplined. None of them was known to snore more than momentarily. If this occurred, it was the duty of the man next to him to stop him. For several years, it was my task to ensure that the Colonial Secretary, who sat next to me, was awake whenever necessary. I never let him down and acquired, as a result, a wholly unjustified reputation for reliability. This stood me in good stead when he was considering his successor.

The officials answered the questions directed at them and sat down swiftly before any supplementaries could be asked. Fortunately for the officials, these were uncommon, and the rigorous and acrimonious questioning of ministers which took place in some other legislatures was considered to be bad manners. If it was thought necessary to pursue a matter further, this was done in private. There, the official was subject to close enquiry as to what had been done and why.

The senior official for many years, a charming Indian named Rhutonjee, fell asleep soon after the Governor had entered. He was followed soon after by Peter Williams, a large man who was chairman of the Jockey Club, and two or three regulars who could be counted on to drop off if they did not have to speak.

It was not customary for anyone to speak off the cuff. There was a rule which prevented speeches from being read. Nobody paid any attention to this. Speakers produced detailed manuscripts, from which they read, some of them managing to sound as if what they were saying was original, even though they had been polishing it for the last fortnight and knew it by heart.

There was one occasion on which the C.S. was given the wrong script. Instead of a worthy and dull statement about the school leaving age, he was handed a speech which he was due to deliver at the opening of a conference of unmarried mothers. It was not until Sir Hugh, the C.S., rose to his feet to make the statement that he realized that he had been given the wrong paper.

'Hong Kong has never suffered from the unmarried mother,' he began. Luckily the microphones had not been switched on and his opening remarks were missed.

'Denys,' he said accusingly to me, 'you've hidden my speech.'

'I assure you, I have not.'

'It's just the sort of thing you would do,' he muttered at me, 'just to get a laugh.'

I searched the area of his seat and found nothing. He was obliged to make his speech without help. He did it well. When I suggested afterwards that he didn't need a crib at all, he replied that he had had to think carefully about what he was saying, instead of reading out what someone else had prepared for him.

I recall with special affection the Commander of the British Forces. The General remained a member of Leg. Co. until about 1972. Throughout the first six years of my membership, he sat opposite to me, smiling broadly and saying nothing, except to murmur 'Aye' when everyone else did. He never fell asleep, however dull the agenda and however warm the room. It was, I thought, not a surprise that we had managed so well in the past with a small standing army. I was sad when the General ceased to be a member of the Council. The fact that he was no use there did not seem to matter. He was removed from the Council in order that its composition could be widened.

'Leg. Co. is not representative,' commented Sir Murray Maclehose, the new Governor, before he had been in Hong Kong for long.

'It isn't really meant to be,' replied Sir Hugh.

'It's full of lawyers, doctors, accountants and businessmen.'

'What do you say, Roberts?' M.M. wasn't really interested in what I thought, but it was possible that I might have different views from Sir Hugh, whom the Governor regarded as shrewd but old fashioned. Sir Hugh looked and sounded shrewd and old fashioned.

'What about the workers?' I replied, helpfully I thought. M.M. glared at me.

'Don't you care that it's not at all effective?'

'Are you sure', Sir Hugh replied, 'that you want an effective Leg. Co.? It would be a dreadful nuisance.'

'It looks bad,' M.M. insisted. 'There's a Tory government in power in London. They send me telegrams asking when I am going to widen the membership. We must try and look more democratic.'

'I wouldn't oppose that for a moment,' Sir Hugh agreed, 'so long as the extra chaps don't try to introduce unarmed combat into the chamber.'

'I think we can let the unofficials take care of that, Hugh.'

After some searching, the Governor found two men with trade union backgrounds who were acceptable to the existing members, the senior of whom was consulted by the Governor before he made the appointments.

'I've asked you to come up, Y.K.,' he said, 'to talk about some new appointments to Leg. Co.'

'I have a list,' Y.K. replied.

'That wasn't quite what I had in mind. I thought it was time we tried to make Leg. Co. more representative.'

'A good idea', commented Y.K. 'Like all your other ideas, if I may say so. I've often said that we should have more members. The unofficials are overworked.'

Umelco dinner in honour of the Governor, 1976

'Yes, but –'

'It's the complaints system, you know.'

'Is it not working?'

'Too well, you might say. Anyone who has a complaint about the way he has been treated comes to see a member of the United Members of Executive and Legislative Councils, or Umelco as it is called.'

'I wondered what Umelco stood for, Y.K.'

'When we agreed to do this, we did not know how many people have a grievance against the Government.'

'I'm sure there are not many.'

'There are thousands. Every time any department says no, the applicant hurries round to the Umelco office and asks us to do something. Yesterday, there were twenty angry hawkers who had been cleared from a road on which they have been operating for years.'

'Illegally?'

'Certainly. But that doesn't make them any less annoyed when someone comes along and interferes with them.'

'Surely hawkers are an Urban Council responsibility, not the Government's,' said M.M.

'It's no use telling that to a group of men with meat hatchets. They don't see the difference between the two. So far as they are concerned, they are being mucked about again by the Government.'

'Surely this has given Umelco an importance it didn't have before? Anyone who wants to get something put right comes to it first?'

'Not first. Only if he can't get any satisfaction after complaining to the department. So this usually means that a more senior officer there has looked at it and agreed. After that it's very difficult to shift them.'

'Does this mean that Umelco is not always successful in dealing with complaints?'

'Last year we persuaded the department to change its mind in fourteen per cent of cases. This is not good for Umelco's reputation. People are beginning to think that we are in the Government's pocket!'

'Are you suggesting that we ought to take complaints away from Umelco and give them to an independent person, like the ombudsmen they have in some countries?' asked M.M.

'Certainly not, but –'

'If your success rate is so low, it shows that the threat of Umelco is making some Government departments act properly.'

'I wish I could persuade the other members of Umelco of that,' said Y.K. 'They see a letter from the housing people which says we regret that we are unable to put Madam Wong at the top of the list of applicants as she already has a flat in the name of Madam Tang. Because the word 'regret' appears, they think they have failed.'

'So you want extra members to help out with these regrets, Y.K.?'

'Yes, we do. What about Lai Sze Kong? He is a lawyer.'

'We have enough of them already.' The Governor shuddered. Almost without exception, they talked too much, even if they had little to say.

'If you want younger men, there's my cousin Chow See Foon. He is only fifty-two and is an accountant.'

'We have two accountants on Leg. Co.'

'Chow isn't an accountant now. He is in business, import and export of shirts. Very successful he is. If you want someone really unusual, there's my wife's uncle who is very popular with young people, because he's made a lot of martial arts films.'

'I am sure they are admirable people, but I had thought we might take this opportunity to introduce a couple of trade union officials.'

'What will people say?'

'I thought it would show that Leg. Co is more representative,' M.M. replied.

'It may mean that to people in England. But here it will prove that the Chinese People's Government is forcing us to appoint left wing officials.'

'I wasn't thinking of anyone from a Communist union.'

'Those are the only unions that matter, though they have been very quiet since 1967.'

'I'm under a lot of pressure from the UK to appoint some trade union members.'

'Why don't you ignore them?'

'I wish I could. But think of the danger. If I don't nominate a couple of union officials, London may call for elections. Then where would we all be?'

'Elections!' spluttered Y.K., to whom this was obviously a very unpleasant word. 'We have managed very well without any for a hundred and thirty years. Why should we have them now?'

'That's what I told them, in effect. They replied that, if I put a couple of trade union members on Leg. Co., they would defer the question of elections for some years. So I thought we had better find somebody. Can you sell this to the other unofficials?'

'It depends on who is appointed. They won't want a left wing rabble-rouser who will turn every Leg. Co. meeting into a platform for a lot of half baked Marxist nonsense. Did you see yesterday's *Wen Wei Pao*?' Y.K. mentioned a Hong Kong left wing paper.

'I only read it when it abuses me or the Government,' the Governor replied. 'Quite often, really.'

'They called me a capitalist lackey and the Governor's running dog.'

'Deplorable,' agreed the Governor. 'Particularly as we seldom agree about anything.'

'That is the sort of thing that will happen in Leg. Co. if you appoint some left wing trade union officials.'

'I didn't intend to do that at all, Y.K. The union officials I have in mind are presidents of the right wing unions.'

'Who are they?'

'There's Mr Yip, who is general secretary of the bus workers' union.'

'When did they last strike?'

'Not since he came to office in 1967, after many of the left wing workers had failed to turn up.'

'Who is the other?'

'Mr Woo, who used to be President of the Junior Civil Servants Union. He retired from Government service last year. Everyone says he is a pleasant chap.'

'I know him,' Y.K. agreed. 'He's been to Umelco more than once to seek out help. Called me "sir". He might do.'

The two trade union members were duly appointed to Leg. Co. Both proved to be pleasant, modest men who said little and soon became accepted by the other unofficial members. They did not really, as the Governor commented later, behave as if they were connected with trade unions at all. They were, however, sufficient to satisfy the Foreign Office ministers that the composition of Leg. Co. was being widened.

During my membership of Leg. Co., I introduced a number of Government bills. Anything of importance was not entrusted to me, but to the secretary or head of the department responsible. I was left with the other measures, which were seldom considered by unofficial members to be worth a challenge. If, however, a bill which I proposed to introduce contained a controversial clause, it was likely that I would be asked to attend a 'working lunch' at Umelco. Here I would be subjected to the hostile attacks and vigorous questioning which were thought to be impolite in a public assembly.

The meeting was chaired by Dr S. Y. Chung, a deceptively mild man who ran a manufacturing business with great success.

'Come in, Denys,' he greeted me with a welcoming smile. 'Would you like a drink?'

'Chinese tea, please.' I hoped that my choice might, perhaps, make my arguments more acceptable. It did not.

Those unofficial members who were interested in my bill sat at a large round table, to which food was brought, while we discussed it. Most of them had business to attend to in the afternoon and wished to get away as soon as they had brought me to heel.

'This bill to substitute life imprisonment for the death penalty. We do not like it.' The other members made the noise for 'Hear, hear' in Cantonese.

I didn't like it either, but I could not tell them that.

'What about the petition?' asked one of the members. 'Over a million signatures asking for the carrying out of the death penalty!'

'There were sixty-four thousand Chans among them,' I remarked. This proved nothing, but might divert them. It did not.

'Public opinion opposes the bill,' said S.Y.

'It's just a recognition of reality. The British Government won't support the Governor if he orders an execution.'

'He did that last year,' a member said. 'He was told that the Queen had commuted the death penalty to life imprisonment.'

'The Queen, my foot,' said another. 'She only did what she was advised to do. And why was she told to commute? Because the Government thought it would not get a majority in the House of Commons.'

'When the Governor in Bermuda was murdered,' S.Y. continued, 'the killers were strung up. So why not here?'

'They say it's because the UK does not like to interfere with the elected assembly in Bermuda, and we don't have elections here,' I replied.

'Nonsense!' commented another member. 'It's because it was a British Governor who was killed in Bermuda, whereas here it was only a Chinese auxiliary police officer.'

'I'm sure it wasn't like that really,' I protested, not being able to think of any other arguments.

'Have you seen the figures of crime in Hong Kong?' an unofficial asked.

'Well, not recently,' I admitted.

'The figures show that in the past fifteen years the number of homicides has increased by almost 40 per cent.'

'The population has about doubled,' I replied.

'That is quite irrelevant. The point is that everybody wants killers hanged.'

'In China there are several thousand executions a year,' another member added. 'No doubt it's more humane there, as they simply fire shots into the head. But the principle is the same. Execute the man and he will not offend again.'

'If you don't he will be out in less than ten years, killing again,' added a member.

'How many people who are released after being convicted of homicide ever kill again?' I asked.

'That's not the point,' S.Y. replied. 'People think they do.'

'Surely many people think that it is wrong to take a life?' I objected.

'Not even the Christians believe that. Isn't there something in the Bible about an eye for an eye?'

'That's not quite the context,' I ventured.

'You can tell the Governor that we shall vote against the bill, if you insist on going ahead with it. Have some more shark's fin soup.'

The bill was not taken to Leg. Co., where it would have been opposed by the unofficial members, even if it had been reluctantly supported by the official members, most of whom thought that murderers should be executed.

Instead, I made a statement that, in future, if a sentence of death was commuted to life imprisonment, this meant that the offender would be detailed for the remainder of his life and not be released, unless he was very old or terminally ill. This rule was strictly observed, though it meant that, fifteen years later, there would be over two hundred prisoners serving life sentences.

The Governor presided over Leg. Co. Fortunately for him, he did not have to control a disorderly assembly. His rulings were accepted without argument, though he was obliged from time to time to rescue an official member who was in difficulty, as happened occasionally when questions were asked.

'Question No. 4, Mr Williams,' the Governor said. Someone dug Mr Williams in the side, waking him up to ask the question.

'Will the Director of Medical Services please say how many abortions were carried out last year?'

The Director was away, no doubt having his annual check-up in Britain. The question was answered by his deputy, an experienced specialist in gastric disorders, who knew little about other parts of the body.

'We do not have the figures,' he replied, and sat down, hoping that this would be sufficient.

'Why not?' demanded T.S. Lo, who enjoyed putting questions, especially if it was unlikely that he would receive a satisfactory reply.

'The returns are not yet complete, sir.'

'Would the Director agree', asked James Madding, who was a lapsed Catholic, 'that abortion is no better than licensed murder of a child in being?'

'I can't say,' replied the deputy, who could not see what anyone was getting excited about.

'Is abortion voluntary or compulsory?' asked a member who was trying to be helpful.

'Of course it's voluntary,' replied the deputy. 'We provide a service in government hospitals. You don't have to use it.'

'Is it not true', asked Mrs Wong, a staunch feminist, 'that women seek abortions because men have taken advantage of them?'

'Sometimes,' agreed the deputy.

'Have you any figures of that?' T.S. Lo demanded.

'I can give you totals for two years ago,' said the deputy. I'm sure I brought them with me.' He began to search his papers, apparently without success.

'We will pass now to Question No. 5. This is also being asked by Mr Williams.' There was silence while Williams was being awakened again, to ask how many horses imported for the Royal Hong Kong Jockey Club had been refused permission to enter because they had not been inoculated, and did the Government realize that this had affected racing? As Williams was chairman of the Jockey Club, his question was taken seriously.

The last time I appeared in Leg. Co. was in August 1978, at the time when Sir Murray Maclehose was taking his annual leave. It was customary for the Governor to mark the last meeting of a member by extolling his virtues. This was sometimes a task of some difficulty, though one invariably tackled by him with some courage.

On this occasion, I was presiding over the Council. I was therefore obliged to speak myself, in the following terms, which I thought suitable to the twelve years I had spent in the Council trying to keep awake:

> This is the last meeting of this Council which will be attended by the Chief Secretary, in any of the disguises in which he has appeared in the last fifteen years.
>
> Not without reluctance, I feel it is appropriate for me to mark the occasion, even if my close and sometimes unsatisfactory relationship with him makes it difficult for me to refer to him with the relentless admiration which is customary when delivering a valedictory address.
>
> However, there comes a point in the life of any ancient survivor when his personal faults, and the catastrophes for

which he is responsible, are charitably shrouded in a fog of respect for his longevity.

The Chief Secretary has been an ex officio member for an uninterrupted period of twelve years, and indeed appeared in this Council as long ago as 1963 for a short period.

Therefore, it is fair to accord to him the same degree of uncritical reverence as is accorded to any octogenarian who can still tie his own shoelaces.

Consequently, I feel obliged to avoid any criticism, however well deserved, of the somewhat obscure and indeterminate role which he has played during this long period. This is another of these frequent occasions on which honesty would be in the worst possible taste.

Instead, I shall confine myself to delivering the kind of innocuous and inaccurate testimonial with which the managing director marks the retirement of an employee who has been asked to retire early because nobody can think of what to do with him – though I must make it clear that I do not imply that the Chief Secretary has vacated his seat in this Council in comparable circumstances.

I can, however, express my sincere appreciation of the consistent and unquestioning support which Sir Denys has given to Government proposals during the years of his membership of the Council. I do not recall any occasion on which he has matched the suicidal bravery of Mr T. S. Lo by voting against a Government motion.

And he has developed a pleasing range of tones when saying 'Aye' which will be greatly missed by members with a taste for music.

During his seven years as Attorney-General, Sir Denys achieved a higher rate of production of legislation, most of it unworkable or irrelevant, or both, than any of his predecessors. It can be fairly claimed, in his favour, that the obscurity of some of the drafting for which he was responsible has contributed substantially to the prosperity of the legal profession.

As Chief Secretary, his main achievement was to increase the number of unofficial members of Council to a point at which it became difficult to see any justification for his own continued membership, unless it is accepted that he performed a marginally useful function in dealing with questions which were either unanswerable or more were too trivial for his colleagues.

Although it is usual on these occasions to refer only to the merits, some of them hitherto undetected, of the retiring official, the Chief Secretary has asked me to depart from tradition and to express, on his behalf, his deep appreciation of the friendliness, tolerance and willing assistance which he has received from all members of the Council.

It is, perhaps, natural enough that official members who occasionally allow their thoughts to wander momentarily from the public interest to the advancement of their own careers should have found it prudent to give the Chief Secretary their diligent and unquestioning support.

It is, however, more unusual, particularly if you study the conduct of other assemblies, that he should have received from members on the other side of the house the patience, understanding and good will, both personally and in the dispatch of public business, which they have invariably displayed towards him.

Chapter 21
Courting

In December 1982, the judiciary had moved back to the old Supreme Court building in the centre of Hong Kong.

The foundation stone was laid some years before it was opened, for various compelling reasons. It was designed to be built on a raised platform, which was too expensive; it was back to front, a mistake anyone could make; the Government ran out of money, which is normal enough; and the Chief Justice and the Chief Secretary were no longer speaking, for what seemed to them, though probably not to anyone else, to be compelling reasons.

This time the building had been evacuated because the Mass Transit Railway, which was about to pass close to it, had undermined it so that it had become dangerous. While nobody minded about members of the judiciary being hurt, there was a deeper concern for members of the legal profession and, a bad second, for jurors and those accused of crimes, who had to appear in it.

The building had been made safe at inordinate cost, so that the High Court was able to reoccupy it, though still obliged to retain half a dozen courts in an office block, because it was not large enough.

I heard appeals from Magistrate's Courts about once a month. I told everyone that this enabled me to keep in touch with what was going on in the lower courts, which 'reflected the society in which they operated'. This phrase seemed to impress those who did not know me better into believing that I had an acute social conscience.

In reality, these appeals did help me to understand better what magistrates did, as I had never been one myself. On the whole, they were easier than the alternative, which was to devote the day to appeals from other courts, which were even more difficult.

There were about half a dozen appeals from various magistrates that day. After reading the records, I kept, as usual, an open mind, in the sense that in one case I had not made up my mind what to do. Most of the appellants were not represented. I noted that a Miss Alexander was supposed to be appearing on behalf of the Crown.

I entered court as the clock in the hall struck ten. It is useful to be punctual, as counsel expect a judge to be late. Miss Alexander was covering her red hair with a counsel's wig as I entered. I am not sure why I thought that I should have waited outside until she had finished.

The first two appellants put forward no argument of substance and I dismissed their appeals, without calling on her to reply. The third did not either, but I thought I should let her say something.

I studied her rather more closely as she did so. Even with a wig, which does not sit easily on a woman's hair, she was an attractive woman. Her gown largely concealed her figure, though as she leaned forward I could see that this was admirable.

'What have you to say about this, Miss Alexander? Isn't the sentence rather severe?'

'No, my lord. The maximum is three years. The appellant got two.'

'Where do you say the burden is?' I was enjoying listening to her. She had an educated voice. It didn't matter what she said.

'Gordon Bennett!' she observed in a stage whisper to the police officer behind her. 'If the old bugger doesn't know where the burden lies, what does he know?'

'You'd better humour him,' the police officer replied.

Acute hearing is not a blessing for a judge, who may catch what he is not intended to hear, as I often did. It is wrongly assumed by counsel that anyone on the bench will be hard of hearing.

Miss Alexander patiently explained to me what a burden of proof was and who had to discharge it. I thanked her for helping me and dismissed the appeal.

Shortly before one o'clock, we were half way through the last of the appeals. It would suit me to finish them off, so that I could return to my chambers and finish off the judgment which had been outstanding for over a month, in defiance of my own circular that everyone in the judiciary should try to deliver a judgment within two weeks of the close of the hearing.

'Would it suit you, Miss Alexander, if we were to carry on for a few minutes in order to finish, rather than resume at two thirty?'

'I think it would be better if we went on,' she replied, guessing that I wanted to go on.

She had not realized, however, that I had found the last appeal difficult and that I should feel obliged to ask her a number of questions, all of which she answered effectively.

It was about twenty minutes to two when the appeal ended, after I delivered an extempore judgment, the main constituent of which was 'Well – er – um'.

I thanked her for her help and left the court, making for my chambers and my lunchtime apple. I did not see Miss Alexander again for some months.

In 1983, the Commonwealth Law Conference was held in Hong Kong. One of the many functions which I attended was a reception for delegates held on the first evening in the ballroom of a Kowloon Hotel. So far, the reception had not all been successful.

I had been closely questioned by a delegate from West Africa, who wanted to know where his Chief Justice was. I was unable to tell him. This did not satisfy him. He suggested that his C.J. might be in detention, because he had spoken out about human rights and everyone knew that there weren't any in Hong Kong. He did not believe me when I said that I did not even know if his C.J. had arrived. He left me muttering about the intervention of his President. Two days later, his C.J. appeared after a short visit to Peking. His ticket had been arranged for him by an aide who believed that Hong Kong was part of China. The Chinese authorities had not been expecting him and did not know what to do with him.

I wandered aimlessly through the ballroom, smiling cheerfully at complete strangers and passing on before they had a chance to speak to me. It was supposed to be a get-together for the delegates to the conference. According to the conference brochure, it was a time to meet old friends and to make new ones. I just hoped that such a dreadful thing would not happen to me, though it was just about to.

The wife of a magistrate took me by the arm.

'I want you to come and meet a friend of mine,' she said. 'She has a serious complaint.'

'If she is from West Africa, I have already dealt with that, by saying that I know nothing about it.'

'She doesn't look West African to me. But make up your own mind.' She tapped the shoulder of a woman who was attacking a pile of potato crisps, who turned to me with her mouth full.

'Fiona Alexander,' the wife of the magistrate said. 'I think you've met the Chief Justice before?'

'Of course,' I replied, though I could not remember meeting this beautiful girl before.

'All right,' she said. 'Tell me where?'

'I expect it was some hotel room.'

'Wrong. Suggest somewhere else which is equally disreputable.'

'The only place I can think of in that class is court. You don't look like one of my defendants. They all try to look unhappy for my benefit.'

'We met in court, in December last year. I was appearing for the Crown.'

'You look quite different in your wig and gown. I mean, I didn't see your legs last time.'

'You were right,' she said to the magistrate's wife. 'He is a dirty old man. And what is more,' she went on, 'you cost me lunch.'

'That is terrible,' I agreed. 'If I had known, you could have shared my apple.'

'I don't suppose you remember, but you sat until twenty to two.'

'A short morning,' I agreed.

'I was due at the Mandarin for lunch at twelve forty-five. When I did get there, it was close to two o'clock. My host did not think I was going to turn up, so he ate his lunch and left before I arrived.'

'That was inconsiderate of him,' I agreed.

'It was worse than that. It was my only decent meal that week.'

'I can see that you are sadly undernourished,' I replied, gesturing at Fiona's admirable and generous upper works. 'In any case, I seem to remember that I gave you a choice whether we went on and finished or came back in the afternoon?'

'That was an Irishman's choice. You wanted to go on, so we would have continued anyway.'

'Probably,' I conceded. It was easy to agree with her, even when she was wrong. She had a charming smile.

'So, you owe me a lunch,' she said.

'And you've just won a five-dollar bet that you wouldn't ask me, I suppose?'

'Ten,' she replied. 'Now that I've aired my grievance, you had better go and say pleasant things to the other delegates, even if you would rather hide here and make excuses to me.'

The following week, I invited her to dinner. My secretary sent her an invitation card. As I was noted for the dullness of my entertainment, I would not have been surprised if she had refused. She accepted.

She arrived late, in a jeep which had no silencer and had been left by one of her colleagues, who was on leave. It was fortunate that the brakes worked as she drove down my drive at forty.

'Am I late?' she asked, as she was shown into my study.

'Only half an hour or so. But please don't worry. I'll tell the police to recall the search parties which are looking for your headless body in all the ravines round here.'

'At least I've come on the right evening. I was beginning to wonder, when I saw there were no other cars in the drive. I must be the first.'

'You are in fact the only guest this evening.'

'Do you mean that there is nobody else to share the listening with me?'

'What listening?'

'I expect you are going to spend most of the time telling me about your career.'

'Not all of it,' I conceded, leering at her and fingering an imaginary moustache.

'Did you ever have a moustache?' she asked.

'I grew one in 1945, when I was the brothels' officer at a leave centre in Belgium. Very well run they were too.'

'I suppose you want to recruit me? I got enough of that in the Legal Department. Some of them seem to think I came out here because I couldn't get a man in England.'

'Like the girls who were called the "fishing fleet" in India, in the old days?'

'I suppose you were there with Dickie?'

'Dickie who? Oh, you mean Mountbatten. Never met the fellow.'

'Well, I didn't. I came out here because I was broke. I thought I should be able to pay all my debts. I was wrong.'

'I could lend you a hundred dollars, if that would help.'

'If you think I am going to let you loose for a hundred dollars, you are mistaken. In any case, you have deceived me. This is supposed to be a lunch. And I would not have come to dinner if I had known I was going to be alone with you.'

'Not quite alone,' I protested. 'There's a staff of six.'

'One of whom is turning down the bed upstairs, I expect.'

'Certainly not. I would not think of taking advantage of you. Not on our first evening, that is.'

I behaved with great restraint throughout dinner. I gave her an avuncular kiss on the cheek, as she left in a cloud of gravel.

As she explained the next day to several members of the Legal Department, she had expected me to make a grab for her during the evening and was sure that I had meant to do so, until she put me off. The D.P.P. asked if she would mind doing some appeals for the Crown in front of me, as this would increase its success rate dramatically.

I did not see her again, until I asked her if she would like to come with me on a walk in the New Territories.

'What kind of walk?' she asked suspiciously on the telephone.

'With feet,' I explained patiently.

'You just want to get me into the bushes, where I shall be too exhausted to resist.'

'I also need a companion, to make sure I don't get lost, which I usually do.'

'I haven't walked for years, except from my car to the beach. Are there any taxis where you are going?'

'None. Not even a food stall. It's empty country.'

'How far is this walk?'

'Quite a short one. A few miles or so.'

'Oh, all right. I'll come. But if I pass out you'll have to carry me.'

'That will be a pleasure.'

'On second thoughts, it might be better if you just left me and went for help.'

There are, of course, not many ways in which a man of sixty can show off his fine physical condition. I tried to impress one woman, when I was about fifty, of my fitness by playing cricket. I had to be carried from the field when I suffered cramp in the right calf. I did not have much success with tennis either, as I dislocated my shoulder when serving into the net.

Walking is different. I had managed to outlast several women companions, all admittedly in terrible condition, in the New Territories. I had no doubt that I would be able to do the same with Fiona.

The driver put us down in a remote place. I asked him to pick us up from another in about five hours.

'Five hours!' Fiona protested. 'Are you expecting to take that long? You promised me it was only a short walk.'

'I'm a very slow walker,' I replied, striding off up the path at rather more than my usual pace. I thought about fifteen miles would be enough to reduce her to acquiescence, though silence was too much to expect.

Fiona talked volubly during the first few miles, mainly about my shortcomings. I did not pay much attention to what she said, making allowance for the fact that walking was something which she had not done for years. When she stopped complaining, as she did after five or six miles, I knew that she was in some discomfort.

'I wish I had brought my cigarettes,' she said at one point. 'It is your fault that I left them in the car. You said it would be a short walk.'

'It is, my dear, it is. We shall be finished by one o'clock.'

'One? We started at eight. You made me get up at six so that you could pick me up at seven.'

'It's a splendid morning! What would you be doing if you were not out here, with the trees and the birds?'

'Lying in bed, reading the Sunday newspapers, drinking coffee and enjoying myself. Did you bring any cigarettes?'

'Of course not. I gave up heavy smoking in 1965.'

'Did you bring any coke?' she asked a few miles later.

'Rather. I never go anywhere without half a dozen tins. They are all gone, alas, but I can offer you some water instead.' She accepted with poor grace.

For the rest of the journey, she said little, except to grumble about the lack of Coca-Cola. She began to limp after ten miles. As we completed the walk, she was putting her weight on one leg, and using language that her mother would not have understood.

'Having trouble?' I asked jovially.

'Only in keeping my hands off you,' she replied. 'I've been five hours without a coke or a cigarette.' She looked at her watch. 'Even my watch is broken, as well as my ankle.'

'Never mind, dear. I expect it was a little too far for you.'

We reached the car a few minutes early. Fiona was soon asleep in the back of the car. I stayed awake. At least I had discovered something which I did better than she did. I did not manage to find anything else.

I realized this when I attended a wedding, at which she was the matron of honour, in England the following year.

It was not my fault that I was late. This was due entirely to Fiona's inadequate directions. I had driven past the church earlier, but thought it was empty and that this could not be the correct one. She should have warned me that all the cars were parked at the back.

Fortunately, I was correctly directed by one of the local police, who saw me driving into a no-entry road and told me where to go. He used quite threatening language. Although I did what he told me, I thought quite seriously of reporting him to his superiors.

The service had begun before I entered the back of the church. I was asked if I was bride or groom by a young man sporting a grey waistcoat and a bout of acne. I replied that I was neither. This did not seem to satisfy him and I was put in the emptier side, which I assume to be for friends of the groom. I knew him to be Scottish as those in front of me were mainly wearing kilts. The vicar pronounced the couple as man and wife, at which happy announcement half the women in the audience burst into tears to mark the event. The bride, followed by her bridesmaids and matron of honour, walked down the aisle, smiling happily as the church organ, which appeared to have two pipes blocked, played the majority of the wedding march, to which at school we sang 'Here comes the bride, short, fat and wide, see how she wobbles from side to side.' I sang the words again to myself, as the procession went past me.

'Try not to miss the reception as well,' Fiona muttered as she went past.

I had been clever in the car park. As I had left my car across the exit, nobody could leave without me. I backed into the road, demolishing a garbage bag which had no right to be there, and followed the other cars to the reception, which was held in a local hotel.

'You were late,' Fiona said as soon as I arrived.

'Yes, but it was entirely due to your confused directions.'

'I drew a plan. I suppose you had it upside down?'

I experienced a moment of panic, remembering the unfortunate occasion when I had mistakenly directed fire at myself in Germany, mainly because the map I was looking at was the wrong way up. I did not correct those who told me how brave I had been.

'Not at all,' I replied. 'I haven't got it. I left it behind. But it is imprinted in my mind and it is misleading.'

'I told everyone here that you may have your faults, but that you were at least punctual. You have let me down.'

'If these are your friends,' I replied stiffly, 'they ought to be used to it.'

'I suppose I had better introduce you to my sister.'

'What does she think I am? I'm not sure what you tell people?'

'I say that you are a dirty old man from Hong Kong, who keeps pursuing me and won't take "no" as an answer.'

I replied that I could not have put it more accurately myself and was introduced to her sister, Morag. She was carrying twins and looked, as she said herself, like a woman called Hattie Jacques, who was an English comedienne of generous girth. She asked me if I had had trouble finding the church.

So did the bride, and the groom, and the latter's father and mother. I repeated to all of them that it was wholly Fiona's fault. This was no time to accept the blame for something for which I was not responsible.

It was about two hours before we were able to leave the reception. Fiona had changed into the clothes in which she intended to return to Hong Kong. I cannot remember what they were, though there must have been some.

She sat in the passenger seat without saying anything, though she did indicate, the second time the car stalled, that there was a handbrake and that the car would probably run better if it was off, though with me driving this was something which she felt unable to guarantee.

I drove to the motorway in what I can best call a dignified silence. I kept well within the speed limit and paid no attention to the cars behind me which sounded their horns. Fiona sat low in the seat, almost as if she was reluctant to be recognized.

I entered the motorway, after waiting on the slip road for five minutes or so, to ensure that it was clear before I entered it. Those who are less familiar than me with the motorways may not realize that there is usually an extra lane on the left, known as the 'hard shoulder'. There is seldom anything on it, except for those cars which seem to have broken down, no doubt because their drivers were attempting high speeds for which their cars were not designed.

'What the hell are you doing?' Fiona asked, in her usual oblique way. I did not take my eyes from the road when I answered.

'About thirty-five miles an hour, and I expect to get the car up to about forty, if your nerves will stand it.'

'My nerves are already in shreds. You shouldn't even be driving in this lane!'

'Why on earth not? It is quite clear. And much safer than the others. Just look at that fast lane over there. It is full of cars going at appalling speeds.'

'Why not let me drive?'

'Certainly not. It's like carving the joint.'

'If you mean that you drive as if the steering wheel was a carving knife, I won't argue with you.'

'What I mean is that driving is a male thing.'

'Like having babies?'

'There's a male contribution to that also, in case you had forgotten.'

'It's not likely that I would, with you reminding me of it every few minutes. Please stop at the next service area. I would like to get a coke and lie down until my nerves recover.'

My good humour was not increased at the café where we stopped for half an hour. I signalled for the bill, while Fiona disappeared to the cloakroom. The bill was brought to me by a plump lady wearing a white mob cap and a pink dress.

'She says you are going to pay this.'

'Who does?'

'Your daughter. Just before she went into the ladies. She told me that her dad would settle the bill.'

When I returned to the car, Fiona was already in the driver's place.

'I know that I only go at half your speed, so it will take us a long time to get to Gatwick.'

I wish it had done. I have to concede that she drove well. If she had not, at the pace she chose we should both have perished.

Chapter 22
The 'weeding'

I consulted a number of people as to whether I should get married again. I did not disclose the name of the girl concerned. I decided that I would keep this to myself. It did not occur to me that everyone I spoke to knew exactly whom I meant.

I first mentioned the possibility to John, a temporary bachelor who had been married unsuccessfully twice. He could therefore be relied upon to give a neutral opinion. He did not disappoint me.

'Don't be ridiculous,' he replied. 'What on earth do you want to get married again for?'

'There's no need to be quite so offensive about it, John.'

'The girl is 33 years younger than you are.'

'Don't exaggerate. For part of the year, the difference is only 32. Hey, I didn't say who it was.'

'I guessed, though I'm sure that nobody else will. The fact that you have been seen out with Fiona for the last six months will fool people. I have your interests at heart,' he went on. This was news to me. 'I don't think it will last.'

'I am young in heart, you know.'

'That is what people say when you have to push them about in a wheelchair.'

'I'm not in one. If I were, she would be skilful with it. Her father has been using one for years and she manages splendidly.'

'The fact that she can manage a wheelchair is not a good basis for marriage.'

'She is beautiful,' I said. 'I suppose that doesn't matter either?'

'Of course not. She'll be as old as you are now in 32 years.'

'I won't be there at 93, so your point is irrelevant.'

'She'll be a widow for years.'

'She would look marvellous in black,' I agreed.

'I would rather not discuss your sexual perversions.'

'She is bound to be a widow, even if she marries someone her own age. The world is crammed with widows.'

'She'll be tired of you in a year and be on the lookout for someone else. Just like my first wife. It's not as if you were particularly attractive yourself.'

'I don't think you are being at all helpful, John.'

'Can she cook?'

'She is absolutely splendid in the kitchen'.

'I didn't ask about that. I only wanted to know about her cooking.'

'It is excellent. The trouble is that I'm not very interested in food. However, we have lots of other interests in common. We have compatible minds.'

'That's an unusual description of what you've got. I advise you not to do it. It will be a disaster.'

On reflection, I decided that his advice was prejudiced and unreliable. It was affected by his own unhappy experiences.

My daughter, then aged 26, lived in California. She visited Hong Kong for a holiday. I thought that I had better ask her what she thought. I hoped that she might be influenced by the belief that someone else would look after me when I became a cantankerous old man.

'You go ahead and do it, if you think it's right for you. That is the usual rule in California. It works sometimes.'

'I wanted to know what you think, Mandy.'

'If you really think you must do it, you should. If you don't, you will always be sorry, even if you are sorry that you did not.'

As she had been living in California for several years, I reminded myself that this was as close as I was likely to get to a definite reply. I took her advice as an encouragement.

I decided that I would propose to Fiona on Christmas Eve. I reckoned that her judgment would probably be adversely affected by champagne and that she might agree to something which she would reject if she were entirely sober.

After lunch, in the house, as I was clearing my throat and preparing to deliver the speech I had worked on for days, mainly about her shortcomings, she fell asleep. I made efforts to wake her up and succeeded in rousing her sufficiently for her to mutter 'Bugger off' and relapse into sleep.

She did not wake for a couple of hours. When she did, she thanked me for the lunch, announced that she would have to be somewhere else at six o'clock and drove up the drive at fifty in the jeep which she had borrowed.

Next time, I planned matters with greater care and took her for dinner to the restaurant at the Cricket Club. Apart from being much cheaper than any restaurant in the town, the chairs were not comfortable, so that the chance of her falling asleep again was poor.

'It's like the Gobi Desert in here,' she observed, soon after we had sat down.

'I don't think that the Long March went as far north as that.' I was being deliberately obtuse. I was determined to keep her awake this time.

'Were you thinking of offering me a drink?' she asked, deciding that an indirect approach was wasted on me.

I ordered her a drink and sipped at a glass of wine. I decided to postpone my proposal to a more suitable moment, preferably when I had done something right, though this might not be an easy condition to fulfil.

'You know,' she said, taking the piece of lemon out of her gin and tonic and dumping it in my wine. 'I've been in touch with Bermuda again. When the A.G. of Bermuda was over here, he seemed to think there might be a vacancy for a Crown Counsel there.'

'You only want to go to Bermuda so that rich dirty old men can chase you,' I replied accusingly.

'I am chased quite enough in Hong Kong by poor dirty old men. Besides, there is not a lot to keep me here.'

This was a good opening. But I told myself I was not ready yet. I emptied my glass absent-mindedly. It was refilled by a waiter, who smiled at me because I had never taken a second glass before. I have never seen a Chinese wink. He managed it somehow.

'Don't you like your work?' I asked. 'Or does it interfere with your sunbathing?'

'Certainly, I like it. Except when I come in front of Mellors!'

'What is wrong with him? Apart from his unfortunate name?'

'He is bloody offensive. Last month he acquitted someone, after paying no attention to the evidence. When I blew my nose, admittedly very noisily, he said it upset him to have to acquit too, but that it was quite right of me to cry for the incompetence of those who prepared the case.'

'You must have been very upset to be crying,' I suggested.

'I was not crying, you idiot. I was much too angry for that.'

'What would you like me to do about it?'

'Just put him in the Labour Tribunal, where there aren't any counsel.'

'I could, of course, speak to him.'

'Not necessary,' she said. 'I just thought you'd like to know. Anyway, he's been fixed. He won't be rude to me again.'

'Why not?'

'The man who was acquitted got the idea that I had let him off. So he slashed Mellors' tyres the next day. Mellors is now convicting everyone. He may not be very pleasant, but he is not a fool and knows his tyres were slashed because he acquitted. He thinks it's a rival triad lot that did it.'

'You have restored my faith in the judiciary,' I said, draining my glass. It made me feel unusual. I tried to take hold of her hand, which was lying on the table, not by itself that is, but at the end of an arm. I missed it by a generous margin.

'Were you looking for this?' she said, stubbing out her cigarette and offering me her hand.

'Oh, was I?'

'If you were not, I cannot imagine why you were thumping the table.'

'Would you like another drink?'

'I have had three doubles. The waiter keeps filling my glass. I imagine that you must have paid him to do so. I'm quite receptive now.'

'You'll need to be, Fiona. I have an important question to put to you.'

'Well, go on then, for goodness sake. If you are going to propose I assure you I shall know exactly how to deal with it. I have had six proposals in the past ten years and accepted all of them. However, I am free now.'

'I was going to ask you if you would care to share a licence with me?' I thought this was cleverly put. Even Fiona must realize what I meant.

'What kind of licence, dear? Dog, motor car or television.'

'With you, I think it will have to be cat,' I replied with spirit. I may have been on the defensive, but there are limits.

She laughed, in the cheerful, bubbling way which I found irresistible.

'Tell me,' she asked, 'why did you bring me here?'

'Because this is the cheapest restaurant in town.'

'In view of the food, that is not surprising. Was there any other reason?'

'Certainly there was. I've already done it.'

'Was that an indecent proposal? I get them all the time in the A.G.'s chambers.'

'Certainly not. I have just asked you to marry me. Though with a chest like yours I'm not surprised that you get a lot of offers.'

'Before I decide whether to put you on the list of my fiancés, I must see the ring.'

'Which ring? I've got a curtain ring at home. I kept it because when I was young you were not let into a hotel unless the girl was wearing one. It doesn't matter now. I never use it anyhow. Would it do? We could go home and find it. I'm sure it's in my stud box.'

'I can hardly regard this as a serious proposal unless you thrust a diamond ring on to my protesting finger.'

'I promise to get one tomorrow.'

'I expect you did not want to get one, unless I said yes?'

'I haven't proposed to anyone for about thirty-five years. So I'm a bit rusty.'

'Please buy the ring at Silva. He knows what I like. And it would be fun if you choose it yourself, instead of sending out your secretary, like you intended to do.'

'I have spoken to the Anglican bishop. He says I can't be married in church, because I was divorced over ten years ago.'

'Not like Wales,' Fiona replied. 'They'll marry anyone there. Especially if they are pregnant and it is a rush job, which it usually is.'

'Are you trying to tell me, as delicately as possible, that you are in trouble?'

'If I was, which I am not, you would not be the father, would you?'

'Whatever you say, of course.'

'Did I say I would marry you?'

'Not really. You just told me what sort of ring to buy.'

'Let's assume that I am willing. What else do you want to arrange?'

'I thought it would be a good idea to keep it a secret.'

'You can't keep anything quiet here. People gossip about things you haven't even thought of yet.'

'That is why I thought it would be a good idea if we were married in Brunei.'

'That's a Muslim country, isn't it?'

'Certainly, but they have registry offices.'

'I know what you're after! A marriage down there won't count. So you'll take me through a false ceremony and you'll discard me when your lust is slaked. Just like an old shoe. My mother warned me there were people like you.'

'Of course it counts. I have already spoken to the British High Commissioner there. He says we can do it in the garden, if we like.'

'Can we indeed! Does he mean before or after we are married?'

'I meant to say that we could get married in his garden. He's got a lovely bank of hibiscus there. I have seen it.'

'Specially grown, I hope?'

'Certainly. It'll be much prettier than most churches. And far more attractive than any registry office.'

'Don't forget to remind him to water the grass, so that I can be certain that my spiked heels will stick in.'

I left for Brunei a couple of weeks later, towards the end of January. I had been going there at least twice a year since 1980.

About 1951, a unified judiciary was formed, to serve Sabah, Sarawak and Brunei. In 1963, when Malaysia came into being, Brunei refused to join. It harboured a suspicion that the rebellion which had taken place the year before in Brunei had been encouraged my Malaysia. The nearest British possession at that time was Hong Kong.

From about 1963, until the arrangement ended in December 1992, Hong Kong provided judges for the High Court and the Court of Appeal of Brunei. The Chief Justice of Hong Kong was ex officio Chief Justice of Brunei. To some of my predecessors, it seems to have been an unwelcome extra burden. I soon became very fond of it.

When I left Hong Kong, I had told nobody of the proposed wedding, except Mayreen Fook, my secretary. Fiona had promised to keep it to herself, except that she wanted to bring some witnesses to Brunei and had insisted on telling her parents and her sister.

I had not yet met Fiona's parents, who congratulated me on the phone, wished me good fortune, which I should need if I was unwise enough to marry their elder daughter, and offered to arrange for me to see a psychiatrist when next I was home. Fiona's father, who was two days younger than me, complained that she had selected as her husband somebody whom he could not call 'son'.

Mayreen Fook, who seldom made a mistake, told one of the judges, in a forgetful moment, that I had gone to Brunei to get married. It was a secret no more.

The following morning, Fiona was interviewed by a reporter and gave an interview to one of the English daily papers. It was sent to me in Brunei. The interview was accompanied by a photograph of her. It made her look so young that I nearly cancelled the marriage, as she certainly looked under age, even if she behaved as if she was well above it. The article presented me in such a favourable way that I thought, at first, that it was about someone else and became unpleasantly jealous.

The article was captivating. It did not, of course, prevent her from being accused of a variety of motives, the most pleasant of which, among a selection of iniquities, was gerontophilia.

Fiona arrived in Brunei shortly before the wedding. I had already obtained a special licence. I had even bought a ring, to impress her with my intention to take the matter seriously. I kept the ring in a safe place, even though I forgot several times where that was.

Hulme House

Wedding photo of D.R. and Fiona

I greeted her warmly on her arrival and congratulated her on the contents of the article.

'You really did very well,' I admitted grudgingly. 'It makes you sound quite willing. There's nothing in it about you being desperate or having to get married in a hurry.'

'If either were true,' she observed, 'I would hardly have chosen you to cover my tracks. Some of my fiancés were both wealthy and young. Ah well,' she concluded, 'we all make mistakes. I've always believed that, if you are going to make them, they might as well be big ones.'

This was an auspicious beginning.

Things did not go so well on the wedding day itself. Fiona had refused to have anything to do with me since dinner the evening before.

'It is bad luck for you to see me on my wedding day.'

'I was rather hoping you might turn up for the ceremony.'

'Don't be dense. I mean before that. And what is more, if you happen to see two magpies, it's all off. That's a terrible omen.'

She had booked an appointment with a hairdresser, who had a headache and did not come. Fiona's hair was therefore prepared by an assistant, who had to be restrained from backcombing and making it stiff with lacquer. She told me to keep my hands off her head, if I didn't want them lacerated.

I drove to the house of the High Commissioner by myself, dressed in my morning coat. This did not fit, as I had bought it thirty-five years before, when I was a marshal to Mr Justice Hallett, who sneered when he saw it and asked me when it was made for my father.

At the house, I waited with the magistrate, Robert Augustin, who was to perform the ceremony. He had once been a member of a seminary, though he insisted that this did not count.

'I suppose she has arrived?' I asked him. This was to put him at ease, in case he was feeling nervous.

'Don't worry,' he replied. 'I saw her come half an hour ago and disappear upstairs.'

'I thought I had arranged for a cameraman to take some video pictures. Fiona seems to want to commemorate the day. I expect they'll all laugh at it when she gets married next time,' I added gloomily.

The magistrate laughed. 'No need to worry about that, C.J. I'm a Catholic. We only remarry when the other party is dead.' I thanked him for cheering me up.

'You look rather warm,' he added. 'Would you like to borrow my handkerchief?'

'I am very cool, thank you.' I wiped a trickle of sweat from my chin. 'But I will just freshen up in the cloakroom.'

'You might care to do up your zip, while you're there,' Robert added. 'We don't want anyone to think you are rushing things.'

In the car park outside the house, the cameraman was taking careful pictures of each car as it arrived, though not of all of its passengers, as this would have been impolite. We thus have a permanent record of all the cars which attended the wedding. I do not know of anyone else who has been so fortunate.

I returned to the house. Robert ushered me into the garden at five minutes to four. It was extremely hot. We stood in the shadow of the hibiscus bushes. They provided an admirable shelter for us. They served the same purpose for the bees. We moved into the sun again.

At ten past four, Fiona had not arrived.

'Don't worry,' Robert replied, when I suggested to him that she must have been fortifying herself with vodka and overdone it. 'Brides are always late. Grooms invariably worry.'

Freddie Shoobridge, who was to give her away, came into the garden and explained that Fiona was having some sort of trouble with her dress. He thought it must be serious, as when he knocked on her door she was using the sort of language which he had heard once before, in a hostel for distressed seamen.

The cameraman had moved into the garden, where he filmed at some length both the hibiscus bushes and Robert Augustin and myself, waiting in the heat and engaged in a desultory conversation about it. It was not surprising that, when Fiona did arrive, about twenty minutes later, he had exhausted his film and was changing the cassette in his camera. This did not seem to be a simple operation.

'Wait!' he shouted. As we did not want him to miss this part, we stood and watched him wrestling with his tapes. When we thought he had finished, we began to move again.

Fiona was wearing a cream dress. As I had been married before, she explained, she could hardly have appeared in white. Whatever had been the trouble with the dress had been solved. It was only later that she explained that it was held together by four safety pins, where the stitching had torn when she trod on the dress. This was my fault, she told me, because she knew how agitated I would become if she was late, and she did not want to keep me waiting.

Robert read out the short form of marriage service, which is used in a civil ceremony in Brunei. There was no reference to endowing

Fiona with all my worldly goods, though she had told me that I could include this if I wished.

I had no best man to remind me when to put the ring on her finger. The magistrate told me, in a whisper which everyone could hear, 'Put on the ring now.'

I had put it, for safety, in a piece of tissue paper in one of the pockets of the waistcoat of my dress suit. I managed, after a moment of rather undignified scrabbling, to push it through the hole in the pocket, so that it fell to the ground.

'For goodness sake, mind your spine,' Fiona urged. 'If it seizes up, I shall find myself married to a hunchback.' I decided that this was an unnecessary risk and straightened up. Fiona retrieved the ring and put it loosely on the top of the proper finger.

'You can push it down, if you like,' she said. 'That ought to be safe enough.'

'You may kiss the bride,' said Robert with a giggle.

'That's very decent of you,' I replied. 'It will, of course, be the first time I have done anything of the kind.'

'And probably the last,' added Fiona.

Francis Cornish, the British High Commissioner, had kindly allowed us to use his house for a reception.

'Don't worry,' Fiona reassured me as we entered the room. 'I have been practising how to be a lady. I'm sure I can manage it for half an hour or so.'

After a few minutes, I made what I thought was a short speech, welcoming the guests. I gathered from Fiona that I spoke at inordinate length, which did not matter as most of the guests were so full of inexpensive champagne that they were prepared to be amused by anything.

As I spoke, the cameraman moved round the room, taking generous pictures of the guests, especially from the rear which, for many of them, was probably the best angle. This made it difficult to decide, in later years, who had attended.

We left it to him to edit the film which he made. It was introduced by a piece of cheerful Malaysian music and began with two minutes of a series of Japanese cars arriving at the house.

It was called 'The Weeding'.

Chapter 23

M.M.

Sir David Trench, the last of those Governors who had spent some years in the Colonial Service, left Hong Kong in 1971. He was not as gifted as his successors, but was a courageous and much liked man, who invariably behaved with dignity.

He was tall, which helped to impress whose who met him. His successor, Sir Murray Maclehose (M.M.), was even taller. This helped, as size was important.

M.M. was the first of the Diplomatic Service Governors, who thereafter presided over Hong Kong for more than twenty years. The Foreign Office was considered an obstructive irrelevance by many members of the local service, who wished to do things their own way, because this was highly successful in the 50s and 60s. M.M. was therefore received with some suspicion by some of his officials.

He arrived at Kai Tak, the airport for Hong Kong, named after a Mr Kai and a Mr Tak, the men who had once owned the land on which it stood. There he changed into the unbecoming white uniform which Governors wear on formal occasions. He was brought across the harbour in a launch, which had broken down the day before during the rehearsal. It disappointed us by running smoothly when he arrived.

As he stepped ashore, a band played the national anthem. It was so far out of tune that many of the audience did not recognize it. Fortunately, Sir Murray did. He produced a credible, if somewhat lopsided, salute until the anthem died away, one of the trumpeters having to be struck in the midriff to make him stop.

M.M. walked down the line, shaking hands gingerly with those who were presented to him. He had some difficulty in not getting his sword, which seemed to serve no purpose, ceremonial or other, stuck between his legs. The Colonial Secretary was somewhat behind with his introductions, so that I was put forward as the Financial Secretary, and the General, who was beside me in uniform, as the Attorney-General.

I took Sir Murray's hand in a firm grip. I thought I should make it clear from the outset that I was a person of some account. He withdrew his hand hurriedly, looking at me with a pained expression.

'You have shrunk since I last saw you, F.S.,' he commented, before moving on to the General, who was not pleased at being introduced as me.

The next time I saw Sir Murray was at a meeting of the Executive Council the following week. He had met us all before, and was therefore expected to remember everybody. As I told myself, it would be quite understandable if he forgot some of the others, but he was bound to know who I was. It impressed me that he did not make any mistakes. I did not know till later that he had a table plan, prepared by the clerk of councils, which showed where everyone was sitting and what he did. I gathered that a blank was left next to my name.

He sat quietly during a discussion about pollution. Several members seemed to want less of it. Others thought the amount was about right. A few wanted an immediate programme to reduce it, in spite of arguments that this would halve profits, drive many businesses to the wall and bring disaster and probably widespread death.

'There is no agreement on this,' he pronounced, 'so we will ask the officials concerned to look at it again and then bring it back to Council.'

I looked at him in surprise. The last Governor would have ignored the disagreement, told us all that we had agreed with what he had said himself and recorded the decision accordingly. I wondered how long it would be before he did the same, since it did not take a Governor more than two or three years before he knew a great deal more about most subjects than anyone else in the room.

Because it was the new Governor's first Ex. Co. meeting, the agenda was sparse and, so it was hoped, largely uncontroversial.

After the ill-disciplined discussion about pollution, there was a simple item of law reform, some small amendments being made to the Interpretation Ordinance. This was mainly intended to correct errors which I had made when I drafted the ordinance a few years before.

At the end of the table sat Jeff Toms, a nervous Australian with thick spectacles. He was the draftsman and was present to help me if I ran into difficulties, which the law draftsman seemed to think was likely.

'Has anyone any comments on this bill? It seems quite straightforward,' asked M.M.

I suppose it was asking for trouble to say that you had. Whatever the reason, C. Y. Kwan, the senior unofficial member, attacked me at once.

'Why have you put in this clause about the male and the female?' he demanded.

'Which one, Mr Kwan?' asked Toms from the end of the table.

'Clause three, which says that the male includes the female.'

'It was left out before,' Toms explained.

'I don't mind that so much,' C. Y. Kwan continued. 'It's the next bit which says "and vice versa". What is that supposed to mean?'

'It only means that if a law has a reference in it to a woman, this includes a reference to a man.'

'Do you mean that we are going to alter a lot of laws to put in references to women instead of men?'

'No, no. It's just that I left this bit out of the ordinance,' I replied.

C. Y. Kwan was not satisfied. As he often did when I had failed to allay his fears, he wagged a forefinger at me.

'It won't do, A.G.,' he said. He then paused, his mouth opened and his head fell forward on to the blotting pad in front of him.

Doctor Rodriguez, an unofficial member and a medical practitioner, hurried round the table and, with the help of Toms, who was very useful, lowered C. Y. Kwan to the floor. After a minute or two, he straightened and shook his head.

'There is nothing I can do,' he said. 'I'm afraid C.Y. has expired.'

'In that case,' the new Governor announced, 'I will adjourn the Council until next Tuesday. I will leave it to the C.S. to call for an ambulance.'

I was sorry to see C.Y. go. He had been a redoubtable opponent. But it would be a lesson to him not to argue with me.

During the disturbances of 1967, some left wing journalists had received substantial terms of imprisonment. Other sympathizers were similarly sentenced for rioting, arson, intimidation and causing damage. In 1972 there were still well over a hundred of them in prison.

The A.G. was ex officio chairman of the Board of Review of Long Term Prisoners. This board considered any sentence of four years or more and recommended the release of prisoners in suitable cases. Its function was that of a primitive form of parole. It had not, however, yet recommended that anyone should be released ahead of his time, except for the very sick or the very old, as it was thought wrong for anyone to die in prison. The Governor mentioned the left wing prisoners to me, at the end of a discussion, during which I had been on the defensive. This was about an ordinance which had recently been published.

'I expect that I have missed it,' said the Governor, who never missed anything, 'but I can't find the section which says the Governor-in-Council can order the taking over of land for public purposes.'

'There's a section which says that compensation shall be paid for anything which is resumed under Section 4,' added Sir Hugh. I think he was being helpful.

I looked at the Ordinance in dismay. There was no Section 4. 'Something is missing.'

'The bill seems to have gone through Leg. Co. without any Section 4,' the Governor added.

'Why did nobody notice that it wasn't there?' I asked, hoping for sympathy.

'I expect they relied on you,' the Governor replied.

'That was a fairly stupid thing to do,' I objected. 'Just because I introduced and explained the bill doesn't mean I am always right.'

'Or even that you have read it,' Sir Murray added with a laugh, in which others present joined, except for myself.

'I accept full responsibility for the error,' I said. 'I suppose I should resign,' I added.

'Don't be ridiculous,' said Sir Hugh. 'We can't have people resigning just because they've made a mess of something. We'd have nobody left.'

'I can do no less that offer you my head,' I said to the Governor, rather dramatically I thought.

'What on earth do you suppose I would do with a thing like that?'

'You could stuff it,' Sir Hugh suggested.

The Governor asked me to stay behind after the meeting. I expected him to revert to the deficiencies of the ordinance, which he did not. I was greatly relieved and happy to discuss something else.

'I don't think I have asked you about your Board of Review of Long Term Prisoners, A.G.?'

'Not yet, sir.'

'How often do you meet?'

'About three times a year. It depends on how much work there is to do. I think there will be quite a lot this year.'

'Why is that?'

'Many of the left wing journalists and protestors are due for review this year as they have served four years.'

'What does your board usually recommend to the Governor?'

'Not to do anything, unless a prisoner is very old or very ill. We think that, if we start making a lot of recommendations for an early release, the Chief Justice would get uneasy.'

'I don't suppose he would get to know, would he?'

'I don't tell him. I don't suppose anyone else would. He keeps complaining to me that nobody tells him anything.'

'According to the figures given to me, there are about a hundred and twenty serving sentences of over four years,' went on M.M. 'And our relations with the C.P.G. on the mainland are a lot better. Unhappily, these prisoners are a bit of a stumbling block.'

'Most of them did not actually hurt anyone,' I agreed. 'Before they could be released, I would have to get the two Chinese members of the board, Lai and Li, to agree with me. They said it was wrong to send left wing supporters to prison in 1967. They think they should all have been shot.'

'Of course, it is entirely a matter for you. I should be the last person to interfere with an independent board like this.'

'Naturally. And what about Lai and Li?'

'Purely by chance, you will understand, I had them both to dinner last week. I told them how valuable the work of the board is and how little it is appreciated. I told them that I had been asked if I could release the left wing prisoners to improve relations between China and Britain.'

'I expect that you told Lai and Li that you could not do so, as you could only act on what the board recommended?'

'I did. They asked me what I would do if the board thought the left wing people should be released. I said I would follow their recommendations.'

'Because they sit on an independent board, over which you have no control, I suppose you told them?'

'Naturally. It's entirely a matter for the board. If it feels that it can take this small step towards an improvement in our relations with the C.P.G., I should be pleased to go along with them.'

'I can't answer for the board, of course,' I replied. 'I don't know how it will decide.'

I was not surprised, at the next meeting of the board, when Lai and Li, apparently independently of one another, agreed with my tentative suggestion that perhaps the time had come when left wing prisoners, if they had been sentenced for political actions rather than for personal reasons, should be released. Nobody mentioned China.

By the end of the year, they had all been released. Lai and Li received awards in the following year for their valuable services to the board. Mine was to come later.

It was the practice of the Governor, from time to time, to entertain members of Ex. Co. on his boat, the *Lady Maureen*, on which he spent most Sundays. He stayed for the weekend at Fanling Lodge, a pleasant house near the Chinese border, built for the Governor before the Pacific War.

I had not been on the *Lady Maureen* before. I joined her, towards the end of 1972, at a jetty which had been built at the end of a road in the New Territories. It sailed towards another jetty, to which there was no access by road, below Sharp Peak.

'I hear you enjoy walking,' said the Governor.

'So long as it is fairly flat,' I replied modestly. I was still fit enough to go uphill if this was unavoidable, though I learned better later.

'There are some pleasant walks around Sharp Peak. I won't join you as my hip is a bit painful. Do you have a map and a compass?'

'Don't need them,' I replied confidently.

'Try and be back for lunch about one o'clock,' he said. 'That will give you a couple of hours to walk. I shall read some papers while you are gone.'

It was about twelve o'clock when I realized that I was lost. When I say lost, I did know roughly where I was. If I had walked in a straight line, I should have reached the boat in less than an hour. But I could not find a path through the jungle.

The one I followed led me to a row of houses which had been a village not so long ago. The roofs had fallen in. Across one front door was a notice in Chinese and English, saying 'Apply Mr Tang, 27, Wilmot Avenue, Hove, England'. The village was deserted.

The next path was well maintained. Even though I had no compass or map, I could see that it was not going to take me to the boat, as it turned sharply to the left. I decided not to retrace my steps. After a mile or so, the path opened out into another village. This was well maintained and obviously inhabited. Outside the first house, sitting in a bamboo chair, which sagged dangerously to its left, was a cheerful looking man.

'Do you speak any English?' I asked. I had discovered, on previous walks in the New Territories, that many people did not. As they seldom met any Europeans there was no need to do so.

The man nodded. 'I am on holiday from Manchester. What can I do for you? Would you like some tea?' I thanked him. He put his fingers to his mouth and made one of those butcher's boy's whistles which I have failed to produce all my life, in spite of frequent instructions from experts. The tea was brought by another man, rather older.

'That's my Dad,' he explained. 'He looks after the village while I am away. I expect you are lost?'

'Do I look lost?'

'Yes. Nobody comes to the village otherwise, as the path ends here.'

'I need to get back to the jetty just below Sharp Peak.'

'The safest way is to go back on the path you came on, until you meet another path at a T-junction. There you go left. You should be back at the jetty in an hour and a half.'

'I'm late already,' I protested.

'There's a shortcut, I believe, though I haven't tried it myself. I'll ask my father about it.'

He came back a few minutes later.

'My father says you take the path at the back of the village and go to the top of the hill. You should be able to see the jetty from there. He hasn't been that way himself for some years, so it may be a bit difficult to find the path.'

I thanked him for the tea and took the shortcut. It did not take me more than twenty minutes to reach the top of the hill. From there I could see the jetty in the distance, with the *Lady Maureen* lying alongside it. I knew that I should be late, but was sure I could arrive there by two o'clock.

I had not allowed for the fact that there was no path down. No doubt there had been one, but it had either disappeared or I was not able to find it. It took me more than an hour to descend the hill. I made slow progress, whistling loudly to frighten off the snakes. Someone once told me that this worked well in Africa. I could not remember if any of the snakes was attracted by whistling, but hoped there were none of them in Asia.

As I descended the hill, I noticed that a helicopter was flying backwards and forwards, as if looking for something. I remembered that newspapers were delivered by helicopter on Sundays to remote villages, as a form of training. It looked as if the helicopter had lost the village.

I arrived back at the *Lady Maureen* rather after three o'clock. The new trousers which I had worn for the occasion were torn and marked. So were my shirt and my face. I apologized profusely and explained what had happened.

'Don't worry about it at all,' Sir Murray said. 'It was my fault for letting you go off on your own. I should have known that you were going to get lost.' He was referring to another occasion, when I had been late for a dinner given by the C.S. because I had become lost on Hong Kong Island. This was a considerable feat, as it was one of the most densely populated areas in the whole world.

'You can tell the air force that they can recall the helicopter,' he said to his police A.D.C. 'The A.G. has been found.'

'Was that helicopter looking for me?'

'Certainly. If your headless corpse was found tomorrow, who would believe that I was not responsible? So I really had no choice. Please don't worry about the expense. A helicopter doesn't cost more than $1,000 an hour.'

Early in 1973, I was told that, when the present Chief Justice retired later that year, I was to succeed him. This was a common colonial progression, from A.G. to C.J. It happened sometimes, even if there were judges who were far better suited to the C.J.'s job, as was no doubt the case here. I was therefore delighted. It would not have surprised me if a judge had been appointed.

When I started to look for reasons, I decided that it must have been because the Governor wanted to get rid of me. The holder of the A.G.'s job was of importance to him. It did not matter greatly to him who the C.J. was, though he had a nuisance value.

I had been told to keep the transition to myself until it was announced publicly. I did so, though I thought that this belief in security was ridiculous.

Soon after I had been told of this appointment, by the existing C.S., I was summoned to Government House. I expected the Governor to congratulate me on my promotion. I was very pleased myself. It looked as if I had continued to make others think I was brighter than I was.

'I suppose', he began, 'you thought I had asked you up to say how pleased I am to offload you on to the judiciary at last?'

'I would not have put it like that.'

'The C.S. has been offered the Governor's job in the Isle of Man. He would like to go.'

'He did not mention that last week, when he told me about my new job.'

'It's only just come through. But it leaves me without a C.S.'

'Are you asking for my advice, sir?' He nodded.

'It depends what you want,' I replied. A splendid answer, I thought, the culmination of years in the public service. Always answer difficult questions with another.

'Well?'

'The best all-rounder is Clinton.'

'He doesn't want the job. He told me so last year.'

'The F.S. isn't ready yet, though he is very able. The Secretary for Home Affairs is charming but won't do. So it looks as though you will have to bring in someone from outside, as we did for Sir Hugh and his predecessor.'

'The service here would not like that, would they?'

'They would realize that we have to go outside.'

'I don't think they would, not a third time. So we'll have to do the best we can with what we have.'

'If you have made up your mind, sir, I will give you my support of course.'

'I'm sure of that at least, as it's you.'

'Me?' I did not take him seriously.

'Certainly. You have yourself eliminated all the other possibilities.'

'Yes, but they'll crucify me! I'm not an administrative officer.'

'I will not repeat your numerous admirable qualities, one of which is the ability to make up your mind very quickly, even if usually you're proved to be incorrect.'

'I must think it over. I shall be out of a job at 55. A judge can stay until 62, steadily deteriorating, but nobody can do anything about it.'

'I will try to ensure that you succeed whichever judge it is that becomes C.J.'

'When do you want an answer?'

'Shall we say two minutes? It should not take you much longer than that to decide whether you want to be the equivalent of a prime minister or not.'

'I accept,' I replied. 'Not only because the job is exciting, but if I leave it any longer you may come to your senses and offer it to someone else.'

What I think Sir Murray needed was someone who would carry out his ideas. He was full of them. He wanted a C.S. who would give effect to them and not argue. I think that is what he got.

Chapter 24
Visits

Each Thursday afternoon, as C.S., I tried to visit a different department, in an attempt, quite fruitless of course, to show that I was in touch with reality, and knew how things really were at ground level.

One of the most efficient, if underused, departments was the fire brigade, known as the Fire Services Department. It managed to retain the enthusiasm of its members, even though they were seldom called out. When they were, the work was often dangerous.

Like most small boys, I had always wanted to do two things: to slide down a smoothly polished steel pole from dormitory to fire engine and to drive an engine through the streets ringing the bell. I was allowed to slide down a pole.

I was wearing a Hong Kong suit, which had been made for me the week before. When I slid down the pole, most of the seams went. Only when I got home did I discover that my yellow underpants were visible whenever I bent forward. This no doubt explained why my visit caused so much amusement.

I did not drive the fire engine, as this demanded a licence to drive heavy vehicles, which I did not have. I did ring the bell, as we entered a street near one of the fire stations. This expedition ended abruptly when a motorist, who thought we were on our way to a fire, drove on to the pavement to get out of our path and demolished an illegal stall. We left the motorist and the stall holder shouting at one another, but united in their criticism of the fire brigade.

The department was inordinately proud of its newest vehicle. This took firemen 200 feet above the ground, enabling them to play their hoses on tall buildings. I was shown this acquisition by Fred Jackson, a senior fire services officer, who was proud of the new toy.

'It just came last week. It's taken us three years to wring the money for it from the finance branch.'

'I don't suppose any of them lives more than fifty feet above the ground. What about the really tall buildings?'

'There is a new 300-footer, which will take us to the top of a thirty-storey building.'

'Have you asked for one of those?'

'Certainly. I expect we shall get one in about ten years, after we've had a fire on the twenty-fifth floor of a building and people are burnt to death.'

I had by then learned that Governments prefer to react, if money is involved, rather than to initiate. When something has gone wrong, the money appears.

'How would you like', asked Fred, 'to have a ride in our new 200-foot machine?'

'Well, I – er –'

'We call it 'the drop-out'. If you are not properly tied in, you can easily drop out of the platform.

Ever since I fell off a rocking horse in the nursery, I have suffered from vertigo. On a number of occasions I have been told firmly that it is psychological and that I can conquer it if I want to. This had not prevented me, only a month before, from dropping on to all fours and crawling into a flat, when I noticed that its balcony, where a reception was being held, was on the third floor.

Before I could explain to Fred that I was sure it was an excellent machine and a great credit to a splendid force, he had strapped me to a spar, which looked insecure to me even if it was steel. It probably had a flaw in it and would fracture at a hundred feet. I should fall from the platform and land head first on the pavement. I should die in agony.

I closed my eyes as this dire picture arose in my imagination. When I opened them, the platform was climbing. Fred was beside me, strapped to another spar and still talking cheerfully. I made the mistake of looking down. We seemed to be about five hundred feet up.

I decided that it would be sensible to drop to my knees. There would then be a smaller chance of falling from the platform. The harness which attached me to the spar was too tight to allow this. The most I could do was to adopt the sort of crouch which is much favoured by hunchbacks.

'You all right, sir?' said Fred. 'Or is the back giving you a bit of trouble?' I nodded in reply. 'Takes a bit of time to get to the top.'

The machine stopped with a jerk. Fred pressed a button. The platform moved towards one of the upper floors of a tall building. It halted outside a window.

An angry face appeared and shouted at Fred, before closing the curtains.

'Sorry about that, sir. It seems as if we are interrupting a bit of the other, if you know what I mean. He seemed to think I might be an enquiry agent. Would you like to stop at some of the other windows on the way down?'

'No, thank you, Fred. I've seen how effective this machine is. Please take it down now.'

We went slowly towards the ground.

'So you can see that we are very well equipped at last,' said Fred, with some satisfaction.

'I've seem that you can deal properly with adultery at a hundred and twenty feet!'

When we reached the ground, a knot of firemen applauded. It was probably the first time they had clapped someone who was green in the face.

I may have found it difficult to retain my lunch when I visited the fire brigade. It was just as hard when I was taken round the abattoir some weeks later.

I was fond of lamb, even though the meat was somewhat strong for the Chinese palate. I had more than once seen it hanging in the butcher's shop, impaled on the sort of hooks which left wing supporters had shaken at the capitalists in 1967. I had, however, not thought about what happened before the lamb arrived at the butcher's.

My daughter had passed through a phase when she refused to eat lamb, because she was doing biology at school and could see that a little woolly animal might end up as a slice of lamb. Fortunately for me, this was not a connection which I ever made.

When I was asked if I would care to see how an abattoir worked, I agreed. I did not expect that live animals would be used.

Outside the slaughterhouse, I was met by the vet who was in charge of the Public Health Department of the Urban Council, which was responsible for the slaughter of animals.

'We bring in from China every day, for the local market, about a hundred sheep, five hundred cattle and seven hundred pigs.'

'I thought we brought in about a thousand pigs.' I had looked hurriedly at the statistics before I left. I liked to give the impression that I was something of an expert in any department's work.

'That is what we slaughter,' he replied, 'not what is brought from China.'

'Do any of the animals walk?' I asked.

'That is not such a stupid question as one might think,' he conceded. 'There was a time, about sixty years ago, when cattle were driven over the frontier from China. Now they all come by rail as far as Kowloon, where they put them into lorries.'

'I know the place. You can smell the pigs as you go past.'

'You won't smell anything in the abattoir,' he said proudly, as he opened the door. 'Everything in here is spotless. I expect you would like to see how we deal with the cattle first? After that we can look at the pigs and sheep.' He sounded enthusiastic.

'What about the goats?'

'We do not have goats. The Chinese don't eat goat meat, which they think is suitable only for poor Europeans who can't afford anything else.'

As he opened the door, a lorryload of pigs arrived. They began squealing.

'They have smelt the blood, I'm afraid, and have guessed that something unpleasant is going to happen to them. Not that it is, of course.'

'Apart from being slaughtered?'

'Yes, but it is done very humanely. Nobody bleeds while conscious.' He shut the door behind him. In a pen to his left a number of cattle were standing. As we watched, one of them was ushered into a narrow passage.

'When he gets down there,' the vet explained, 'a stun gun is strapped to his head.'

'What happens then?'

'The gun is fired and a steel bolt hits the cattle in the head, knocking it unconscious. It collapses on to a moving belt, which takes it along to the next room. We call this the preparation room. That is where we cut the throat.'

'But the cattle are still alive.'

'They don't feel a thing. That is why we have the stun gun. In the old days, they were prepared while they were still conscious. They did not like it at all.'

'I suppose this new procedure is very popular among the cattle?'

'If they could talk, I am sure that they would tell us that it is a great improvement over the old method.'

In the preparation room, men wearing white coats spattered with blood were playing hoses on to the drains. They waved cheerfully at us as we walked past.

'I expect you would like a drink before we look at the sheep and pigs? The pigs do make rather a lot of noises. They seem to sense what sort of a place this is.'

'If you are going to offer me a cup of warm blood, I'm not sure I can manage it.'

He led me to the office attached to the abattoir. There he talked of his long experience of the slaughterhouses of Asia. He told me how primitive these still were in parts of China, how improved the facilities were in South Korea and Singapore, and of the special methods which had to be adopted in Muslim countries.

From time to time, I asked him questions, which were sufficient to remind him of how they disposed of animals elsewhere. I did not want to return to the abattoir. I was feeling odd. The sight of blood has always disturbed me, since I was punched in the nose by Wilkins at the age of 7. I never really understood why he hit me, as all I had done was to ask the headmistress why Wilkins kept playing with himself.

'Good heavens,' said the vet, looking at his watch. 'It's nearly four o'clock. Shall we go and see the pigs?'

'Four o'clock! I promised to phone my office then. There is a bit of a crisis.'

I telephoned my secretary, a splendid woman who had been lent by the Foreign Office to try to keep my affairs in some kind of order.

'Mary,' I said, 'what has happened to the crisis?'

'Oh,' she replied, knowing where I was, 'it is worse. In fact the Governor would like you to return as soon as you can. It is very urgent.'

'What a pity,' I shouted back at her so that the vet could hear. 'I was really enjoying myself in the abattoir. Please tell His Excellency that I will be with him as soon as I can manage it.'

I apologized to the vet for having to leave in such a hurry, and before a fascinating and rewarding visit was finished.

'Come back later,' he insisted. 'I know how much you wanted to see how we get rid of the pigs.'

I managed to get home without being ill, though I was close to it more than once. The visit had, however, left its marks on me. The cook did not understand why I was unable to eat the steak which he offered me for dinner.

One of the tasks of the Marine Department was the staffing and maintenance of lighthouses, which were placed in the principal approaches to the Colony, mainly on barren outcrops of rock which were useless for any other purpose. The lighthouses were supplied by sea, but those which were still manned by keepers, which were in a minority, had a helicopter landing pad constructed on a levelled space below them.

I suggested to the Director that I ought to visit the lighthouse on Waglan, which lay to the east of Hong Kong Island. He arranged for me to go by helicopter. When I arrived at the helipad in the Central District, the plane had not arrived. It did so a few minutes later, landing heavily and bouncing. I climbed aboard, ducking my head beneath the blades, which were still rotating.

'Sorry, I'm late, C.S.,' said the pilot, whom I recognized as Ross Penlington, a cheerful New Zealander. He had been a Crown Counsel and prosecuted with some success between flights. He was now a district judge. I did not ask him how he managed to take the afternoon off. At that stage, I believed that nobody in the judiciary worked very hard.

'Glad you kept your head down, when you walked across,' he added when I had been strapped in and provided with an earphone by his co-pilot. 'We lost a chap last month when he walked into one of the blades. He was a tall bloke, mind you. I hope I can get her up again. I'm a bit rusty at flying these things. What is more, they've changed the model since I learned. This is full of avionics, but I'm not sure which button to press. Where did you want to go?'

'Waglan. To look at the lighthouse. Didn't anyone tell you?'

'I expect they did. Is that the place with the sheer drop into the sea off the edge of the pad, Jack?' His co-pilot nodded. 'Do we have any maps of it?' The co-pilot shook his head.

'OK, then. Off we go. Are you all right back there?'

'No,' I replied. 'Firstly because I have no confidence in the pilot, secondly because I want my mummy and thirdly because the door is still open and I expect to fall out.'

'How are you for heights? Whoops,' he added, as the helicopter rose, veered sideways and narrowly missed a crane in the nearby naval basin.

'So why not shut the door?'

'Regulations. We have to keep the door open for safety,' said the co-pilot.

'Safety. It's very dangerous! What happens if I fall through it?'

'Depends how high we are. If we're over ten feet, I'm afraid you would have a nasty accident. The door has to be left open in case we have a fire. If we do, you can jump out, of course. Dear me, I must watch where I am going.'

He seemed to have missed a tall building by about ten feet. I clung with determination to the back of his seat. I did not rely on my belt. It could easily come loose, and I would be sucked out through the open door. My knuckles were white when we landed at Waglan. It took a while to prise them loose and for me to walk to the lighthouse, where I was met by the Director, who had come in a boat, and the keeper, named Fong.

'How long have you been here?' I asked him.

'Fong is a bit hard of hearing,' the Director explained. 'It's because of the silence. He's been here about forty years. He should have retired about five years ago, but he doesn't want to go.'

'Why is this island called Waglan?'

'As far as I know,' the Director replied, 'we built the lighthouse shortly after the Crimean War and named it after Lord Raglan.'

'It is not spelt the same.'

'As a lot of Chinese found trouble with the "R", it became known as Waglan.'

Mr Fong grinned happily and made for the narrow staircase, which led in a spiral to the lighthouse. By the time we reached the top, I was out of breath and my legs were hurting. Mr Fong was untroubled.

As I sat with my chest heaving, in the only chair, Mr Fong showed me how he cleaned the mirrors. The light had not gone out since he came to the island in 1936, he said, not even when the Japanese were here and wanted him to turn it off to mislead the British ships, if they came back.

Mr Fong gave me a cup of tea before I left. He had, he said, used a fresh tea bag. This he did not do very often, as supplies had been short in 1943 and he had learned to use tea bags as often as possible. He waved goodbye as I left for the helicopter. He was past the usual retiring age when I visited Waglan. He was still in charge of the lighthouse ten years later. Successive directors did not like the idea of moving him forcibly.

On the way back, Ross Penlington asked me if I would like to see where I lived. I said that I would not, which he apparently regarded as enthusiastic agreement. The house looked impressive from the air. The roof was in good condition. Green shoots were growing from one of the chimneys. I refused an offer to land on the lawn.

The door remained open on the return journey, which I enjoyed as little as the outward flight. I went straight home and shut myself in my bedroom, indulging in deep breathing until I felt better.

'You must go and visit the Customs Department,' I was told. 'It will be very good for morale.' Nobody seemed to consider mine, which was poor after my trip in the helicopter and my visits to the fire brigade and the abattoir.

Customs officials face a difficult task. Apart from the usual evasions, such as describing a consignment of dutiable articles as something free of duty, they were obliged to search incoming ships for heroin. The smugglers were ingenious, and customs officers often did not find the drug unless they had received a warning beforehand.

I was taken out to the quarantine anchorage, where incoming ships were stopped for clearance. We went in one of those motor-boats which travel at outrageous speed, with the front in mid-air and the rear just above the water. Every few yards, the front end slapped the water. I had not been a good sailor since I was sick playing with boats in my bath. The customs officer, named Watson, had been in the merchant navy. He seemed to enjoy the voyage to the anchorage.

He was equally at home as we climbed the rope ladder which had been lowered from the main deck. Half way up it, I looked down. The boat in which we came had left, in a cloud of spray. The harbour below looked green and unattractive. If I fell into it, as seemed likely, I should almost certainly choke to death on the plastic waste which surrounded the *Arethusa*, as the visiting ship was called. The unpleasant alternative spurred me to the top of the ladder.

I asked Watson where the *Arethusa* was registered, as the name sounded British.

'Liberia,' he replied. 'Most of the ships are registered there or in Panama. It's much cheaper than going to London. We have found most of the drugs on ships that have come from Thailand, like this one.'

He offered me some blue overalls, of the kind worn by garbage men.

'Surely I don't need these,' I protested.

'Best way of keeping the oil off your suit. That is, if you want to see what it is like to search a ship. It's a pretty messy business. Just follow me.'

Watson clambered down a steel ladder into what looked like an engine room. Here, other men in boiler suits, some heavily stained, were searching vigorously. I watched as they became dirtier, without finding anything.

'Anyone found anything suspicious?' shouted Watson. Nobody had.

'Is that all?' I asked hopefully.

'Not yet, sir. We next search the cargo.'

'You mean, we started in the engine room?'

'That's right. We don't often find much down here. We have to look just in case. Look out, sir,' he shouted as I stepped back to allow one of the stained suits to pass me.

Unfortunately, I had caught my boiler suit in some piece of machinery, which must have been put there especially to trap people like myself. It took some minutes to extract me. I must admit to having moved, when I was told to keep still. As a result, the sleeve of my suit was torn. I asked Watson not to let it bother him as I was sure it could be repaired.

I was taken to the front of the ship to have a look at the cargo.

'We can't do more than random checks,' Watson explained. 'This ship is supposed to be carrying tomato sauce, cooking oil and pineapple rings.'

He opened a packing case. Inside were two dozen bottles of ketchup. He extracted one and dropped it to the floor. It smashed satisfactorily and splashed my boiler suit.

'There you are! Nothing in that bottle.'

Watson next opened a carton marked 'cooking oil'.

'We will test that too,' he announced.

'Please don't smash it for me,' I protested. 'Why not just pour it out?'

'Very well,' Watson agreed. 'Though it isn't quite the same thing, you know.' He undid the screw top and poured the oil over the floor.

'Just oil,' he said. 'What a disappointment. Now let's try the pineapple rings. There are cases of them. We'll just prise open one or two and have a look.'

He extracted a tin and used a can opener on it. He poured the contents to the ground.

'Nothing there either. We'd better try once more and then give up. Would you like to open a tin yourself, sir?' He handed me the opener and a can of pineapple rings.

I suppose the ship was moving up and down a bit. It may have been my desire to impress Watson. Whatever the reason, I cut my thumb on the opener.

I did not mind my failure to find heroin in the pineapple tin. I did not mind having to bind up my thumb. I would not have objected to my boiler suit being spattered with a mixture of tomato sauce, oil, cooking liquid and pineapple juice. I did, however, feel unhappy when I returned to the deck to find several photographers waiting for me.

Mary greeted me with a smirk when I went to the office the next morning.

'An interesting photograph', she said, 'all over the front pages of the Chinese papers.'

'They were waiting for me, Mary. The customs must have tipped them off.'

'I liked your boiler suit. I didn't know you had one!'

'I don't. It was lent to me. And I hurt my hand.' I shook the plaster covering my thumb.

'I'm glad it was only your hand. Next Thursday, you are supposed to watch an operation. I do hope you won't be asked to try out the scalpel.'

Chapter 25
Trial judge

I returned to Hong Kong in May 1979 after more than seven months away. This long period, for which the Hong Kong Government generously paid, was mainly occupied by a series of visits to Commonwealth countries.

In these I learned that in most courts there was a long delay in dealing with both criminal and civil matters and that it was difficult to secure money for more judges and courthouses since there were other projects which seemed to the local treasuries to be a better use of scarce resources. Fortunately for me, Hong Kong was not a democratic regime and the unofficial members, who approved all expenditure, did not owe their positions to votes. I was therefore able to secure, during the next few years, the majority of what I sought. In addition, the Hong Kong officials may have decided that it would be sensible to keep me quiet; otherwise I might have made a nuisance of myself, by persistent lobbying of those unofficial members with whom I had dealt for some years about other matters.

When I returned in 1979 it was about twelve years since I had appeared as an advocate and six since I had last given legal advice. Since 1973 I had tried to do so once, when I argued with the A.G. in Executive Council about something he had said.

'Tell me,' he said after Ex. Co., 'what is your position?' John Hobley was a quiet, determined man, who had been retrieved hurriedly from Bermuda, to which he had been lent for a couple of years, when I ceased to be A.G. I thought he was being rather slow and somewhat out of touch, even though he had been away.

'The Colonial Secretary, though I am hoping to change the title. Do you think that's a good idea?'

'I thought you were still the Attorney-General,' he went on.

I looked at him closely. He was smiling at me, though only just.

'Certainly not. That's you. And very well you do it,' I added, hoping that this would divert him.

'I'd do it better if you did not argue about the law.'

'What, me?' Hobley nodded. I thought back. I had.

'Please remember that you don't know any.'

'That won't be difficult.'

'But it will be difficult for you to keep quiet when I give the Governor advice you don't like.'

'I will try to say nothing in future.'

'That won't be easy. Remember what you said when you were A.G.? That one of the important parts of the job was to tell the administration that it can't do something that it wants to do.'

'Unless it changes the law first?'

'That's not too hard while you still have an official majority in Leg. Co.'

After this, I did my best to forget the little law that I had learned. I left it to Hobley to advise, as he continued to do with much ability for some years. No doubt this prevented me from intervening, when I should not have done as C.S.

When I became C.J. in 1979, the Supreme Court was sitting in a building which had been built, some sixty years before, for a group of French monks. It had housed the Education Department for a time, but was allocated to the Supreme Court when an alternative courthouse had to be found hurriedly for it.

The old Supreme Court building had been undermined by the Mass Transit Railway. The Chief Justice had reported on several occasions that the building was unsafe. No action was taken by the administration, which, apart from regarding judges as expendable, had received similar reports along the line of the underground railway. It was obliged to do something only when a large piece of cornice broke off and fell on the desk, in the chambers, of one of the judges. Fortunately, or unfortunately, depending on the point of view, the judge was in court. However, this fall could not be ignored, as a massacre of judges would cause establishment difficulties and probably give rise to an enquiry, from which the Government could hardly emerge with credit, even if it agreed that the loss of a few judges was of lesser importance than the building of a Mass Transit Railway.

The Supreme Court was therefore transferred to the monk's building in Battery Path. The Court of Appeal sat in a long, narrow room which had served as a chapel when the brothers had occupied the building. The judges, as I suppose was appropriate, sat where the altar had been. Counsel, though unfortunately not required to kneel, occupied the space where the pews had been placed.

The Chief Justice's secretary was a Chinese girl with a strong Welsh accent. She had been brought up by her parents in Cardiff and had returned to Hong Kong only when she was an adult. She was an admirable secretary, often reminding me of things I did not even know that I had forgotten.

'I think,' she began, as she always did when she was sure, 'that we have a jury trial tomorrow.'

She was being tactful, as she had typed out four different versions of my summing up. She did not think a great deal of my insistence on presiding over trials with a jury. This meant extra work for her, usually late in the evening, and much of it wasted as I kept changing my mind.

Because I had been away from the law for somc years, I thought it would be sensible if, in addition to sitting in the Court of Appeal, I took part in jury trials, civil trials and appeals from magistrates, though my two immediate predecessors, who had much experience of work as puisne judges, had not sat outside the Court of Appeal.

I had been provided with an experienced court clerk. It was his task, so he was told by the Registrar, to see that I made as few mistakes as possible. My first jury trial tested him severely. The clerk's name, fortunately, was S. K. Wong. At least I could pronounce it correctly, except for getting the tones wrong. He brought me the papers in the case, which had been sent for trial before the High Court by a magistrate, after a 'paper committal', in which the statements of witnesses had been tendered but the latter had not been called to give oral evidence.

'Are you sure you want to do this, sir?' Wong asked unhappily. He knew that I would make a mess of it. He would be blamed for it. So long as I sat on the Court of Appeal, with two other judges, he did not feel responsible. If I insisted on conducting trials by myself, he did. He would lose face if I was reversed on appeal.

'Certainly,' I retorted. 'I want to have a shot at everything!'

Wong cringed. Usually, he was a plump, happy man. Now he looked miserable and thin.

'There might be a plea of guilty.' Wong brightened as he said this. 'Shall I get you the book on sentences?'

'If that happens, I'll take another case. What is this one about?'

'It's robbery,' he replied gloomily. 'The Registrar says it's very easy, sir. So you need not worry.'

'What happens if the jury can't make up its mind and has to be kept somewhere all night?'

'You sent out a circular about that last month.'

'I'm always signing pieces of paper the Registrar says I need not read. What did that one say?'

'You asked all the judges to finish summing up by three in the afternoon or save the last few minutes until the next day, so that the jury would have plenty of time to reach a verdict without anyone having to put them into a hotel.'

'Sounds a rather sensible circular, S.K.'

It also said there was no accommodation arranged for the jurors, though you hope to find some soon.'

'Have I?'

'Not yet, sir. The circular is quite new. Meanwhile the Registrar has kept some camp beds in his office.'

'Has he used them?'

'He did, before you sent out the circular. You may remember that Mr Justice Brown finished summing up to his jury about eight in the evening. As they had not agreed by midnight, he put them all on camp beds, the men in one court, the women in another. They did not like that.'

'I suppose it was being segregated. Didn't they acquit?'

'They did. When the court clerk, who looked after them, asked one of the ladies why they had let off the defendant, who had obviously done it, she said that she wasn't going to risk another rotten night's sleep, even if the others did.'

'Was that the only reason?'

'Some of the members of the jury did not like the judge. They said that he wanted them to convict, and that they were not going to do what he wanted. As the judge had a wart on his neck, that was very bad luck. So they acquitted.'

'They won't like the mole on my head. I suppose I had better cover it up.'

'Moles are all right, sir,' S.K. replied soothingly. 'It's just warts that are bad luck. Besides,' he added, 'it must have been a very superstitious jury.'

'Just warn the Registrar, then, that we may need the camp beds.'

'I have done so already, sir.'

I was not, of course, at all worried. The fact that I had not been involved with a jury trial for the best part of twenty years did not matter. I had been criticizing other judges for their summing-ups for a couple of years. So I knew what ought to be done, even if I did not do it.

As I could not be sure of what I had said, I read again all my judgments in criminal appeals. I was glad to find that I had repeated several times that a summing-up only had to be fair and that an appellate court should not pick at it like a vulture over a corpse.

To ensure that I was not waylaid, during the trial, by a clever defence counsel who knew more than I did about the rules of evidence, which would not have been difficult, I took a copy of

Archbold on Criminal Pleading and Practice and a number of other books to bed each night. I could not rely on prosecuting counsel to correct the defence. I had been a prosecutor myself.

It was entirely the fault of this text book that I did not sleep well the night before the trial was due to begin. Several times, as I dozed, I remembered a point of evidence to which I did not know the answer. By the time I had found passages which dealt with the point, another hour or so had passed and I found it difficult to get back to sleep.

What I found even more disturbing was that either the textbooks did not deal with the matter at all or, as often occurred, merely cited several decisions, which appeared either to ramble about in all directions or to contradict one another.

I spent three hours, for example, in trying to discover why a witness should be allowed to say how old he was, as he was only repeating what his mother had told him, which was hearsay and not admissible. I found no answer in the text books.

S. K. Wong entered my room with a worried look, about five minutes to ten. I was already dressed for court in my red robes. I had tried the wig at several angles and chosen that which I thought most attractive. I hoped it would project an image of firmness and compassion.

'Have you come to fetch me, S.K.? You must not be nervous. It is not time yet.' I thrust my hand into my pockets, so that he would not see that I was trembling.

'Not yet, sir, please. Mr Justice Baber is having a bit of trouble selecting a jury. As soon as he has finished, he will send up the others to you.'

'How many did we ask to come?'

'We thought we would be safe, sir, so we've got about fifty of them for only two juries. Usually we manage with less.'

'Why is Mr Justice Baber having trouble, do you know?'

'I am told that his trial is likely to last a month. When he told the waiting jurors this, half of them said that if they were away from work that long they would lose their jobs. So he let them off. And a lot of others hurried out too without permission. I will let you know when we are ready, sir.'

It was about a quarter past ten when S.K. returned.

'Please don't let it worry you, sir. But we've only got about fifteen jurors left.'

'Why is that?'

'Because the others have gone. As soon as Mr Justice Baber told them he did not want them, they left. It was quite a stampede.'

'How can I manage with fifteen? There may be challenges by the defence and the Crown may ask some of them to stand down.'

'Don't worry, sir. I'm sure we'll manage.' S.K. did not actually pat me, though he would have liked to do so. He had been dealing with nervous judges for years.

I followed Wong into the Chapel (as the Main Court was called), a few minutes later. At the back was the Registrar, with two of his assistants. I thought that this was entirely unnecessary, if he feared that I would make some mistake, though permissible if he wanted to see me preside with some precision over my first jury trial.

The accused, as expected, pleaded not guilty. He was a villainous looking man. Nobody, I decided, could be innocent and look like that. I reminded myself that I must remain neutral and that anybody who looked as guilty as he did must be innocent.

S.K. addressed the jurors and asked them to come to the jury box as their names were called, reminding the defendant that he had the right to challenge any of them before they were sworn. The defendant nodded his head, and spoke in Cantonese to S.K.

'What did he say?' I asked. I did not have enough experience of Hong Kong defendants to keep quiet.

'He said that he did not like the look of the first juror, sir.'

I asked his counsel, an eager Chinese named Chan, if he wanted to challenge the first juror. I did not much like the look of her either.

Chan turned to the dock and spoke to his client.

'We challenge this juror,' he said. 'I've told the defendant to leave it to me in future and not upset Your Lordship by speaking when he should keep quiet.'

'Is that all he said?'

'Well, no,' admitted Chan, 'but I would rather not repeat his other words.'

'Please do, Mr Chan.' I saw S. K. Wong was shaking his head, but ignored him.

'He said he did not want to upset Your Lordship, who is going to tell the jury to release him and who looks so handsome in his wig.'

I revised my first opinion of the defendant, who was obviously a man of discernment, however he looked.

Chan challenged two more of the women who were called to the jury box. Counsel for the Crown remained silent, no doubt because he thought his case was so strong that it did not matter how the jury was composed.

Before the trial began, I saw a juror whispering to Wong, who had collected the cards from which the jurors had read out the oath. More than once, from a juror's inability to read the card, it had been discovered that he could not understand English, though all jurors were supposed to be able to do so.

Wong was shaking his head, when he spoke to me, in a stage whisper, which must have been heard by everyone in spite of the fact that the room had been built as a place of worship.

'It's the juror at the end, sir. He says he knows the defendant.'

'That doesn't matter, does it?' I started to look at *Crown Court Practice* to see if there was any reference in the index to 'friend of the accused, disqualification of juror'. I could find nothing.

'It's not that, sir. He says that he was on the jury for the defendant's last trial for robbery, when he was convicted and his record was read out.'

'What shall I do, S.K.?'

'Better let the juror go.'

'We haven't got any spares, however?'

'I'm afraid that we have used up the fifteen that came from the other court. We will have to find some more jurors elsewhere. It's called praying a tales, I think.'

'You mean, we use that?'

'Mr Justice Baber has, twice.'

'That's his sense of humour. So what will we do?'

'Please go back to your room and leave it all to me, sir.'

As I left, I saw S. K. Wong speaking to the Registrar, who appeared to be giggling, which I thought to be in poor taste in the circumstances.

I paced my room for half an hour. My desk carried a pile of annual confidential reports. These had been placed there every morning for the past month by my conscientious secretary, with a note that they were late. She had spent some years in business and still worried about that sort of thing.

Once a year, I am supposed to report on my colleagues, drawing to their attention any defects which I thought they could rectify. The temptation, to which I succumbed regularly, was to write something nice, or nothing at all. I did not think that anyone read them. To my surprise, a man from the Foreign and Commonwealth Office told me, some years later, that he greatly enjoyed reading my reports. Even if they bore no resemblance to my subjects, he thought that they were literary works of a high standard.

I decided to fill the waiting time by writing a report about Featherstone. I had got as far as recommending that he would probably do better in the Solomon Islands, as the Hong Kong climate did not seem to suit him, when S. K. Wong returned, smiling happily.

'We have them, sir!' he announced. 'We could not find anyone in the building, so we went into the street and brought some people in from there.'

'I hope they came voluntarily?'

'Except for those who thought we were the police. They ran off.'

'I hope they are all qualified.'

'Don't worry about that, sir. We told each of them that they were. We'd better go in now.'

There was an unhappy group at the back of the court, presided over by the thin, tubercular looking police officer who was supposed to guard me. Much to my relief, I was never attacked by an unhappy litigant. If I had been, I would have been obliged to try to defend the constable as well.

'Please answer your names and come to the witness box,' S.K. announced. 'Mr Oriyashi.'

After many years in the Far East, I kept mistaking Chinese for Japanese. But the name made me suspicious. It was like a Chinese being called Smith.

'Just take the card in your hand and read what is written on it,' said S.K.

Oriyashi beamed back at him through his thick glasses.

'I think we may have made a mistake, sir. He does not look right to me. I will ask him.'

S.K. directed several questions at Oriyashi, in English, Cantonese and Mandarin, all of which S.K. spoke well. Oriyashi smiled in reply, bowed several times and used a language which nobody could follow.

'Oh, dear,' conceded S.K. 'I don't think this juror will do, sir. He does not understand what is happening.'

The prosecutor, a clever and pleasant counsel named Alderdice, asked if he could help.

'As I come from New Zealand, I am quite good at broken English,' he said.

'We seem to be rather desperate,' I agreed.

'You come see Hong Kong?' Alderdice asked him.

'Ah so,' replied Oriyashi.

'You tourist?'

'Ah so.'

'You stay hotel?'

'Ah so.' Oriyashi produced a card, which was one of those electric affairs with which you are unable to obtain entry to anything. It bore the name of a prominent hotel.

'You come seven days from Japan?'

'Ah so' replied Oriyashi again. His supply of English seemed limited.

'I don't think he'll do, my lord. He seems to be on a package tour, which probably includes sex and that's what he thinks we are going to provide.'

'Ah,' I said. 'I expect the robes have done it.'

At the word 'sex', Oriyashi clapped his hands together and pointed at the female court reporter.

'Might I suggest that it would be better if Mr Oriyashi was removed,' I said to S.K. 'He obviously thinks that you are the pimp he was expecting.'

'That's the tour guide's job, sir, not mine. I've seen one of them lead a party into a brothel with a flag, sir.' Wong gestured at the constable, who removed Oriyashi from the room.

Another of those who had been found in the street was called to the jury box. This time it was a grim faced Chinese lady.

'Challenge!' said Chan.

'You can't do,' protested Alderdice. 'You've had your ration.'

'I used three on the proper jury. I've got three more on the talesmen, or whatever they're called.'

'Why do you object, Mr Chan, to this lady?' I asked.

'I don't like the look of her,' he replied with surprising honesty. I didn't myself, but I would not have had the courage to say so.

'So it is a peremptory challenge, and not one for cause?'

'Whatever Your Lordship says,' conceded Chan, who had obviously not heard that there was any difference. Nor had I, until I had looked it up a few nights before, just in case.

I turned to the relevant pages in the text books, which filled the trolley standing beside me on the bench. None of them contained anything about challenges to talesmen. I have found that most of the difficulties which occur during the trial were either not mentioned by any of them or were carefully mis-indexed, so that I was only able to discover them the following day when I had already decided wrongly.

I adopted what I described as 'the practical approach', when I could find nothing to guide me.

'How many did you pull off the streets, S.K.?'

'Only the four. They seemed enough for one vacancy.'

'If we allow Mr Chan two more challenges, that would exhaust them, now that we've let Mr Oriyashi go?' S.K. nodded gloomily in agreement.

'I will have to go out again and get some more,' he agreed. 'Next time I'll get twenty.'

'Don't worry, you'll probably bring in a group of Austrian visitors, who only speak German.'

'But –,' replied Chan.

'I have considered your point, Mr Chan. It's a novel and interesting one.' Mr Chan beamed. 'I rule that there will be no peremptory challenges of the talesmen. Please swear the last juror.'

I noticed that she seemed to have some difficulty in reading from the card. I preferred to believe that this was due to nerves. The last juror folded her arms and glared at counsel, and then at me. I wanted to tell her it was not my fault.

As Alderdice opened his case for the prosecution, I began to think of what I would have said if I had been sitting in the Court of Appeal, when this case came before it.

'We regret to have to say that the trial judge failed to follow those elementary rules, established 400 years ago, which govern the right of defence counsel to challenge potential jurors. If this essential safeguard is removed, the defendant will be severely prejudiced throughout his trial. The strong protests of his counsel were overruled by the judge. We have no alternative, in view of this serious defect, but to quash the conviction.'

The case proceeded at measured pace. Chan cross-examined each witness at inordinate length, mainly about matters which seemed to have nothing to do with the case against the defendant. Alderdice dozed quietly throughout, so that I could not count on any help from him. I decided not to intervene myself, as Chan would have argued that this showed that I was biased against his client. I was determined to appear neutral in my first jury trial, even if this meant that an obviously guilty man was going to be acquitted. I had, of course, retained an open mind.

On the fifth morning, S. K. Wong entered my office. He never wrung his hands. If he had acquired this habit, he would have done it then.

'Sir, sir,' he announced, 'it's all my fault.' I nodded in encouragement. That was a good start. 'It's the woman juror. She's just spoken to me.'

'I don't suppose that's a ground of appeal, is it? I'd better look it up.'

'No, no, sir. It's not that. She asked me when she could go home, because her husband does not like her being away each day.'

'Jurors don't often listen to anything much until the summing-up, apart from deciding if they like the look of the witness or not.'

'She says that she does not understand any English, and why do you wear that funny thing on your head?'

'She read the card, didn't she?'

'She nodded her head when I asked her if she was on the jury list too,' replied S.K. 'She says that she can read a little English and knew what was on the card because a friend of hers was on a jury last year and told her all about it.'

'Ought we to see if she's on the jury list?'

'I have, sir. I got someone in the Registrar's office to look. She isn't.'

'I suppose that I had better stop the trial, S.K.?'

'It's a pity, sir. You won't be able to sum up.'

I shook my head sadly. It would not do to let him guess that this was an attractive argument for not continuing.

As soon as I entered court, I questioned the lady juror.

'How well do you understand English?' I asked her.

'Good day,' she said.

'Mr Yuen,' I said to the interpreter, 'I think we should ask her the same question in Cantonese.' David Yuen did so.

'She says that she doesn't understand English at all. She did not know that she was supposed to do so. She was arrested on the pavement outside, brought to court and put in the jury box, where she has been ever since. She wants to know how much longer she has to sit there.'

'How does she know when to come back?'

'She asks the other jurors, who speak Cantonese among themselves.'

'I'd rather nor get into that,' I replied hastily.

I announced that, in view of one juror's lack of knowledge of English, I had no alternative but to stop the trial and order it to take place before another jury.

The defendant protested, insisting that, as the trial had stopped, he should be acquitted. I rejected this attempt, as I described it, 'to interfere with the due process of justice'. I discovered later that he had paid one of the jurors a considerable sum to vote against his conviction. The money was wasted.

Chapter 26
The judicial image

It is insufficient merely to be a good judge. Wisdom, learning and intelligence are wasted if those who benefit from them fail to recognize them for what they are. So a judge must seek to project himself in as favourable a manner as possible, even if this involves a battle with his natural modesty.

The ordinary citizen knows little or nothing of jurisprudence, of the virtues of civil and criminal proceedings or of the intellectual niceties of the law. If the judge is wise, tolerant and sympathetic, the citizen will assume that the system is. If the judge is short tempered, ill mannered or inhuman, the citizen will not think much of any system which allows this to happen.

As Lord Trott, L.C. once observed, 'It is more important to appear to be a good judge than to be one.'

Good temper

A judge must soon realize that, unless he develops a calm and detached manner, he is unlikely to retain his temper in the face of the procession of human incompetence which is paraded before him. If he does not adapt, he will be affected by bouts of ungovernable range, apoplexy, strokes and premature death, at best. Unless he is able to maintain a relaxed outlook in all circumstances, his sagacity and learning will be drowned in a sea of bile.

Analysts agree that any man in a prominent public position must be able to relax completely in his own home. A judge who causes serious physical injury to his wife would probably be obliged to resign. He must, therefore, adjust his domestic life.

Among the expedients which have been successful is the noise-proofed room. A variety of sounds attacks the judge's ears during a working day. These include the human voice, in its least attractive forms, the creaking of courtroom furniture, the thump of heavy boots worn by police officers and warders. There is also a variety of emotional sounds, such as gasps, cries of anguish, muttered curses and the protesting screech, coming from those who have been convicted. It is therefore desirable for the judge to build some room, into which exterior sounds can penetrate only with difficulty.

With a disregard for the well-being of those who sit in them, courts are usually sited in the centre of town, where the fumes of cars are at their most lethal. Nor is it any longer fashionable for judges to walk round the court. So the judge must rely on his garden for exercise. Indeed, he has often been heard to tell prisoners that Satan always finds some immoral use for idle hands.

The judge should equip himself with a potting shed, to which he can retire to meditate, an exercise which incorporates a period of sleep.

A judge who wishes to maintain a high standard of good humour may do well to install in his home a number of special items. Among these is a rocking chair, much in vogue in the USA. It is a soothing experience to see seven of the nine Justices rocking themselves to sleep in the American Supreme Court in Washington, during counsel's address.

A writing table should be as uncomfortable as possible, so that the judge may be spurred to complete whatever task he has been obliged to bring home in the shortest possible time.

A library containing humorous works is essential. They can, if necessary, be used for other purposes, such as propping up chairs which are short of a leg, as shredded material for paper chases or to meet sudden hygienic demands. The judge should make sure that the library includes those works which amuse him.

He must remember that he is a member of a group which is supposed to be without a sense of humour. This is unfair, as most judges like nothing better than to crack a little joke when passing sentence, or when explaining why a female plaintiff who lost a breast in a mincer cannot obtain damages from the manufacturer.

If a judge feels depression descending, he should retire to his soundproofed room and read risible passages aloud, until the gloom is dispelled by healthy laughter.

Cheerfulness under pressure

A judge will find his bonhomie severely strained in a number of situations, such as when dealing with reporters. The accepted way of dealing with them is to appear helpful and say as little as possible. If these two objectives appear to be in conflict, this is because they usually are. For example:

Reporter: What do you think about flogging, sir?

Judge: It depends who is about to be flogged.

Reporter: What about juveniles?

Judge: I regret that I cannot answer that.

Reporter: Why not?

Judge: Now that the power to flog the little sods – I mean, since the legislature in its wisdom has decided that this power shall no longer be available, its restoration is a political matter.

Reporter: Yes, sir, but do you favour bringing back the cat?

Judge: I regret that I cannot answer that. I am glad to have been of service to you.

The wife

She knows that her husband wants her to show an interest in his work, without asking a lot of questions, especially those which he cannot answer. She has made up her mind before she speaks to him, as to what he should have done:

Wife: Well Cedric, what did you do?

Judge: I gave her twelve months.

Wife: All she did was to chop the scrotum off her lover. He asked for it.

Judge: I thought I was being lenient.

Wife: You should have bound her over, like you promised.

Judge: I did not.

Wife: When I suggested it, you kept quiet. That's the same thing. How the poor girl must have suffered with that beast.

Judge: A refusal to buy a mink is not a proper excuse for using a ham knife, and a blunt one at that.

Wife: This judicial work is making you very crude, Cedric.

Members of the legislature

A Member of the Legislative Council (M.L.C.) seldom asks questions in public about the conduct of a judge, knowing that he would receive little support from the Attorney-General, who will be hoping to become one himself. Instead, he would try a personal approach to the judge. The approved technique for dealing with an enquiry of this kind is a careful blend of deference and honesty:

M.L.C.: Su Su Wong's father came to see me last week.

Judge: You are in demand. Everyone turns to you for help, don't they?

M.L.C.: Mr Wong is very angry. You let off the man who attacked his daughter.

Judge: How embarrassing for you. Where did it happen?

M.L.C.: On Lamma Island. What has that got to do with it?

Judge: Nothing at all, I expect. Was this near the new power station?

M.L.C.: Look, Judge, I'm a plain man.

Judge: Go home, Mr Tai. You are not doing yourself justice.

M.L.C.: What do I tell him, then?

Judge: What a difficult position you are put in. I don't know how you fellows stand it.

Friends

A judge's friends (using the term in the widest sense to include anyone who is still speaking to him) will display a marked interest in certain aspects of his work and ask questions about them:

Friend: I hope you don't mind if I ask you a question.

Judge: It depends what it is.

Friend: There's no need to be technical. I was going to ask you how you feel when you sentence someone to death.

Judge: Relaxed.

Friend: What! You mean you enjoy it. You must be a pervert!

Judge: Nobody has been executed for twenty years.

Friend: But you enjoyed it then?

Judge: I wasn't a judge when they hanged people.

Friend: That's got nothing to do with it. Let me ask you another question. How often have you convicted an innocent man?

Judge: Never. I only do jury trials. They do the convicting.

Friend: You've often said you can make the jury do just as you want.

Judge: I was boasting.

Friend: And what about Mr Justice Stone? Is it true he's an alcoholic?

Judge: He has port at breakfast, but that's quite normal, isn't it?

Friend: What about Judge Perkins then? He gets a kick out of collecting lady barrister's bands.

Judge: They must be better looking than in my day. I mean the lady barristers, not the bands.

Personal first aid

A judge should resort to a suitable personal first aid, whenever he feels a bout of tantrums stirring within him.

Deep breathing is helpful, even if this involves throwing back the head or raising the arms to shoulder level. It will attract attention in court, but this is more desirable than a display of ill temper.

Prayers are helpful to the atheist as well as to the believer. The content of the prayer doesn't matter, so long as it makes no reference to the wrath of God. The object is to calm the subject, not to frighten him. Among subjects which have been found successful are:

1 The restoration of the Stuarts, for active fantasists.
2 The moral condition of the bishops, for those who like fantasy with an erotic element.
3 The progress of Prince Jack, twenty-second in succession to the throne and a notorious wencher.
4 The recovery of a sick relative. This can be combined with the hope that, if she does not recover, her property will be left to the judge.
5 The guidance of judges. He will be thinking of his colleagues, who need divine intervention more than he does.
6 The miracle. This is a good humoured, though serious, plea for counsel to suffer paralysis of the voice box or for a witness, who has been lying for days, to be struck by a thunderbolt.

Cursing is often efficacious, if prayers fail. This diverts the anger to someone else. Among the many serviceable targets are:

1 The appeal court, which keeps interfering with the immaculate judgments of lower courts.
2 Mr Justice Bones, who always takes your special chair at the Club, with its view of the bedrooms in the adjoining hotel.
3 The Kaiser. Still very popular with senior judges. The younger ones seem to prefer Adolf Hitler.

4 The Prime Minister, a target which has returned to favour in recent years.
5 The judge's wife. One of her many sterling services is that she acts as a mental punchbag. Your ill temper can be attributed to her incompetent housekeeping or to some other matter for which she is responsible, like the squeak in your shoes, the hole in your sock or the frayed cuff. It is courteous to inform your wife that you intend to use her for these purposes, when you leave home that morning.

Good health

The most important single judicial asset is good health. Learning, wisdom, wit and intelligence are of little use to a judge who coughs claret into his silk handkerchief.

1 *The big toe.* This may become weakened as a result of buckle shoes, which fall off unless the big toe is used as a lever. Or it will be subjected, with other limbs, to extremes of temperature on the bench. It may have been damaged by a furious kick at the wooden panel in front of his desk, or have set in the wrong position when wriggled to keep the judge awake.
2 *Elbows.* For several hours a day, the judge is writing in a cramped position, which throws most of his body weight on to the point of his right elbow. When he is not writing, he cups his jaw, partly to stay awake and partly because it is good for his double chin.

   Bathing in warm molasses, tying the member (the elbow) in a loose bandage, or a plastic operation to alter the shape of the elbow, so that it may rest easily on the desk, have all been tried with some success.
3 *Deafness.* The judge is placed at a significant distance away from anyone else. No doubt this was to lessen the risk of assassination by outraged peasants in mediaeval times. The tradition has persisted, so that anyone who wishes to be heard by the judge must shout. It is likely that, unless he takes precautions, he will be deaf in ten to twelve years.

   It is, especially at the end of the day when the speakers are too exhausted to shout, better not to strain your ears by trying to hear what is said. In a court where shorthand writers or a tape are provided, this does no harm. Perhaps it may help to wear a hearing aid, as its mere presence will make people speak at a higher volume.

4 *Short sight.* Many courts are lit by electric bulbs planted where gas mantles once flourished. The judge's raw material is the written word, even if some of it is in his own hand and difficult to decipher. The best method of preventing damage to the eyes is to shut them. Unfortunately this quickly induces sleep. Since little can then be done, the only resort is to more powerful glasses, to a handheld magnifier and, eventually, to several sets of glasses, which fit into one another as required. Hallett J. wore four sets of glasses, when studying photos of partly unclothed ladies.

5 *The bladder.* A judge must train himself to eat only dry food during the day. This enables him to sneer at counsel, prisoners and witnesses who seek adjournments to relieve themselves. The judge must accept that he may suffer from constipation, acute wind or severe thirst.

6 *Sleep.* No judge can hope to avoid the occasional struggle with sleep. This may be due to advancing age. Judges serve until 70 in England, though ambassadors are thought to be too old for organizing garden parties in Lima at 60 and airline pilots are likely to overshoot runways at 55.

The judge may also be affected by the reflection from the head of bald court officials, by bees and by heavy robes, often red in colour. These remind judges, sub-consciously, of winter dressing gowns.

It is wise for the judge to take a precautionary nap in his retiring room for half an hour or so before the trial. If he finds that, even so, he is beset by the onset of sleep, there are last minute expedients, such as crossword puzzles, best glued to the inside of his notebook. Doodles ought not to be left on the bench, as Sturt J. was obliged to retire when his doodles of the accused, naked and sexually aroused, chasing a policewoman wearing only a helmet, were sent to the Lord Chancellor. Counting games are useful so long as they are not difficult, like adding up the buttons in court.

Other attributes

A judge is unlikely to be held in general esteem unless, in addition to his good health and to his warm, human character, he develops other qualities as well:

1 *Discreet dozing.* Even if the judge applies the various methods of avoiding sleep which are described above, his disinterest in

some of his work is likely to be such that he is overcome with drowsiness. He must learn how to doze inconspicuously.

This demands the acquisition of various basic skills. Prominent among these is keeping the eyes open while asleep. This depends upon self-hypnosis, though this requires the judge to tell himself to wake up after a given time. Pront J. omitted to do so and slept for eleven days, being fed through a series of undignified tubes.

He may also, using the 'Cry wolf' method, pretend to be asleep early in the trial. When this is noticed by counsel, the latter may cough loudly or drop a heavy object from a substantial height. Observe him with some amusement. Do not ask him why he is throwing heavy weights on the floor. Open your eyes and ask him if he is feeling well enough to continue. It will thereafter be assumed that the crafty old sod, which is a term of affectionate respect, is playing possum again.

2 *Humility.* The judge should accept the need for this, not for any moral reason, but because of its practical benefits. A reputation for modesty has many advantages.

Recommending a colleague is one approved method. The judge who is asked to take a six-week company fraud trial and says Titmarsh J. would do it much better will gain much praise. It may also acquire the unexpected bonus of making an enemy of Titmarsh. You should not, if you are worried about the terms of your obituary notice, place too much emphasis on humility. You do not want to be described as a 'quiet, modest man who never made the impression which his abilities would have justified'.

Do not challenge the cases. Fairness and good sense may suggest that a case should be decided in one way but precedent requires you to decide in another. You should, if this arises, pretend to follow a supposed principle established by a higher court, when it considered a totally different set of facts about ninety years ago.

You will have to resort to the process known as 'distinguishing the authorities on the facts' and protest that you are adhering to the earlier principle, while having nothing to do with it.

The humble judge makes full use of the 'nutshell', a series which sets out the law. The latter is composed of disordered and contradictory principles. The nutshell presents it as if it were logical and simple. This is done for examination purposes and is not intended for any other employment.

Judges are, traditionally, expected to know little of matters of common knowledge. For a judge to ask 'What is a chorus girl?' gives an excellent impression. Litigants do not want their cases tried by the sort of man who spends his evenings in a smoky cellar plucking at stocking tops.

It is wise to be diffident, which will not be difficult. There will be frequent, and ill informed, criticism of his judgments by an appellate court. Articles will appear in law journals, using the phrase 'with respect to the Learned Judge' as an introduction to a savage attack on his mishandling of a trade mark case. And pressure will be applied by other judges suggesting that he should try not to be clever, as they have to read his cases when they are reported.

3 *Controlling the voice.* The judge is in a unique position, shared only with royalty, that whenever he speaks everyone else will stop talking and simulate interest in what he says. This opportunity should not be wasted. The judge must develop a firm, pleasant voice and eliminate a number of unfortunate mannerisms which may mar the effect.

The stutter, thanks to the baleful inference of Mr Bertie Wooster, is associated with stupidity. This is best overcome by the 'filthy word mechanism'. The sufferer, when he feels a stutter forming in his larynx, must 'think dirty'. The possibility of, for example, the word 'ordure' being enunciated from the bench is usually sufficient to overcome the stutter.

If you are cursed with a high pitched voice, it is desirable to attend a speech therapist, in an attempt to lower it. Gargling is not, by itself, likely to help.

Try not to gabble. The problem of co-ordination is difficult and the judge will find that he has to write at high speed. This will, unless corrected, affect his speech patterns and make him gabble. However, if something else is done at a slow pace, this will affect the voice. Some judges have found a rhythmical scratching at an imaginary spot on the thigh most effective in slowing down the speech.

4 *Self-defence.* A judge is not as vulnerable to physical attack as police officers, night club bouncers and trade union officials. Few judges are trained in unarmed combat, save for that which they have learned in the rough and tumble of marital life. They should be equipped to deal with such assaults, as there is nothing more undignified than a judge being hurled into a horse trough by an angry plaintiff.

Among those likely to launch a physical attack is the litigant. He has asked the judge to decide in his favour a dispute between himself and another citizen. If the judge does not carry out his duties properly and does not find in his favour, he may well exercise his right to protest by daubing obscene words on the walls of the judge's garden, by scratching with a sharp object on the paintwork of the latter's private car or by picketing his house. Physical attack, other than tomatoes at the judge's wife, about which most judges are able to take a philosophical view, is unlikely.

The prisoner often reacts sharply when sentenced. It is well for the judge, at this moment, to be on the alert for a variety of missiles. Among these is a policeman's hat, which is powerful but inaccurate. A shoe is more likely to strike its target, especially if the defendant has been practising in his cell. As food, if thrown, is likely to disintegrate in the air, the clerk of court is more vulnerable than the judge. It the clerk is struck by a decomposing hamburger, the judge can react in a calm manner, which will be widely acclaimed.

An insensate prisoner may try to fight his way to the bench, evading police and warders and trying not to collide with counsel, who will be going in the other direction. A prisoner has only reached the bench twice in England (and sixteen times in Australia) since 1960. It is better, in such circumstances, for the judge to leave the court, even if this subjects him to criticism in the press for discourtesy to the prisoner. The alternative, a numbing blow by the judge to the prisoner's thyroid, would be described as an overreaction and is thus best avoided.

Women do not like courts, which they still regard as male dominated. This is largely their own fault, due to their reluctance to commit crimes as often as men. They may therefore be expected to display some sensitivity and to react in different ways to males.

A female witness may, for no apparent reason, emit a muted cry and fall senseless in the box, in as elegant a manner as is consistent with a loss of consciousness. The judge will be assumed to be responsible, as having bullied her. He can lessen criticism by having her inert body treated by the first aid personnel who should be available in all court buildings.

In theory, women can hurl a handbag at the bench. However, about 90 per cent of handbags are so full of useless objects that the catch will not do up properly. The bag will open within a few feet of being launched, scattering a selection of soiled personal trivia in all directions and ruining its aerodynamic qualities.

It is a long time since a judge in Hong Kong was faced by an angry mob, though this is more common in parts of Africa and the USA. It is not to be expected that such a decadent attitude will persist in Hong Kong. A judge who is faced with an ugly mob, outside his courthouse, should react in the same way as that recommended for football referees.

He should remain cheerful, as the majority of the crowd does not know why it is there. If they see the object of their protest laughing, they may decide it can't be him. Without the help of the police, you cannot control a mob. It is better to wait cheerfully and make your way into the crowd, shouting 'Follow me.' If they do, you will have to think of somewhere to lead them.

Do not ignore the mob. A judge who stalks past the front row with an air of disdain is asking to be torn to shreds. If you cannot be cheerful, and it is conceded that it is not always easy to laugh at a large crowd which is demanding your blood, it is wise to appear to be terrified, which should not be difficult. Most mobs will be appeased if they see the purpose of their execrations looking frightened.

5 *The press.* It is unfortunate that the achievement of a press favourable to yourself is not dependent upon your own sterling qualities, but upon your ability to ingratiate yourself with reporters.

It is first necessary to overcome a latent hostility to those in the press box, described inaccurately as 'ladies and gentlemen of the press'. Because a court reporter is expected to report what actually takes place, rather than what he would like, the more experienced reporters are seldom used for this work. Those in the press box are likely to be young, underpaid, bored, long haired, dressed in jeans and a grubby T-shirt and worried about the spread of acne.

Self-presentation demands that you should develop a tolerance of reporters. Any reporter knows that his readers much prefer public figures to appear to be sadistic, inhumane and, if possible, sexually deviant. You must at all times address them with the respect reserved for your clerk, your wife or (to take a nineteenth century example) the Lord. If this tolerance demands preparation, a form of self-hypnosis, during which you tell yourself how much you love the press, has often proved effective.

To demonstrate your attachment, public flattery can be used. The reporter who is representing the *Evening Gazette* will be impressed by a judge who refers to 'our friends in the press', 'gentlemen reporters', 'those bastions of liberty' or 'the representatives of our great newspapers'. These remarks should be accompanied by a simulated bow from the sitting position, or a friendly smile which suggests that judge and press form a team, with the joint task of educating the public.

In order to save court reporters trouble, the judge should make full use of the hand-out. This contains a summary of the evidence given so far, in the hope that it may appear correctly in the papers. The hand-out should contain passages, which ought not to be too oblique or the readers will miss the meaning, showing that the judge is wise and tolerant, that the trial is fair and that the press plays an important role.

Phrases such as 'the judge observed that the press, as usual, had made a decisive contribution' or 'the judge commented that there were those who wondered if the press served any useful purpose by attending trials but he was not among them' will be well received by editors, who do not believe in self-criticism.

A certain way of enlisting the support of the papers is to launch an attack on somebody, The safest target is a fellow judge. A sharp criticism of a recent judgment of Moult J. is a certain success. Use the words 'tendentious', 'semantic' and 'disingenuous'. Such slang phrases are much in use in bars and on the factory floor. Even editors will know what you mean.

Photographs are important in forming the public's prejudices about the judiciary. Unless the judge takes precautions, the papers will use one photo throughout his career. The wife of a judge of 70 may be upset if she is asked why he has aged so fast recently by someone who has only seen a photo taken when he was 50.

The model photo, if taken on the day he was appointed, may show him with a broad smile. This is not appropriate for publication when the judge has been trying an unpleasant murder for the last three weeks. Of course, it may have been taken on Remembrance Sunday and show the judge in sixteenth century costume, looking grim because his buckle shoes are pinching and his tights are laddered and descending.

It is usual for the judge's clerk to distribute contemporary and flattering pictures of the judge to reporters. These will probably be used, even if the wrong name is attached to them.

It is to be hoped that a judge, by following the above advice, will achieve the excellent reputation which he could not hope for without it. He must never forget that, like serial killers and income tax assessors, he has few natural friends and must work hard if he is to be admired.

Judges, 1985

Chapter 27
Buildings

Even my admirers, of whom there are few others, agree that I am least at home with intellectual concepts. If, for example, you were to ask me to define a 'reasonable man', a mythical creature who frequently appears as a guide to what the law permits, I should have difficulty in answering.

I am much more at home with buildings. I do not mean that I have any understanding of how to design them. I only stated what was needed and complained if this was not provided. I was fortunate in joining the judiciary at a time when money was being spent quite freely on public projects. This did not mean that it could be wrung easily from the Treasury, only that the latter did not refuse to provide any for essential buildings.

The Registrar, however, believed that I could secure anything for which I asked, because I had been one of 'the enemy' myself and knew how their minds worked, if they had any, which he doubted. I was pleased that he saw my transfer to the judiciary as an advantage, even if his reasons for doing so were not those I would have liked. My fellow judges muttered about lack of experience, and the members of the administrative service thought that I must be desperate for a job to have joined the judiciary.

It was not long before my attitudes changed. Previously, I had been somewhat critical of the judges, looked at from the outside.

About 1974, the Secretariat decided that it would be a way of silencing the unofficial members of the Legislative Council for a few weeks (though nobody expected it would be effective for much longer than that) if the precedence list was altered.

This list was seldom changed, so that it often contained references to offices which no longer existed. This was thought to be preferable to making the slightest amendment. However innocent or desirable the changes might be, long forgotten grievances came swiftly to the surface. What had started as a minor matter bloomed into a full scale conflict. Those who had gained a place in the list were convinced that they should have got more. Anyone who moved down the list attributed this to malice, bad faith, ignorance or all three.

In 1974, I put the draft revision of the precedence list at the back of my bottom drawer, where I put the papers which were too difficult for me, but could not be passed on to someone else. I had already attempted to shift the burden to the Governor, on the ground that the Secretary of State would have to approve any changes. In such a case, I had suggested, the matter should have the benefit of his experience and wisdom. He denied, for this purpose only he said, having either and was sure that I would do the job splendidly.

My secretary, who was fully aware of the drawer, kept retrieving the file and putting it on my desk. Eventually, as was usual with matters which were virtually insoluble, I asked the Deputy Chief Secretary to convene a sub-committee. This often put off a decision for some weeks, even if the resultant report contradicted itself in so many places that it was difficult to find out exactly what had been recommended.

The Deputy Chief Secretary was a cheerful man, his optimism undimmed by his experience of past disasters.

'It's about the precedence list,' he said, putting a bundle of papers on my desk. 'I thought you'd like to read those. You don't look too busy.'

There happened to be nothing on my desk. My safe, cupboards and drawers were full of files which I had not dealt with. But I had read somewhere that a clear desk signified an uncluttered mind and made the visitor think you were concentrating only upon his problems, to the exclusion of all else.

Rather later, when the habit of having a clear desk was so established that I could not change it, I read in another magazine that an empty desk showed that I did not have enough to do.

'I have plenty to do, thank you, without the precedence list. What are all these papers you've given me?'

'They show what is done in other Commonwealth countries. There's a very helpful list from Burma.'

'Even I know it hasn't been in the Commonwealth since 1947.'

'This is pre-war. There's some interesting information from Sierra Leone, before it became independent.'

'I take it, then, that the committee you set up has not recommended anything.'

'Indeed it has. It thinks that the members of councils ought to go above judges.'

'Why should they do that?'

'Because judges are somewhat overgraded at present.'

'What you really mean is that you meet the unofficials quite often, but not the judges.'

'That's not how it will look,' he replied. 'The unofficials say that they perform a greater public service, for which they are not paid, than the judges, who are.'

'Have you asked the C.J. what he thinks about it?'

'I thought I had better, though I knew he would not like the idea much. So I tried it on him.'

'Go on,' I said encouragingly.

'I could hear the C.J.'s lips tightening over the phone when I told him what had been suggested. His reply was quite mild. He merely said that the proposal was a disgrace, that the unofficial members were a lot of useless ruffians (I have paraphrased his actual words) when compared with the sterling service given by the judges to the public.'

'Did he say that the judges were underpaid?'

'Certainly. He added that, if we were going to mess about with the list, judges ought to be put above bishops. He told me that the bishops were not off their knees long enough to be in any list at all.'

'We have a clear difference of opinion between the judges and the unofficials, haven't we?' The D.C.S. nodded.

'Do you think we could lose the file?'

'No. I am phoned twice a day by the unofficials' office to ask what has happened to their very reasonable proposal, and once a week by the C.J.'s secretary, who says that he hopes that no more will be heard of my wholly unreasonable suggestion.'

'In that case, we had better ask the Secretary of State to approve the change. Can you do anything about the bishops?'

'Not without a clash with the Church. I spoke to the Anglican bishop, who said he didn't mind in the least for himself, but thought that any downgrading of bishops would inevitably be seen as a sign that the Government no longer believed that religion in Hong Kong was of any importance.'

Some months later, the revised list was published, placing judges below the unofficial members of the Legislative Council. I imagined that it would not matter greatly, as the number of occasions when the list was used was small. I was wrong.

Several years later, when I joined the judiciary, it was still a subject which aroused the judges. Most of them were cynical men who had spent years listening to human frailties at their most unpleasant. This did not obstruct them.

'I sat next to Rosie Baxendale last night,' one of my colleagues told me.

'Was she sloshed?' I enquired. She usually was. She was married to a successful businessman and was doing her best to drink her way through his profits.

'She was. What is more, she attacked me.'

'Lucky you.'

'I don't mean physically. She told me I was stuck-up, remote, unfriendly and that I didn't drink enough, just like all the other judges.'

'I hope you agreed with her. It usually saves trouble.'

'I was outraged. And it is largely your fault.'

'Why me? I didn't slip anything into her glass. It isn't necessary.'

'If it hadn't been for you messing about with the precedence list, I shouldn't have been next to her. I was only there because you put the legislative councillors above judges. There were three councillors there and I found myself next to Rosie. I hope you are pleased with yourself. I suppose you did it just to make sure there was no trouble with them over some of those awful bills the Government enacted and we now have to make sense of?' I had not realized before that angry judges snort.

After a few weeks, however, what he had said seemed quite sensible. By the end of the year, I found it hard to believe that anyone in his right mind could have thought that councillors were more important than judges. I could see that the latter were overworked, underpaid and did society's unpleasant work for it. They were rewarded by being put lower in the precedence list than legislative councillors, who did little.

It was not long before I started to regard the administration as being on the other side, rather like the motorist who becomes a pedestrian and regards all drivers as a menace.

The principal need was for a new Supreme Court, the building of which started about 1980, though we did not move into it until 1984. The foundation stone of the building was laid in 1983, by Lord Hailsham, the Lord Chancellor, when he attended the Commonwealth Law Conference, held in Hong Kong. When he did so, the shell of the building was complete, though the main hall, at the entrance to which he was to lay a stone, was festooned with wires. It looked dangerous when I visited it, a few days before, to have a look at its progress.

'There is no need to worry,' insisted Mr Soo, the main contractor. 'We shall make sure that everything is safe when the English judge comes.'

'The electric wires do not look safe to me, Mr Soo.'

Lord Hailsham, foundation stone of New Supreme Court, 1983

'Very safe,' he relied. 'I will show you. Chan,' he shouted at one of the workmen, 'take hold of the wire and show Sir Roberts that he need not worry.'

Chan smiled cheerfully, took a firm grip on several of the wires and was hurled thirty feet by an electric shock. He recovered consciousness ten minutes later, still smiling.

As I was not sure that Lord Hailsham would think it amusing if he were hurled thirty feet, I insisted upon all loose cables being put beyond his reach. Chan stood by, on the day of the opening ceremony, to take hold of anything which came loose. Lord Hailsham duly laid his stone without mishap. Chan was only electrocuted once, towards the end of the ceremony, which was fortunately not affected.

The new Supreme Court building, a fine modern structure clothed in concrete, looked from the outside like a warehouse. It was first occupied by the judiciary in 1984. It was built on the site of an abandoned army ammunition store, which had not been used for about thirty years. There were those who thought it an appropriate place.

About three months after we had moved into it, we held an Irish opening, a device invented in Dublin so that anyone who forgot to celebrate an opening could do so at any time. It was attended by the Governor, Sir Edward Youde, a wise man who had succeeded four other Governors who had all been over six feet tall. As he was only five feet seven, the Chinese decided that he must be very clever, as indeed he was.

As this was a ceremonial occasion, the judges, under protest, put on their robes and sat in mutinous silence while I spoke, with the exception of Moult J., who slept through most of the proceedings and had to be elbowed sharply by his neighbours whenever he snored.

'It is of interest', I began (this is a phrase which is often used by speakers who are about to introduce a subject of unrelieved boredom) 'to note the history of the Supreme Court.'

A photographer's bulb broke with a loud bang. This ensured that I had everyone's attention for the next five minutes or so:

> In the last century, successive Chief Justices, whose influence, hard though it is to believe this, was even less than it is today, complained, at their usual inordinate length, both publicly and privately, about the inadequacy of the Supreme Court building in which they had sat since 1850.
>
> Finally, worn down by words, the Governor agreed to the construction of a new courthouse. Its foundation stone was laid in 1903. It was not occupied until 1912.
>
> This long interval was not due only to the natural reluctance of any proper bureaucracy to spend money on courts. There were other factors. The Government of Hong Kong insisted that it had run out of money. There was a shortage of stone masons. The granite quarry was exhausted. The Chief Justice interfered on a number of occasions with the architect and the consulting engineer, who replied by ignoring him.
>
> Most important of all was the constant stream of letters addressed by the Chief Justice to the Governor. The latter passed them, with his best wishes, to the Colonial Secretary, who decided that the only way of preventing the Chief Justice from renewing his complaints was to lose his letters.
>
> In spite of these matters, the Supreme Court opened it doors in 1912. It was constructed the wrong way round, though this did not seem to matter at all.
>
> The building contained three courts. It was therefore much criticized, as a gross overprovision, as for the next twenty-five years it was occupied only by the Chief Justice and one judge, and of course by the large staff without which they were incapable of operating.

As is widely appreciated, judges are modest, patient and undemanding men, interested only in serving the community and seldom mentioning that they are grossly overworked and sadly underpaid. Even this long suffering group became discontented, by the 1970s, with the further division of the Old Supreme Court building, until it housed about eleven courts, in conditions which would have shocked a warder in an overcrowded prison.

The Chief Secretary of the time, which I happened to be, with a degree of wisdom and foresight not often found in the holder of that office, established a committee. This masterstroke showed that he was taking the judges seriously, something which had not happened for a long time.

The committee recommended that a new Supreme Court building was overdue and that a site in the Victoria Barracks area would be suitable. The move was bitterly opposed by members of the legal profession, mainly because the new site was close to a district called Wanchai, which was already known for providing other pleasures. As the site was employed in the nineteenth century as a store for damp ammunition, it was thought to be historically suitable for its new purpose.

The lifts, which were the slowest in South East Asia, have been designed to ensure that nobody using them is likely to suffer from divers' bends, however sensitive he may be to abrupt changes of depth at sea. The building is, however, incomplete, in that it makes no provision for solicitors in wheelchairs or for members of the public who wish to take large dogs into the toilets.

However, the courts themselves were welcoming. It was our object to make all of them, and especially those in which criminal trials will take place, light and cheerful. There is, as is generally accepted, nothing as heartening as a really happy felon.

The Bar has been consulted in the internal design of the courts. If all its suggestions had been followed, the courts would have been triangular in shape and ten feet higher on one end. It was also necessary to ignore its proposal that all counsel should be provided with armchairs.

The air conditioning which has been installed will keep courts at the sort of temperature that produces ice cubes. This will make it easier for judges to remain awake in the afternoon, though not all of them can be expected to meet such an exacting standard.

> The acoustics have been much improved, so that it will no longer be necessary for a judge to sit with his hand clapped to his ear like a primitive ear trumpet, if he is to hear anything. In future, he will have no difficulty in hearing counsel speculate, in loud whispers, as to his hereditary disease, his advanced age or the failure of his mother to go through a ceremony of marriage before, or indeed after, his birth. The judge's ability to hear this will assist the atmosphere of mutual distrust and tension, between the bench and the Bar, which is such an important feature of the common law system.
>
> It is said that Mad King Ludwig of Bavaria once observed, when opening a court which had been designed to look like a railway station, 'I hope that everyone who enters this building will be successful.'

About three years later, I learned that the current Lord Chancellor, Lord Havers, was looking for an excuse to visit Hong Kong. He had come there in 1982, on his way back from a meeting in Singapore, and had enjoyed himself sufficiently to want to return.

I had by this time opened new courts in Fanling, Sha Tin and Wanchai. Sir Alan Huggins, a clever and perceptive judge, sent me a memo saying 'It's about time we asked someone of reasonable distinction to open the new court.'

I therefore asked Lord Havers if he would be prepared to open the new courthouse at Tuen Muen. I did not tell him that it had been operating already for some weeks, as nobody seemed to mind a retrospective opening ceremony. This was to be the most important part of his visit, the rest of which was to be devoted to a rest for him and his wife after a tiring visit to the USA. I cannot pretend that everything went as it should have done.

A large number of invitations were dispatched, in the expectation that there would be many refusals, as the courthouse was to be formally opened at four o'clock and Tuen Muen was over twenty miles to the west of Kowloon. I was not disappointed. Most of those for whom seats had been reserved in the front row said they could not attend.

'I think', I said to the Registrar, who had delegated the organization of the occasion to one of his deputies, 'that we ought to make sure that there are no vacant seats in the front row. It will look as if a lot of people have not even bothered to reply, and he may not like that.'

He didn't. When he arrived, the front two rows were empty. As I later discovered, my message had become garbled on its way down the line, until those in charge of the seating believed that I had insisted that the front two rows should be left unoccupied. Lord Havers looked with some distaste at the empty chairs and observed, in a loud whisper heard by most of the guests, that he supposed that few people had come because his visit was of little consequence. My reply that it was a mistake and entirely my fault did not seem to convince him.

The Registrar had arranged for the Lord Chancellor to be taken to and from the court by helicopter, thus shortening the journey by about half an hour each way and giving him an excellent view of Hong Kong from the air. About three days before the ceremony, he told me that Lord Havers would have to go there by car, though he could have a helicopter to come back. This was, he explained, because one of the helicopters was out of action and the one in which the Lord Chancellor was supposed to go out to Tuen Muen was booked for the Director of Public Works, who wanted to look at the construction of a maximum security prison on Lantau Island.

I rang the Chief Secretary to complain. It did not help.

'Jack,' I said, in a wheedling tone, 'you've got to help me with Lord Havers.'

'Who is he?' Jack asked.

'He's the Lord Chancellor. A very senior man in England.'

'What is he worried about?'

'He isn't getting a helicopter to go to Tuen Muen on Thursday, because it is booked for the Director of Public Works.'

'I know that. He's got to go and look at a prison on Lantau.'

'How can I tell Lord Havers that the D.P.W. takes priority over him?'

'I'm sure you'll find a way, dear boy. You're good at giving bad news to somebody.'

'What about outriders? I want to be sure that he gets there on time.'

'The Commissioner of Police deals with that. Why not write to him?'

I did. I sent a letter that same afternoon. I received a reply, several days after Lord Havers had left, saying that the police would be pleased to provide outriders and would I let them know when these would be required.

Lord Havers came by road, in a Government car which only broke down once on the way. Apart from this, the traffic was heavy. When I met him on arrival at the courthouse he was twenty minutes late.

I introduced him, in the sort of short speech, devoid of interest or content, which is expected of a speaker whose job is to 'warm up' the audience for someone else. The microphones worked perfectly when I spoke. They broke down soon after the Lord Chancellor began his speech.

He had told us what a great privilege it was for him to be there, how much he admired Hong Kong and its many achievements and how he and his colleagues on the Privy Council knew of the high standards of the judiciary, when there was a strangulated sound from one of the amplifiers. Probably somebody had pulled out a wire. The microphone went dead.

No doubt Lord Havers, who had been a Member of Parliament for many years, was used to speaking in a building where the acoustics were poor. In this case, they were dreadful, as the opening ceremony had been held near the entrance to the courts, but outside them. The Lord Chancellor himself did not seem to notice that the microphones were dead. He continued to address his audience in the sort of tones which are suitable for microphones but ensure that nobody more than thirty feet away can hear anything if the microphones are no longer working.

The audience was well away from him, thanks to the two empty rows, and could hear little. This did not particularly matter until Lord Havers made a joke. There was a burst of laughter from the platform, but no reaction came from the audience, which did not hear it. The same thing happened with his next two jokes, which were very amusing if you could hear them. I laughed as loudly as possible in an effort to sound like the people at the back. I found myself still laughing at a serious part of the speech and shut up when he glared at me.

He ended his address, which lasted less than ten minutes, and was steered to the red curtain which concealed the plaque which commemorated the visit.

'I declare this courthouse open,' he said, and pulled the string. Nothing happened. He tried again. 'The bloody thing is stuck,' he said. 'Nothing seems to be working today.'

'For God's sake, cut it loose,' I whispered to the Registrar, who was struggling with the rope, which had broken in his hands. There was a rending of cloth, as he tore the covering from the plaque.

This announced that the court had been opened by Lord Hoovers, the Lord High Chancellor of England. The phantom stone carver had struck again. Lord Havers, who was not amused, seemed to think it should have been corrected.

'What is more,' said Lord Havers, 'the audience was dead and failed to react to the jokes I told them.'

'Perhaps they didn't hear them,' I suggested. 'The microphones were not working properly.'

'Nonsense,' he replied. 'They have no sense of humour, that's all. Do I have to take refreshments now?'

'Please. I'm sure that everyone will be delighted if you mingle with them for a while, before your helicopter comes.'

Lord Havers was a good mingler. For the next twenty minutes or so, he circled the reception, talking to those who had come and telling again the jokes which had fallen flat during his speech. They were a great success, as he was himself.

I saw one of his staff pluck at his elbow. He nodded and came towards me.

'I'm told the helicopter has arrived, so I'll slip out quietly.'

'What about the dragon's eyes?' I asked. 'Aren't you going to stay and dot them? They should be here in half an hour or so.'

He did not, I think, appreciate the importance of dotting. It was essential to the future success of the building that the dragon's eyes be dotted. Otherwise, there would be a great difficulty in finding staff to work in a building that was quite likely to collapse without warning if the proper ceremonies had not been carried out. I had been in Hong Kong long enough myself to believe that this superstition might be true.

'I was not warned about this. Nobody said anything about it to me. If I don't go now, the helicopter will leave without me and my car has been sent back.'

I escorted him to the helipad, which was not far from the court, and saw him fly off in the direction of Hong Kong as the dusk began to descend.

I thanked him for coming so far to open the court. 'Only about 8,000 miles,' he replied, 'and it was worth it.'

I doubted if he believed it, but when I returned to the building I was greeted with a chorus of approval. All those who had spoken to him, and many who had not, told me what a charming and unassuming man he was and how impressive he had been.

'What is more,' they added, 'the least you could have done was to make sure that he had a proper microphone which worked.' It was a disgrace to Hong Kong and probably my fault, they suggested.

As I dotted the dragon's eyes, a few minutes later, I began to wonder if perhaps I had been negligent. By the time I had finished, I had persuaded myself that I had.

I met Lord Havers at a dinner the following evening, shortly before he left. I apologized for the various matters which had marred his opening of the courthouse at Tuen Muen.

'How did the counting of the dragon's teeth go?'

'Dotting its eyes, actually. It was fine, though we missed you. You could have done it better.'

It was not long afterwards that he resigned as Lord Chancellor, on the grounds of ill health. He died about four years later. I remain grateful to him for coming. It gave me much face.

Chapter 28

The Sixth Commonwealth Law Conference

'What do you want to go to Lagos for?' enquired the Registrar, a man with a long black beard. He later became a successful High Court judge. Nobody could guess what he was thinking, underneath the beard.

I was heartened by my reception at Lagos airport. As I walked from the plane towards the customs and immigration desks, I saw a handwritten notice on crumpled cardboard, reading 'Delegates to the 6th Commonwealth Law Conference. This way.' Underneath was an arrow in red coconut matting.

I turned a corner and found a double door, which was shut. I tapped softly, and then more firmly as there was no answer at first. The door was opened by a large Nigerian police officer. Before I could say anything, he shouted 'Security area' at me in a distinctly unwelcoming way.

'Yes, but –,' I began.

'Security area,' he repeated. 'Nobody can come through here. Did you not see the notice?'

'I didn't look,' I confessed.

'That is no excuse,' he replied. 'I am here to make sure that nobody comes this way and to arrest anyone who tries.'

'Yes, but –,' I began again.

'You are arguing with me.'

'No, no, I assure you. It was my mistake.'

'Go back, before I take you to the police station.' He pointed to the handcuffs at his waist. I scuttled, which is the proper word to describe my hurried retreat to the main corridor. The police officer was correct. At the entrance to the side corridor, which led to the double doors, was a notice which said 'No entrance. Security Area.' The word 'No' had been removed from the notice.

I hurried along the main corridor. About thirty yards further on was a harassed looking Nigerian, with a large metal buttonhole reading '6th Commonwealth Law Conference'.

'Are you coming for the conference?' he asked me.

'Not if you are going to arrest me,' I answered. 'How did you know I was going to attend it?' I expected him to say that I looked wise or learned.

'I ask everyone,' he answered. 'I did have a notice, but somebody has lost it.'

'Was it a cardboard one?' I described what I had seen. He was delighted. 'I've been looking everywhere for it. It's in the wrong place, you know. You ought to have turned right here, not there.'

'I have not been to this admirable airport before,' I agreed, thinking that I ought to say something pleasant about Nigeria, even though I had just been threatened with arrest.

'Admirable airport!' he replied. 'It's nothing of the kind. What happened when we wanted to build a proper airport at Kano, in the north?'

'Are you from the north?' I asked. He nodded in reply.

'We were told that there was no money, because it was all being spent on the infamous airport at Lagos.'

'Oh,' I replied. A non-committal answer seemed to be the only safe reply for a visitor.

'If you give me your baggage ticket, I will get Mr Inegu to collect it and take you to your car. This is Mr Inegu.' I shook hands with a young man, who responded with a nervous smile. 'Please go with him. He will look after you and see you get to your hotel.'

As I left, accompanied by Mr Inegu, a puzzled looking cleric was being asked if he was attending the conference. There was a paper called 'When is the victim dead?', so I supposed that the cleric was to deliver it.

Mr Inegu accompanied me to my hotel, a large rambling building which must have been there since colonial times. He left me in the lobby to return to his books, because, like most students, he was convinced that he would fail his exams.

There was a Swiss businessman in front of me, engaged in a furious row with the receptionist. He had a confirmed booking. This seemed to have no effect.

'Very sorry,' the receptionist explained, with a laugh that was either nervous or the result of genuine pleasure. 'The hotel has been taken over for the conference.'

'Why was I not told?' the man in front of me demanded. 'I have a letter from this hotel telling me I have a room. Here it is. My name is Schwarz.'

'That was written over two months ago, before the hotel was taken over. I'm afraid it has been cancelled.'

'What do I do now?' asked Schwarz. 'Where do you suggest that I go?'

Most of us are like that. We shout and bluster at a minor official, hoping that this will move him. When it does not, we cringe. We become quite polite. We try flattery. We resort to bribery. The latter seemed to work well in Lagos.

'I have a cousin who runs a small hotel not far from here,' replied the receptionist. 'Would you like me to see if he has a room?'

Schwarz nodded. He had come from Basle to sell lavatory seats, of which Nigeria was chronically short, since wooden ones made excellent fuel for cooking if chopped into small pieces. He did not intend to be thwarted now.

'£50 or US$100 a night,' the receptionist told Schwarz, who nodded his head. 'Rooms are very short in Lagos this week. It's the conference. You may have to share a room.' Schwarz nodded again. 'There may be several people in it. That will be £10 booking fee. You will need a taxi,' the receptionist went on. 'You can't walk that far with your case. My uncle has a car outside. He will take you to your hotel for only $10. You had better pay him before you get into his car, as he has been cheated more than once in the past year.'

Schwarz left the hotel carrying a suitcase in one hand and two sample plastic lavatory seats in the other.

The receptionist returned to his desk, which had been unoccupied while he introduced Schwarz to his uncle.

'Can I help you?' he enquired politely.

'I think you have a room for me. My name is Roberts.'

The receptionist looked at a list, before shaking his head. I decided that he felt a genuine pleasure in refusing to give me a room.

'Not here, I am afraid. All the bookings were cancelled for the conference. I could try and persuade my cousin to take you in, if he has any room left.'

'I'm sure he would have at four to each bed. Just have another look at your list. I have come here for the conference.'

The receptionist looked again. 'There is no Roberts here.'

'Why not try Sir. See if you've a room for him?' The receptionist re- examined his list, running his fingers down it slowly.

'Ah ha,' he announced. 'There is a room for Sir Roberts. Is that you? Why did you not give me your proper name before?'

'I'm sorry. I travel under a false name. It's a good protection against being attacked.'

'Does that happen often?'

'Frequently. Can I please register?'

'How long will you be here?'

'About six nights, I think. Unless you have sub-let my room. Then I might go earlier.'

I should not have spoken flippantly to the receptionist. He was annoyed.

'The deposit will be £300, or US$600.'

'Nonsense,' I said.

'I'm afraid that I cannot give you a room without a deposit.'

'According to the organizing committee of the conference, all major credit cards are acceptable here. Would you like Visa, American Express or Diners Club?'

'We don't take credit cards.'

'I do not have £300 in cash.'

'I only do what my employers tell me. I can't let you have a room unless you pay in advance.'

'Very well. I'll give you £50 now and the rest tomorrow. Will that satisfy you?'

'It will only do for one night. You can have Room 264. It's on the third floor but the lift does not work. I'll ask Cedric to take your suitcase up. Please make sure that you pay the rest tomorrow if you want to stay. There's a long waiting list, because of the conference.'

'Please may I have a receipt?'

'Didn't I give you one. Dear me, I'll write it out at once.'

It was for £40. 'I just gave you £50,' I protested.

'Forty for the room and ten for my commission.'

I did not argue. I was very pleased to get a room at all. I followed Cedric up the poorly lit stairs. A lot of bulbs were missing from the stairway. Cedric was about 70 and a heavy smoker. He was puffing when we reached the first floor. I carried my case for the rest of the way, Cedric trailing behind me.

'Stop,' he shouted. 'Room 280 is on the left.'

'Good,' I said. We'd better not enter it, as I have been given Room 264.'

'Room 264 is Room 280, sir. When someone took the number plate away, the hotel had no 264s. As it had a dozen 280s, it used one of them.'

I apologized. It's the sort of thing I should have been prepared for. I saw that beneath the number 280 on the door, somebody had gouged '264' in the paintwork.

Cedric pushed open the door and held out his hand. I grasped it, pumping it up and down a couple of times to show I was free of racial bias. Cedric held out his hand again. I was not surprised that I should have to pay for carrying my own suitcase.

In my pocket were some crumpled French notes, the remnant of a recent holiday in France. I gave them to Cedric.

'Sorry. No Nigerian money.'

'Never mind. My nephew at the desk knows where to get any foreign money changed. He gets a good rate, as he married the money changer's sister.'

Inside the bedroom was one dim light, under a plastic covered lampshade. The lamp was standing in a copper pot with a piece missing from the side. The ceiling light did not work. Nor did that in the bathroom. The beside lamp had an empty socket.

I realized that Cedric had not given me a key. When I examined the door, I understood why. There had been a lock at one time. It appeared to have been wrenched out.

I took some more money, this time US dollars, from the money belt which I wore under my shirt. I knew that I should have to pay for bulbs.

I made my way to the hotel lobby on the ground floor. The rest of the Hong Kong delegation had arrived. It had come by a different plane to me, but seemed to have received a similar reception.

The delegation was led by John Griffiths, the Attorney-General, a good looking but rather excitable man. I do not think that he enjoyed Lagos, in which endless patience seemed to be required. With him were Bill Turnbull, an able Hong Kong solicitor who had undertaken to give up a lucrative practice to concentrate on organizing a conference in Hong Kong if our bid was successful. The Hong Kong delegation was sitting along a wall of the lobby, eight of them on a sofa designed for four.

'Just calm down,' Turnbull was saying. 'They'll be along with the money soon.'

'How much did he ask you for?' I enquired. 'It must have been a lot for eight of you for a week.'

'He asked for three thousand, but I beat him down to two-five. How did you get on?'

'Not very well,' I conceded. 'I paid him for one night in advance.'

'Fortunately, I have some Chinese friends who will bring the money along when they can get it.'

'Isn't it a bit late for the banks to be open? It's nearly seven o'clock.'

'They don't put it in the bank. They hide it where it's safe, which means a metal cash box in the garden, I expect. So we will have to wait until they dig it up.'

'You may need some extra cash,' I warned him. 'The receptionist seems to have the concession for most things here.'

He certainly had for light bulbs. I was able to buy four from him, three of which actually worked when I tried them in the sockets in my room and the bathroom. I rejected his offer of a further relative to install them.

After a bath in lukewarm water, about which I decided not to complain in case I was subjected to an expensive plumber, I went to bed early, wedging my door shut with my suitcase.

I was awakened by a soft tap at the door.

'Room service,' said a voice.

'I can manage till morning, thank you.' I did not want anyone to punch the pillows, while I was on top of them.

'I'm sure you can't,' said the voice.

I saw the door opening.

'I'll scream,' I replied.

'Of course you will, before I have finished with you.'

I switched on the bedside lamp. I am not a suspicious man, but I had begun to wonder what sort of room service I was being offered. I saw the door pushed open. A young, slim Nigerian girl in jeans entered the room.

'It's quite all right,' she said. 'Chuck sent me.'

'I don't know anyone called Chuck. And if I did, he's made a mistake.'

'Of course you know Chuck. He works at the desk. He is my uncle. He said you were lonely and needed someone to look after you and stop you being miserable.'

'I am married,' I protested. 'My wife would be very angry, if she knew.' At that time, I had not been married for more than ten years.

'The married men are the worst,' she agreed, coming further into the room and loosening the top button of her blouse.

'I assure you that I am not lonely. I do not need company. I have my teddy bear to look after me.'

'So you prefer your bear to me?'

'It isn't like that,' I protested. 'It's just that the bear got here first.'

'I expect you have to report to your uncle?' She nodded. 'How much do you have to pay him for the concession?'

'A pound a room,' she admitted. 'I've already paid him £10 for this floor. I've only had one customer. And he was from Estonia and paid me in roubles.'

'I'll give you £5 for talking to me for a few minutes,' I said. 'But you'll have to tell your uncle that I have had a nasty accident and am no longer interested in girls.'

I think she did, as I was not approached in the hotel again, though other members of the Hong Kong delegation were.

Three days later, I was one of those who had indicated that he would like to fly to Benin, about 150 miles from Lagos. Here we would be received by the King of Benin and entertained to a display of tribal dances and music. I duly arrived at the private aerodrome near Lagos, from which a plane with forty-four seats was to fly us to Benin. When the plane was full, there were still about thirty of us waiting in the lounge.

'Oh dear,' said Mr Ojokwu, the cheerful solicitor who was in charge of this part of the programme. 'It looks as though we did not get our numbers right. I should have said only forty can go.'

'You did,' I replied. 'Unfortunately you did not say who the forty were. Why not ask them if they all want to go?'

He followed my advice. Nobody withdrew.

'We will have to wait until the plane comes back,' he said. 'It won't be more than an hour and a half. I'll just have a word with the pilot. The phones to Benin aren't working,' he explained. 'Otherwise we would ring up and tell the King there are some more visitors to come.'

I found myself sitting next to a man with his arm in a sling. He did not look happy.

'Is that arm hurting you?' I asked.

'No more than you'd expect after you'd been pushed down a flight of stone steps into a police cell,' he replied indignantly.

'How did you get there?'

'I've come here for the conference. I was supposed to speak on human rights. That's my job. I'm the commissioner for human rights in my country. I read a paper about human rights a couple of days ago. Do you know there were only about twenty people at the lecture? It's almost as if there was very little interest in the subject, though I can't really believe this.'

'I expect it was just bad advertisement,' I said soothingly.

'It was just after a free buffet lunch. I wonder if that had anything to do with it.'

'Probably,' I agreed. 'People prefer the stomach to the brain.'

'The day after the lecture, I took some pictures, with my new camera, of parts of Lagos. I thought I would use them for my next illustrated lecture.'

'Perhaps that was a mistake?'

'The police seemed to think so. I had only taken half a dozen pictures when a police jeep drew up and I was asked what I thought I was doing. I told them I was taking photos for a human rights lecture.'

'Did they say anything?'

'One of them, an inspector, I think, said "We'd better take him to the police station and lock him up until he's deported." Then they took me to the police station and asked me who I was. I was a bit angry by then, about being arrested for nothing. So I refused to give my name. They took away my camera, which was returned to me later, without any film in it, and shoved me in a cell. I fell over on the way down, though I can't say it was their fault, as I was not looking where I was going.'

I looked at him with respect. 'You must be a sensible man. You haven't blamed the police for your injuries. How did you get out?'

'I kept saying that I was there for the conference and demanding that they should phone the secretary. So they did, the next day, though they took their time about it, and he told them who I was. They let me go. Did you go to my lecture?'

'I'm afraid I did not. I did not realize you would be talking.'

'Are you interested in human rights?'

'Certainly I am.' There is, after all, no other answer. Nobody can say he is not interested in human rights, even if it is up to someone else to do something about them.

'I will give you a copy of what I was going to say. I have a spare one in my rucksack. I have brought several, in case the King of Benin is interested.'

I spent the next hour or so reading the commissioner's paper, while I was waiting for the Benin plane. This arrived soon after ten o'clock. If it took off in a quarter of an hour, we should be in Benin by about eleven, less than two hours late. As the pilot had warned them that we would be coming, it should not matter too much.

I was unduly optimistic. It was not only necessary to refuel the plane. It was also considered essential to carry out repairs, before it took off again. It was, in consequence, about eleven fifteen before we took off from Lagos and midday when we landed at Benin.

'Everybody out, please,' shouted Mr Ojokwu. 'There will be a bus waiting for us.'

Outside the only hangar at the airfield was a battered minibus, which seemed to have been partly repaired since a major collision. The words '13 passengers' had been altered to '18 passengers'. There were about thirty of us.

'This seems to be the only bus,' Mr Ojokwu explained. 'It's only a few miles to the city, so we shall have to squeeze up a bit.'

There was a rush for the bus, during which I was elbowed aside by a large man from Sierra Leone, who trod on my feet, put an elbow in my face and apologized so disarmingly that I said nothing. He was, in any case, much bigger than me.

I jumped into the bus and sat on the floor of the corridor, in front of the human rights commissioner, who told me that he had just visited the prison in Nuara and that they kept their detainees in much better conditions than the bus passengers.

After about five minutes, during which the driver ran over two chickens which committed suicide by running in front of the bus, there was a shout from the back.

'Please stop the bus.'

'What for?' asked Mr Ojokwu. 'We are late already.'

'I must urinate,' replied the voice.

'You should have used the plane,' replied Mr Ojokwu severely.

'I did,' replied the victim. 'There was a notice saying "Out of order".' Several others, facing the same problem, agreed with him. 'What is more,' someone added, 'there was no place at the airport.'

'All right then,' said Mr Ojokwu. 'We'll stop the bus.'

He had not realized that those in the gangway would have to leave the bus, if the voice from the back was to get out. Half a dozen of us stood by the side of the bus. The man who had complained ran to the side of the road, holding himself, and disappeared into a banana grove. This must have reminded many of the other passengers that they could not hold out much longer. They also entered the banana grove, emerging some minutes later with expressions of relief on their faces. They began climbing into the bus again.

Mr Ojokwu was talking to the driver, who was shrugging his shoulders.

'The bus won't start,' Mr Ojokwu announced. 'The driver says that the battery is dead. I would be grateful if you would push at the back. If we can get the bus over the next hill, there is a long slope where the driver thinks he can start the engine.'

Half the passengers assembled round the bus and pushed. Among those pushing the bus were one justice of appeal, three puisne judges, an attorney-general and a law draftsman. The attorney-general, giving orders, went to the front to speak to the driver, but went silent when the bus rolled over his foot.

By the time we had reached the rise, we were panting, except for the human rights commissioner, who said it was good for us to behave like ordinary people.

The bus went silently down the slope, slowly at first and then faster. It jerked several times, as the driver thrust it into gear, without result. Then it spluttered into life and carried on for another hundred yards before it stopped.

Those who had pushed it sat by the side of the road and waited for the bus to come back.

'I did not tell you', Mr Ojokwu announced, 'the bus has no reverse gear. Or rather it has one but it is not working at present. This means that we shall have to walk to the bus. It is not far. Follow me!'

It was about twenty past twelve. The sun was shining. We were all in suits, as it had been thought proper to wear them for an audience by the King. By the time we reached the bus we were warm. The commissioner, no doubt in an attempt to cheer me up, informed me that the detention camps in Cambodia were better than this.

The bus arrived at about half past twelve at the King's palace in Benin. This was a wooden building of moderate size. We followed Mr Ojokwu to a long room, while we waited for the King. It was to be a long wait.

Mr Ojokwu disappeared through a door at the back. This was beside a raised platform on which were a number of chairs with long backs. He returned a few minutes later with an elegant young woman, who described herself as the King's secretary. The commissioner showed that human rights were not his only interest by dribbling.

'Ladies and gentlemen,' said Mr Ojokwu, forgetting that there were no ladies in the group, 'I am afraid that the King is not here. He was here at nine thirty to receive the other party. He waited for you till half past eleven and then left. Will you please remain seated, until we find out when he will come to meet you.'

At roughly half hour intervals the young woman informed us that the hunt for the King was still in progress. At two o'clock, Mr Ojokwu announced that the King could not be found, that the plane for Lagos was due to leave at three and that, if we wanted to be on the plane, it would be wise to leave.

We returned, in the same discomfort as that in which we had arrived, in the same bus. The driver had kept the engine running the whole time we had been in the audience hall, in case the batteries went flat. He did not run out of petrol until we were within a hundred yards of the airport. We were content to walk the rest of the way.

We arrived at Benin airport before the first party. We waited by the door in the hangar, in which the temperature was about 120. At three o'clock a plane arrived. It was a large plane, which held a hundred passengers. We entered it and waited. At three thirty, the other group arrived.

Bill Turnbull, from Hong Kong, sat beside me. He had been with the earlier group. 'They said you were not coming,' he commented. 'Did you have a good lunch?'

'We had no lunch.'

'We did rather well. The King received us, showed us the town and provided us with a splendid barbecue. A very pleasant chap. Been educated at Oxford,' he said. 'Weren't you there?' I nodded. 'Pity. He would have liked talking to you.'

'Did John Griffiths come with you today?' I asked.

'He has had a rough time here,' Bill replied. 'He had a row with the receptionist when we arrived. You remember that he wanted £3,000. John did not take that and told the man what he thought about it.'

'Told him he was a swindler?'

'More or less. Anyhow, the next day, poor John had sharp pains all over his body. Somebody called the hotel doctor, who is Western trained, to look at him. The doctor examined him and said he could do little for him, as a witch must have put a spell on him.'

'You mean he believed in witchcraft? What would they say in Barts?'

'The doctor said that pains all over the body were the usual signs of witchcraft and that the only way of getting cured was to bring in a witch doctor, who knew how to deal with the spells. He warned John that it only worked in half the cases. In the other half, apparently, the patient lapses into a coma and dies.'

'What happened then?'

'The next day the Western trained chap brought in a witch doctor, who wore a suit and spoke excellent English. He called himself Dr Benjo. He looked at John and told him that he was suffering from a spell and must have upset someone.'

'Ah ha! The receptionist?'

'John said that he could not imagine who it was, though he had had a mild disagreement with the receptionist.'

'Ah, him,' said Dr Benjo. 'I've asked him not to do this to hotel guests. I will first of all recite a prayer. Then I will give you some medicine, which I want you to take three times a day. I will leave my card, in case you need me again. That will cost you £50.'

'Wasted, I suppose?'

'A complete success. John was up the next day. No pains, no fever. But I don't think he has enjoyed Lagos so far.'

It had not been an easy arrival. It might have been a difficult departure. I had retained some £5 notes, in local currency, in case I needed them. I had been advised to do so by Mr Ojokwu, who said that it was a wise precaution. Of course he had never come across anything of the same kind himself, but he had heard that there was a lot of bribery in the public service.

The immigration officer looked sadly at my passport, which had been stamped for seven days.

'It is out of date,' he said. 'You will have to fill up another form if you want to leave.'

'I thought the stamp was valid until the 28th,' I suggested.

'Anyone can see it expired on the 26th. That was yesterday. So you have been in the country illegally for a day.'

I had left Mr Ojokwu at the entrance to the airport. I had nobody to protect me.

'If you will just give me back my passport for a moment, I will fill in the form.'

The officer handed it to me. I put a note in the passport and gave it back.

'I think', I said, 'you will find the necessary visa at page 14. It is my fault for not drawing your attention to it before.'

'You are right,' he said. 'It was not clear before. I will put a new visa in it. You may now leave the country. Have a nice flight.'

This is how I came to have two visas for Nigeria in 1980.

The airport departure lounge was full of passengers. I took a seat with relief and waited for my Pan American flight to Nairobi. I had not expected that, at this stage, there would be a further obstacle.

Half an hour later, a Nigerian, wearing the uniform of the Civil Aviation Department, according to the words stitched in blue above the left hand upper pocket of his jacket, walked round the lounge, asking for the departure cards for the Pan Am flight. I admitted that I had one.

'I'm sorry to say, sir, that we have overbooked on the flight. We have just heard that there are so many passengers flying to Nairobi that we are obliged to take off half the passengers who are due to join the flight here. What is your name?' I told him. 'Oh dear,' he sighed. 'I'm afraid that we have decided that we should take off all those who have names beginning with a letter in the bottom half of the alphabet. I'm afraid the "R" is near the bottom.'

'Is there anything I can do?'

'It's my superior officer's decision. I could ask him, but I'm sure he will say he cannot help.'

'I hope he can change his mind. He will see that I have an onward ticket from Nairobi. It is in this envelope.'

The officer looked inside the envelope, which contained a £5 note.

'I will see what I can do,' he replied. 'Just let me write on your departure card. Then you won't be bothered again.' He affixed the word 'Examined' and left, with the envelope.

Shortly afterwards, another officer called for Pan Am departure cards. I showed him mine. As soon as he saw the signature, he passed on. I found that I was relieved that they were only collecting once.

The Pan Am flight to Nairobi was half empty. I was the only passenger in the first class section.

It was eleven at night when we arrived at Nairobi. By the time I had collected my suitcase, hired a taxi and arrived at the Kenya Hotel, it was after midnight. Fortunately, I had a confirmed booking at the hotel. I also had some Kenya currency. I could therefore foresee no difficulties. I should have known better. I put down my suitcase and made my way to the reception desk. Behind it was a smiling young man, who greeted me cheerfully.

'What can I do for you, sir?' he asked.

'I have a booking for two nights.'

'Is it confirmed?'

'Certainly. I have a letter to that effect from Thomas Cook.'

'Do you see those other people?' He pointed at a dozen or so others sitting about the hotel lobby, most of them asleep. 'They all have confirmed bookings too. I am trying to find other rooms for them, though some of them say they will just stay here until we have a room vacant.'

'Have you a cousin in one of the other hotels in Nairobi who will take me in?' I was getting the hang of the African extended family.

'I think I can get you into the Bestotel,' he replied. 'I've just spoken to my cousin there. If you go to the front of the hotel and take a taxi, the driver will take you to the Bestotel. Just stand outside and shout "George". Then the taxi will come. Say that Arthur sent you. That's me. George is my brother.'

I did as I was told. George drove me to the Bestotel. I paid him a hundred shillings, for what I later discovered to be a thirty-shilling journey. I carried my suitcase into the lounge of the Bestotel. It was empty. My spirits rose. Although it was after one o'clock, I was not far from a bed. Behind the desk was another happy man. I was beginning to dislike people who smiled at me.

'Arthur sent me from the Kenya,' I began.

'It's a pleasure to see you, sir. If you will just sit down over there, I will find out which room is free.'

I waited in a comfortable seat, dozing off as I did so. I was awakened by a touch on the knee. In front of me was the bellboy, with the name 'Bernard' on a metal badge fixed to his coat. Bernard ushered me to the lift. I was surprised to find that this was working. On the sixth floor he led me to a room. He unlocked the door, switched on the light and waved me into the room. When I entered the room there was a shout of 'Burglars' from the double bed which it contained.

A large man, who was naked, at least to the waist, sat up angrily in bed. Beyond him was a girl, similarly unclothed. I had time to notice that she was richly endowed, before I backed out of the room, saying 'Sorry, wrong room.'

I closed the door behind me. Bernard was laughing so much that he had some difficulty in carrying my suitcase. We went back to the lobby, where he explained to the clerk at the reception desk that the room was already occupied.

'I know, I know,' replied the receptionist, who seemed to find this as amusing as Bernard. 'I've just had a call from Room 653, saying that there is a prowler on the floor. The caller was not sure if he was a burglar or a pervert. By the way, sir, was there a girl there?'

'Certainly there was. A rather good looking girl at that, though I only saw her chest.'

'Ah ha,' said the clerk. 'That's my niece. So she's working in the hotel again without asking me first. If you will just sit down for a few minutes, I will let you have another room.'

'All I ask is that there is nobody else in it.' It was nearly two o'clock. 'Try to find an empty one this time.'

He woke me again, half an hour later. 'We have got another room! Number 322. There is nobody there.'

Bernard led me to the lift and paused outside Room 322.

'Are you sure you have the right key?'

Bernard looked at the one in his hand.

'Sure,' he said. 'Room 822. Oh dear, I am so silly.' He took me back to the lift and to the eighth floor, laughing quietly as we went.

He paused outside 822 and tried the key. The door opened.

'You go first this time,' I suggested, 'just in case the receptionist's niece is working in it.'

'Which niece?' asked Bernard.

'Never mind. You go first.'

Bernard disappeared. I waited in the corridor.

'It's empty,' he announced, as he emerged. 'So I've put your case inside. Have a good night. Please call me if you want anything else.'

It was half past two. I was tired. I hastily donned my pyjamas and pulled back the top sheet. The bottom one was badly crumpled. There were black hairs on the pillows. There was an ashtray beside the bed with several cigarette butts in it. The room had been used that night. The bed was still warm. I did not mind. I had a room at last.

Chapter 29

The Seventh Commonwealth Law Conference

It is not very difficult to persuade the audience, at the end of a conference, that the next one should be held in your country. Everyone is so pleased that the last one is over that they will readily agree to any proposal for the next.

John Griffiths, armed with the necessary authority from the Government, was able to persuade the delegates at Lagos that the Seventh Law Conference should be held in Hong Kong.

Bill Turnbull, an experienced solicitor, set up a limited company, so that he should not be personally liable for any of the debts which might be incurred. He next suggested that I could help in raising sufficient funds from the Hong Kong Government to pay the preliminary expenses. The Hong Kong Government had already agreed to pay the rent of an office for Bill Turnbull and to provide him with a staff of public servants, who were to help him make the necessary arrangements. Even so, a large sum was required to be spent before the conference took place.

Turnbull phoned me one morning. I was in a good humour, having just refused to give an interview to a reporter who wanted me to explain my recent decision that there was nothing indecent or obscene about pictures of unclothed women in the papers.

'We need some money for the conference,' he said, 'or we should not trouble you.'

'What do you want me to do?'

'We thought you might be able to get a couple of million dollars out of the Financial Secretary.'

'What! He was a businessman. He will probably only lend you money if you can persuade him that you're going to make a profit.'

'We are. I'll send up some figures today. They show that if we get 2,000 delegates and accompanying persons, we shall make a profit.'

'Who are accompanying persons?'

'Wives and girlfriends, I expect.'

'Why on earth should we get so many? There were half that number in Lagos and only a few hundred came from abroad.'

'Our shopping is better, even if the subjects for the speakers are not. What is more, we shall get lots of Australians and New Zealanders, because they can get a tax rebate for the expense of coming.'

'All right,' I agreed. 'I will try, though I am not likely to succeed if you have failed.'

'We shall, of course, consult you about the opening ceremony. Meanwhile, we need some money. Please try to get some for us.'

I decided to speak to Sir Philip Haddon-Cave, the Chief Secretary of the time. He had been Financial Secretary throughout the 70s, when he turned down a number of my requests for money, all of which seemed to have been more compelling than the law conference.

'I say, Philip,' I began.

'You want something,' he replied.

'As it happens, I do. How did you guess?'

'Because you only phone me when you are after something.'

'That is not possible. You are much too alert for that.' Even with him, I tried compliments, though they seldom seemed to work.

'What about the huge new courthouse at Tsuen Wan? Seven courts for a hundred thousand people! Who is going to use it?'

'We are looking ahead. Or rather, you are. In twenty years' time, when the courts are very busy there, people will ask who the percipient Chief Secretary was when approval was given for them.'

'What lost cause are you hoping to get money for this time? You'll have to speak to the Financial Secretary about it.'

'I thought you might say that. You are very persuasive.'

'As persuasive as you were with the Attorney-General, when you were the Chief Secretary?'

'Much more so than that, I hope. It's the Commonwealth Law Conference. It's going to be held here in a couple of years.'

'The place will be crawling with lawyers. I shall take my annual leave at the same time.'

'Bill Turnbull is going to be in charge of the conference office. He tells me that he badly needs some funds.'

'Lawyers have plenty, judging by the fees they charge. I had a bill last month with an item saying 'For informing you that I was not available to speak to you on the phone, $50'.

'Bill was hoping that the Hong Kong Government would prime the pump, as he calls it.'

'Just tell me how much profit did the last conference make?'

'It didn't actually do that. But there were a number of factors against it, which will not apply here, like location. Everyone wants to come here.'

'They do,' he agreed. I have four M.P.'s arriving today. I have to entertain them to dinner tonight.'

'Try not to be rude to them this time.'

'What, me? I disagree with them most politely.'

'I remember an M.P. called Cocks storming out of a dinner I gave for him, because he said you had insulted him.'

'I remember him. He didn't like me using his surname in the singular. He said it was time Hong Kong increased its taxes to help the underprivileged. I suppose he meant the poor.'

'What are the M.P.'s doing this time?'

'You ought to know. When you were C.S. you agreed that we should have a dozen of them a year, so that they could learn a little about Hong Kong.'

'I did. What a wise, far sighted and statesmanlike decision.'

'You said that they were going to stand up in the House of Commons and talk about Hong Kong anyway, so they might as well speak with some knowledge of the place, instead of having to find it on the map before they said it was being badly run.'

'I knew I would find you in a good mood. Will you try to persuade the F.S. that it would be good for business to advance money to Turnbull? It would not do Hong Kong's reputation much good if the conference was cancelled or the organizers went bankrupt.'

'I promise nothing,' he replied. 'I will speak to him.'

Turnbull telephoned me the following day.

'You will be glad to know that I got a call this morning from the F.S.'s office. He has agreed that the conference can have a Government loan of a million dollars. We will have to repay this out of any profits we make.'

'I'm sure that won't arise, if previous experience is a guide.'

'Hong Kong always makes a profit,' he replied. He was correct. The conference made a large profit, repaid the government and set up a substantial fund, to be used for the travelling expenses of delegates to future conferences who could not find the money.

'So you see,' Turnbull added, 'we do not need to trouble you to speak to Sir Philip. The A.G., Michael Thomas, had a word with him and the F.S. yesterday.'

'I have hired the Coliseum for the opening ceremony,' announced Bill Turnbull. 'It will hold at least twelve thousand, or fourteen thousand if they put seats in the arena where the tennis courts go.'

'That seems a generous provision for the two to three thousand guests, even if they all turn up with their accompanying persons.'

'There's no other place we could find which would hold two thousand. We're bound to get that number. It's early in the conference and most people will feel obliged to come. We've made it ten o'clock so that everyone will be awake by then.'

'It depends on what the accompanying person looks like,' observed the Bar representative, who had a new fiancée.

'How are you going to fill the Coliseum?' I asked. 'You can't have lions eating Christians in it. You will have to fill the place artificially. Whom are you going to ask?'

There is nothing which depresses a member of the audience more than a half empty auditorium. The ranks of empty seats leave him with the conviction that everyone else has stayed away on purpose. The organizers must have expected a much larger number to attend, or they would not have booked such a big hall. The alternative, which occurs to the member later, is that most of those who were meant to attend are too ill to do so. They must be confined to their rooms with amoebic dysentery or malaria, both of which he knows to be endemic to all tropical countries, because his Uncle Bert caught blackwater fever and bilharzia in Uganda in 1920.

A similar malaise is likely to affect those on the platform. As any actor will tell you, it is difficult to give of your best to a half empty house. It is a serious occasion. Somehow, the seats must be filled.

'I have arranged for four thousand or so schoolchildren to attend, from nearby Chinese schools,' said Turnbull. 'They won't understand all that is going on, but they may learn something about the Commonwealth from the video.'

'What video?' asked the President of the Law Society.

'I just heard today that Mr Ramphal, the Secretary-General, will not be coming. Instead, he will send us a video. I have not seen it yet. But I have allowed for their taste,' replied Turnbull. 'At the end of the ceremony, they will stay behind and see *Snow White and the Seven Dwarfs*. That will stop them leaving early.'

'Is anyone else attending?'

'I've managed to persuade the Commissioner of Police to send five hundred from the police training school. They will be the smart ones, with a short haircut.'

'It will still be half empty.'

'The Commander, British Forces will supply a thousand soldiers.'

'I'm afraid the delegates will stand out,' I commented. 'They will be the only ones in crumpled suits, who look as if they need a wash.

What about prisoners? Couldn't we get a thousand of them to come? They would love a day out.'

'They could rattle their chains, if they like the speeches,' added Thomas.

'What about some factory workers?' suggested the Chairman of the Bar Association. 'We could pay them $20 a head and ask them to applaud everything, just as if it was a union meeting.'

'Now that we have discussed who will be invited,' Turnbull continued, 'I must tell you that I have asked the Hong Kong Tourist Board what would be the best piece to play when the Lord Chancellor arrives.'

'What about something from *Iolanthe*?' Thomas suggested.

'I wanted something which was unusual and would be associated in everyone's mind with Hong Kong. The Law Society promised to provide a Chinese orchestra to play *The Three Legged Chicken Fugue*. May I have everyone's approval to this?'

He did not get it. Apart from himself, and he had not heard it, nobody was prepared to risk the fugue.

There was a similar disagreement as to who should speak from the platform. The President of the Law Society and the Chairman of the Bar Association insisted that their members would be much offended if they did not extend a warm welcome to the delegates. The Attorney-General explained that he felt obliged to say a few words on behalf of the Hong Kong Government, which would expect him to do so. Turnbull, as organizer of the conference, felt that he should inform the delegates of the main functions which were to be held. He added that there would have to be a speech from one of the Nigerian delegates, as the last conference had been held there.

'So far,' he concluded, 'there will be six speeches, which will take an hour to and hour and a half.'

'The children will be piddling all over the stadium by then,' interposed the President, who had a child of school age.

'Then there is your speech,' said Turnbull to me. 'We wondered if we could possibly manage without that.'

'I have already prepared three drafts,' I protested. 'Short, medium and long. Each is full of resounding sentiments, wise thoughts and wind. Will the delegates not be upset if I do not deliver one of them?'

'No, certainly not,' said Turnbull, in what I thought was an unnecessarily forthright manner. Apart from myself, everyone agreed with him.

'But,' said Turnbull, like a father giving his son an ice-cream after a visit to the dentist, 'we would like you to preside over the closing ceremony.'

'Where is that to be held?'

'We don't think quite so many will go to that, so we have booked a hotel ballroom. It will hold five hundred and we expect it to be quite full.'

'What you mean is that it does not matter much what I do at that stage?'

'Not at all. We've got you down to make an after dinner speech and to talk at the law reform lunch. You will be very active. We did not think you would want to deliver a paper as well.'

'Does anyone think I ought to speak at the opening ceremony?' There was silence, broken only by embarrassed coughs.

'People can prepare their speeches as soon as we have agreed on a theme for the conference,' said Turnbull.

'Why must there be a theme?' I asked. The others looked at me in surprise.

'Any conference with intellectual pretensions must have a theme. There was one in Lagos.' Nobody could remember what it was, though they were sure that there had been one.

'I thought "Into the 1980s" would be suitable,' Turnbull suggested. 'It is nice and broad.'

'And meaningless,' commented Thomas. 'What about "Hong Kong and Tomorrow's World"? Very subtle, don't you think?'

'No,' said the President. 'It's too political. The Chinese won't like it at all, while negotiations are in progress about Hong Kong's future. I think we ought to have a safer theme, like "Whither the Law?"'

'I don't much like that,' said the Chairman. 'It implies that the conference is only concerned with law, which is not so. What about "Reforming the Law"?'

This was rejected as being Marxist. Anyone who wanted to change something that had been working perfectly well could speak at the end of the paper on law reform.

'Perhaps I could suggest something, as you don't seem to agree about a theme? I accept that it will give no indication of the subjects to be discussed. So what about "The Commonwealth and the Changing World"?'

'It's the perfect conference theme!' said Turnbull. 'It is vague, unobjectionable and will include anything which is to be discussed.'

'And it will satisfy the few old fashioned delegates who prefer a theme to have some relationship to reality,' commented Thomas.

'It is important', I added, 'that we should make as little reference to the theme as possible, or people might start asking what some of the papers have got to do with it.'

'I'll bear that in mind,' said Turnbull. 'Do we all agree with the C.J.'s suggested theme?' They all did. It was probably my only positive contribution to the conference.

The theme was never mentioned again, though it was inscribed on a banner for the opening ceremony. This had to be hastily hidden when it was discovered that the 'C' had been left off the word 'Changing'. Some of the delegates were sensitive about capital punishment.

There was another committee charged with the preparation of papers to be delivered by various delegates. These papers were printed and a copy of the volume containing them was handed to each delegate on arrival. Before this, however, it is necessary to arrange for papers to be written. This is not simple.

Most organizers of a conference begin with the firm intention that, whatever the theme may be, the conference should concentrate on two or three main topics, to give an initial impression of intellectual unity. The final list of subjects will contain a wide variety of matters, some of which are wholly unconnected with any other paper.

A fine example of this could be seen in the title 'The Right to Live and the Right to Die'. Allied to this were papers on the definition of death, transplant surgery, test tube babies, the duties of a coroner and what were cleverly described as 'allied problems'.

There are a number of matters which have to be taken into account before the list of writers of papers is complete.

Firstly, it must be remembered that many delegates hope to claim tax relief for their attendance. This they can do only if some of the matters to be discussed at the conference are of marginal professional relevance. For this reason, the Hong Kong committee included papers on unprofessional malpractices, in which all lawyers may be assumed to have taken part, and 'computers and the law', which few understand but sounds important to the practitioner.

Secondly, a decision must be made as to whether you will choose a speaker and ask him to talk on anything or select a subject and search for someone willing to discuss it. Most conferences start by selecting their subjects first. This is likely to fail, because you will find eleven distinguished guests who will be pleased to discuss negligence in head-on collisions between stationary cars, but nobody will talk about the equity of redemption. The Hong Kong system, which has since been followed with success at other conferences, was to assemble a cast of distinguished lawyers, let them choose their own subjects and assemble these under a general heading, which is wide enough to cover almost anything.

For this reason, under the title 'The Art of Advocacy', there was included 'Damages for Personal Injuries'. Nobody objected that the connection between the two subjects was not immediately obvious. Under 'Migratory Divorce in a Mobile Society', a subject somewhat surprisingly not confined to those who live in trailers, appeared the subject of 'Child Stealing'. There are likely to be children involved in both.

Thirdly, the list must contain a number of subjects which do not require too much thought. It has to be accepted that many of the delegates will attend to enjoy themselves, rather than to improve their minds. The committee decided that it would be unwise to place an asterisk against those subjects which were likely to be intellectually less demanding.

Fourthly, as this was a conference of about fifty different nations, the opportunity to speak had to be shared. The object of a Commonwealth meeting is not achieved if there are eleven panellists from Vanuatu and none from the UK. The Hong Kong conference managed to persuade representatives of sixteen countries to present papers. Even though half of the papers were submitted by speakers from the UK or Hong Kong, no objections were raised. The committee had taken the precaution of writing to each country, months before the conference began, to ask for volunteers. There was little response, except from Professor Jones, who offered to deliver his illustrated lecture on pornography. This was rejected by a small majority.

On such occasions, there are some delegates and most 'accompanying persons' who will show an unhealthy interest in the activities outside the lecture room. It is for this reason that the committee feels obliged to organize a number of outside diversions for visitors, some of them free and some at an immoderate cost which, it is hoped, will not be noticed by those grappling with the subtleties of the exchange mechanism.

The harbour ferry tour was included because, if carried out at night, it showed Hong Kong at its dramatic best, with lights glowing half way up some of its peaks. The New Territories visit, in chartered buses, was staffed by hostesses who fed inaccurate but dramatic information to the delegates. 'This is the place where six men were shot climbing the fence in 1967', even if wholly without foundation, sounds more exciting than 'This is where Wong cut through the fence during the Cultural Revolution.'

Lunch was provided by the Jockey Club, at its racecourse near Shatin. The member of the committee who asked if the main course was to be old horses was told to keep quiet. He was excused because of his French blood on his mother's side.

With regret, the committee decided not to employ the 'Topless Escort Service', which offered, at a reduced rate for quantity, to provide company for those delegates whose sexual impulses were not sufficiently sublimated by four days of non-stop oratory. It was left to the bellboys of each of the hotels in which the delegates were accommodated to provide these services if they were required. It was thought that this could safely be left to competitive enterprise.

Red Cross teams were discreetly stationed at all lectures, partly for the benefit of those delegates who were of an age when overexcitement may lead to heart attacks. One of them became so incensed, during a debate on crime, that he had to be removed from the room, muttering 'Flog them all.' This was thought to be in poor taste, as the speaker had just informed the audience that theft was rife in the Royal Navy in 1800, when the lash was freely administered. The presence of medical orderlies has also been shown to be useful to subdue delegates who resort to fisticuffs. As this had happened during previous Commonwealth Law Conferences, it was thought that there might well be violence during the debate on the law and the press.

On the evening before the opening of the conference, the hosts arranged what was called a 'get-together'. It was supposed to afford an opportunity for delegates to get to know one another. One man was found in tears in a corner. He explained, in broken English, that nobody would speak to him. When he was escorted to the hotel lobby, it was discovered that he was a Japanese tourist who had entered the reception room by mistake.

On the Monday evening, a reception was held for two thousand, in a ballroom designed to hold half that number in maximum discomfort. The committee adopted the principle that friendships are likely to blossom if it is not possible to raise your glass without indecently assaulting your neighbour. An unexpected bonus was that the waiters with trays of drinks found it so difficult to circulate that they gave up, greatly reducing the bill for alcohol.

In spite of warnings to the contrary, the committee insisted upon organizing a 'hospitality evening' on the Tuesday. As many as possible of the delegates were to be entertained by the Chief Justice, the Attorney-General, the President and the Chairman, as well as by various judges and members of the legal service and private practitioners.

Some delegates found themselves asked to three dinners and accepted all, not wishing to upset any of their hosts. Others decided that the only wise thing to do was to pretend they had not been invited to anything and stayed in their hotel rooms. Some arrived without having answered an invitation. As a result, some hosts, who had expected a dozen, invited twenty and received six acceptances, were faced with fifteen hungry guests, for five of whom there was no fish. Others, who had laid a dozen places, were left with three guests, two of whom were dedicated vegans and refused to eat the main course.

On the Wednesday morning, some of the delegates were still hungry; others were feeling bloated, after helping their hostess to eat the spare portions. Some had been forced to eat standing up; others had faced empty chairs and a tearful hostess.

This was the perfect recipe for disaster. It did not disappoint and gave rise to many long term grievances and enmities which were, in the years to come, the main recollections of the conference.

A time and a place were given for the closing ceremony. Unlike for all other events, no details were stated as to who would preside over the ceremony or what it would consist of. I raised the need for such a ceremony at one of the meetings of the organizing committee.

'I shan't be ready in time,' Turnbull complained. 'Couldn't we put it off for a month or two?'

'There, there,' replied Thomas. 'You've been asking that for a year. I'm sure it will be splendid on the day.'

'I want to raise the question of the closing ceremony,' I said, 'now that we have all decided that we are going to hold the conference.'

'You promised to preside over that,' said Turnbull. 'It's your big moment!'

'You only asked me because nobody else would do it,' I replied, hoping that somebody would contradict me. They did not.

'I've been to a dozen conferences,' Thomas interposed. 'There is always a closing ceremony.'

A closing ceremony is not an occasion which attracts volunteers. On the opening day, usually a Monday morning, most delegates are fresh, eager and determined, out of character, to be friendly to everyone. They even look with a benevolent eye on those professional colleagues for whom they usually harboured varied emotions, ranging from dislike to enmity. By the last afternoon, the initial fervour of many has gone. Some are surfeited by intellectual discussion; others cannot absorb another speech without succumbing to a bout of nausea. Those who have brought 'accompanying persons' with them are likely to be engaged in bitter recrimination about the amount of money spent by them in the purchase of useless souvenirs.

'Look,' said the Chairman, deciding, in desperation, to try logic. 'If you have an opening ceremony, you have to have a closing one as well. Otherwise, the conference is left in the air.'

'Does it matter?' I asked.

'Well, really,' commented Thomas. The others glared at me in hostile silence.

'It's a very dangerous ceremony,' I protested. 'Look what happened in London!'

'I do realize that the closing ceremony of an international conference there was disrupted, when a judge from Burma ran amok, but that is not going to happen again,' Turnbull assured me.

'Who else will be on the platform with me, then?' I asked. 'Will I have a fung shui man?'

'What for?'

'To tell us if the next conference is to be in a lucky place or not.'

'He's been in the Far East too long,' muttered Turnbull. 'And what do we do if he advises against it?'

'He won't,' I replied. 'Just mention to him that you will double his fee, if he does what you say. If he won't, tell the delegates, especially those from the place of the next conference, that it was intended to be a joke and not to be taken seriously.'

'Look on the bright side,' said Thomas soothingly. 'A closing ceremony is the best part of many conferences.'

'Why not have the closing ceremony in the middle before anyone has left?' suggested one member of the committee. It was his only contribution.

'Surely symmetry is more important than reason?' I asked.

'Let's move on to the lunch,' Turnbull said. 'Does anyone disagree that a buffet lunch should be in a room nearby?'

This would probably ensure a good attendance, as many delegates, it was believed, lived only for the next free meal. If some came with plates of pudding or cheese and munched throughout the ceremony, it was a price worth paying to secure their attendance.

'Has anybody thought about how we should fill in the time?' I asked. 'Unless you would like me to speak for an hour or so.'

Turnbull blanched. He was obviously prepared to go to any lengths to avoid that. 'I thought we would ask three judges to sum up, in a quarter of an hour each, all the lectures and discussions in the three hotels.'

'They will find it hard to say enough about them to last fifteen minutes,' I suggested, to be helpful.

'They are all judges,' Turnbull replied, 'so they are used to making things last as long as possible.' Turnbull had recently lost a High

Court action, after a fifty-page judgment delivered some months after the hearing.

'What about questions?' asked a member.

'Certainly not,' I replied. 'There will be no time.'

'I think it would be a good idea if we also included winners of the moot competition. We could ask the Lord Chancellor to present the prizes to them, couldn't we?'

'In any case,' Turnbull added, 'I'll have a couple of students standing by to receive the prizes, just in case there is no competition. After that we propose to call in the Chairman of the Commonwealth Lawyers Association, to describe what it has done since the last conference.'

'What is the C.L.A.?' I asked.

'Don't ask me,' replied Thomas. 'You are a vice-president. Don't you know?'

'It has a fund,' said Turnbull. 'I can't tell you anything else. So we can ask the chairman of it to tell us what is done with the money. Then there are the delegates from the place of the next Commonwealth Law Conference. They can tell us about the pleasures of wherever they come from.'

'There is not supposed to be any time for pleasure,' I replied, 'only for intellectual thought, improving if possible.'

'So that will give us a closing ceremony of about one and a half hours, quite enough. If you keep your speech to about five minutes, we shall all be grateful.'

'And surprised,' muttered Thomas to himself.

The closing ceremony began only twenty minutes late, as many of the audience were engaged in sustained attacks on the buffet lunch. As the chef explained apologetically to Turnbull, he had expected 200 guests, who would pick at the food, not 500 who appeared to be ravenous, though happily they were prepared to eat anything so long as they were not charged for it.

I began with a five-minute speech. This was well received by those members of the audience who were not snoring throughout like a herd of pigs. It was followed by three learned summaries of the discussions. This was punctuated by bursts of clapping from those who had been sleeping and had been nudged awake when the summaries began. They felt it was time that they took an active part in the proceedings. The winners of the moot received prolonged applause when they appeared to receive their prizes.

The Chairman of the Commonwealth Lawyers Association was also accorded a warm welcome, mainly because the delegates had not heard of the association. As members of it, they clapped the

Chairman generously when he sat down. He was clearly pleased. It helped to compensate him for a terrible week, during which he had had to explain what his association did, to assorted audiences and to his own committee. It did not soothe him to see the final programme, on which he was described as Chairman of the Commonwealth Fund.

The optimists commented that this good attendance showed that the conference had been a success, as otherwise so many would not have stayed until the end of it. The pessimists said that the attendance at the closing ceremony showed how desperate the delegates were for anything of interest and that the conference itself must have been an outstanding disaster.

As I listened to the Jamaican delegates describing the attractions of their country, I realized that these were more important to most delegates than the content of the lectures. You can assemble a devoted audience of twenty for a discussion of the legality of killing cabin boys for food in open boats, but most delegates have not come to have their minds stimulated.

On this test at least, the conference was a great success. Most of the guests (if not the organizers) enjoyed themselves, so long as they did not attend too many lectures.

Flagstaff House, 1979–80

Chapter 30
Visit to China

I visited China on my own about 1982. Before I went, I was asked to see the Political Adviser. He thought that my visit would cause him trouble. He was a shrewd man, who understood the Chinese well. He was seldom wrong.

'So you are going to China.'

I nodded. It was a statement, not a question. He knew all about the visit. He had already told me that it would be unwise of me to wear my Mao jacket or carry the little red book containing some of Mao's sayings, as Mao was out of favour.

'Tell me why you are going.'

'Because the Supreme Court of China asked me. I do not want you to think I'm a volunteer.'

'Our discussions with the Chinese about Hong Kong's future have reached a delicate stage. It would be better if you said nothing.'

'I do not know anything.'

'Of course not, but nobody will believe that, will they? Please don't make it up, like you usually do when you are stuck for an answer. You'll upset the Chinese if you do and we shall have another walkout.'

'Is there anyone who *is* popular in China?'

'There is a wide choice. If you can, say something pleasant about the North Koreans, *not* the South Koreans, please, the Albanians or Vietnam, it will be well received.'

'What about the Cubans?'

'They are pursuing the class struggle in Africa and are hostile to the USA. But they are lackeys of the Russians, who are not liked in China because they left more than twenty years ago. So you'd better keep off the Cubans.'

'What about the Americans?'

'When in doubt, abuse them. They are, as you will soon realize, mainly responsible for China's isolation in the world. Apparently it started with the American missionaries, who were all intelligence officers in disguise.'

'What about Chinese interpreters?'

'They are excellent. Sometimes they are not necessary, as many of those you meet also speak good English, though they prefer to use the interpreter. It is a reminder that those who come to China must be ready to use its languages. It also gives the man you are speaking to rather longer to think of his reply.'

'I promise to be as dull as possible.'

'Good. I'm sure you will not find that too difficult. And please keep your hands off the interpreter. The girls wear shapeless clothes and have short haircuts, but you may find some of them quite attractive, after a week of meetings in China.'

'You need have no fear,' I replied with a quiet dignity which I had been practising for my visit.

'That's what Smithers said. He is a junior minister, so I should have known that he couldn't restrain himself for long. He pinched a lady interpreter's bottom.'

'At least it wasn't a man.'

'You can't always tell, I agree. That did not help him.'

'Thank you for your advice. I shall keep my mouth shut throughout my visit.'

'If you do open it, try not to put your foot in it,' he urged. 'It will give me a mound more paperwork to do. I have had enough for a month already from Smithers' visit.'

In Beijing I was accommodated, as a guest of the Chinese Government, at the only modern hotel in the capital at that time, though many excellent ones have since been built. On the first morning after my arrival, when I was on my way to a meeting, I was stopped in the lobby of my hotel by a group of Hong Kong journalists. Several of them, before I could say anything, thrust microphones under my nose, and shouted 'Testing, one, two, three'. I waited until there was a fair chance that I would be heard and replied, before I was asked any questions, that I had nothing to say.

'Why have you come to Beijing?' asked one reporter, an earnest looking girl with thick glasses and ragged jeans. She had a pad of foolscap paper on which she was scribbling.

'Because I was asked,' I replied, deciding that I had better say something. This was fatal. Once you start to talk to reporters, it is difficult to stop. The best way to get rid of them is boredom. If you can convince them that your replies will become steadily duller and be of no interest to their readers, you have a chance of escaping from them.

'Who asked you? Was it the Chinese Government?'

'No. It was the Supreme Court.'

'You are here to talk about the handover of Hong Kong to China,' asserted one of them.

'I assure you that I am not.'

'Then why have you come here when the talks are going on?'

'It's a coincidence.'

'They are going to talk about the courts next week.'

'First I've heard of it.' It was, though nobody believed me.

'You are supposed to be the expert on the Hong Kong judiciary,' the girl with the thick glasses asserted.

'Only supposed, I assure you.'

'And yet you are asking us to believe that you know nothing about the talks next week on the judiciary in Hong Kong?'

'That's right.' It did not sound convincing to me, either.

'What do you say about progress in the talks?' asked another reporter, thrusting a microphone at my chin. 'Please speak up,' he added. 'My batteries are not good.'

'Can't you get any here?' I asked.

'Only Chinese ones,' he answered. 'They don't last.'

'I expect you can get some American ones on the black market.'

'It's not like Canton. It's very easy to get American goods there. Hey, what about my question?'

'No comment,' I replied.

'What are you going to see here then?' asked another newspaperman.

'No comment,' I answered. I had recovered. 'I am glad to have been such a help to you,' I added, as I left the hotel.

It is still believed by many people, particularly when something goes wrong, that I made a special visit to Beijing for the purpose of the talks about Hong Kong's future, and that my presence had been a factor in the treaty which resulted.

I was taken to see a court in operation in Beijing. The day before, I had been asked by an official from the Ministry of Justice if I would prefer to see a criminal or a civil case.

He was a middle aged man in thick glasses, who had worked in the same ministry for 20 years, except during the period of the Cultural Revolution, when he was sent for re-education to a rural area. Here he learned the best way of growing green vegetables, a skill for which he found no use in Beijing. His English was excellent.

'What kind of court would you like to see tomorrow?' he asked me.

'I thought I would like to see a criminal trial, Mr Chau.'

'Why is that?' he replied.

'Only because I spend a lot of time doing criminal work.'

'You can see a criminal trial in Shanghai, if you like. Better to listen to a civil case here.'

'Whatever you choose, Mr Chau.' It was apparent that this was the correct answer, as Mr Chau beamed.

Next day, he took me to a small room in a building which was shared by the courts and the police. This was explained to me by Mr Chau as a matter of convenience, not of principle. As most of those who were taken to court had already been in police custody for some time, it was sensible, he said, for the courts to be in the same building as the police.

'Won't that make it look as if the courts are influenced by the police, Mr Chau?'

'They are. Aren't yours?'

'No. Our courts are independent. Sometimes, they do not believe the evidence of a police officer.'

'Then he should be sacked,' agreed Mr Chau. 'If the courts do not believe him, he must be corrupt or incompetent or both.'

'Surely the courts must stand between the state and the citizen and make sure that justice is done.'

'The police ensure that only the guilty are brought to court. If you are innocent, the police will find that out too and discharge you.'

'Surely that puts too much trust in the police?'

'The police are serving the state. So are the judges. Who pays your judges' salaries?'

'The Government of Hong Kong does.'

'There you are! The judges are only state workers too. If they do not perform properly, they can be sacked.'

'We don't sack our judges. Once they are appointed, they remain for life. They can be removed, but it's a very difficult procedure.'

Chau was appalled. 'Do you mean to say that you have got to put up with a judge who is very bad at his job until he gets to the retiring age?'

I nodded. I was beginning to feel uncomfortable.

Chau shook his head. 'I did not realize', he said, 'that you had to keep on bad judges for life. Fortunately, we are not obliged to do so here. It's just as well, too. We got some very poor judges during the Cultural Revolution. They have all gone now, thank goodness. Some of them were Red Guards of not more than twenty or so. Even the party got fed up with them.

'Are the present judges all qualified lawyers?'

'Not many,' Mr Chau conceded. 'During the revolution, they shut the universities and sent the graduates to the countryside. They've only just opened them again. We didn't get any lawyers for about fifteen years.'

'What a splendid idea!'

'Most of the courts have managed without lawyers. It doesn't seem to matter, except that a lot more cases seem to be tried than when we did have them.'

'Who will be on the court tomorrow?'

Mr Chau pulled a piece of paper from his pocket. 'The President is Captain Fang.'

'Why is he called Captain?'

'We have just restored the ranks in the army. It didn't work very well, when everyone was "comrade soldier". It made it quite difficult to give orders. It was, nevertheless, a splendid army,' added Chau loyally.

'You mean he has retired?' I was thinking of a cousin who was still called 'Major Tomkins' twenty years after the First World War, although he had never been a regular soldier.

'Certainly not. He is a member of the People's Liberation Army. He gets three months' leave each year to sit in the court. The rest of the time, other officers preside. Last year a president who had protested about being sent shot his colleagues and then himself. He made his point, so we only have volunteers now.'

'I expect there are plenty of those?'

'Anyone who refuses does not seem to get on very well. Captain Fang has sat before.'

'His colleagues seem to be in more danger than me. Who are they?'

'One is a woman. You'll see the difference.'

' Are you sure there'll be any?'

'You are making a joke!' Mr Chau laughed loudly. I wasn't. If everyone is in a boiler suit and has a unisex haircut it is not always easy to tell.

'The second member is Lau Kit Sze, from the Women's League of Young Mothers.'

'Will the baby be there?'

'It's just a name. She isn't young and she is not a mother. On the other side of Captain Fang is Ho Hung Lee. He is a member of the party, which nominated him three years ago.'

We duly attended the court, which was on the second floor of what seemed to be a police station, full of men with solemn faces in uniform. There were several men in handcuffs, who were rather more cheerful than their captors. At one end of the court were two wooden tables. Over them was draped the People's Republic of China flag. Behind the tables were four chairs.

'Who has the fourth chair?' I asked Mr Chau, who had come with me.

'That is for the secretary. He makes the notes and records what the judges have decided to do.'

The remainder of the room was filled with benches. These were rough and uncomfortable.

'Very democratic, these seats,' I said to Mr Chau. I carefully avoided the bloodstained nail on the bench to which Mr Chau ushered me.

On the front benches were two couples.

'Those are the parties in the case,' Mr Chau explained. 'The rest of the court is open to the public.' There wasn't anyone else there, except an amorous couple at the back, who were much more interested in one another than in the case.

'Don't worry, Mr Roberts. If this was a criminal case, the benches would be full. People are very interested to know what happens to criminals. Sometimes they stand up and applaud the court!'

The three members of the court entered. The secretary, who preceded them, shouted at the audience to stand. The couple at the back unwound themselves long enough to do so. All the judges were wearing a uniform, with a cap. It was of a brown colour, like that worn by soldiers.

'Which is the lady?' I asked Mr Chau, who replied that he would tell me later, as he could not be sure just from looking at the court.

The secretary put a paper in front of Captain Fang and called loudly 'Poon against Yin' in Mandarin. Mr Chau explained to me what was happening.

'Stand up, Poon', shouted the President. 'I see you claim 2,000 yuan and your flat against Yin. Tell me about it.'

Poon was a determined man. His wife, who sat next to him, tried to restrain him several times. Poon told her to keep quiet, as Captain Fang wanted to hear what he had to say.

'I read this circular,' Poon began. 'It was put up on all the notice boards. It said that a lot of flats had been seized illegally in 1949 and the owners should claim them back if they wanted them, or get some rent for them.'

'Is there such a notice?' Captain Fang asked the secretary, who nodded and handed him another paper. The President read this and passed it to his colleagues.

'Ah ha,' said one of them to Poon. 'You are a capitalist roader.'

'I think Mr Poon just wants his flat,' said the third member of the court. Either she was a woman, or she was a man with a football injury. I thought it more likely that it was a woman. What was clear, however, was that there was a serious disagreement between her and Mr Ho, the party nominee. They appeared to have lost interest in the parties and were shouting at one another.

'He is a landlord!' Ho screamed. 'We exterminated them in 1949. Are a million deaths to count for nothing?'

'He has been told to claim his flat back by the party,' retorted Madam Lau. 'Haven't you, Mr Poon?' Poon attempted to resume his narrative.

'Imperialist exploiter of the poor!' shouted Mr Ho. Yin, the defendant, exclaimed 'I agree.'

'Speak when I call on you and not before,' interposed Captain Fang severely. 'This is a court of law, not a party meeting,' he added.

'He often says that,' Mr Chau explained. 'He means it too.'

'I was put out of my flat in 1949 by the soldiers,' Poon explained. 'They told me that I did not need four rooms for myself and my wife, and that I had better leave.'

'Did you say anything to them?' asked Captain Fang.

'You do not argue with armed soldiers,' Poon replied. 'When I said I didn't want to go, one of them shouted "Capitalist" and pointed his rifle at me. So I left quietly and stayed with my brother.'

'You see,' Ho interposed. 'A landlord. He was fortunate not to have been shot.'

'I agree,' observed Captain Fang. 'The discipline in the army was dreadful then. Fortunately the Chiang Kai Shek bandits were even worse and, with the help of the people, we were able to overcome them.'

'Perhaps you would like to hear Yin?' the secretary suggested.

'I certainly would,' Ho interjected. 'He is being exploited by Poon. Aren't you, Yin?'

Yin nodded. He found the procedure puzzling. He had been a loyal party member for about forty years. Now they were thinking of taking his flat away.

'Tell us how you got the flat, Yin,' said Captain Fang.

'My house in Taiyan had been set on fire by the Chiang Kai Shek bandits, so I had nowhere to go. I was told the flat was empty, when I left the army in 1949, and I could have it. So I took it over with my wife.'

'All four rooms?' asked Madam Lau.

'My wife had two. Mr Jang and his wife had two. Then they died and I had four. Now there are two other people in the other rooms.'

'They pay you rent,' shouted Poon.

'How much?' asked Captain Fang.

'Only a hundred yuan a month.'

'You've been living rent free for over 30 years,' accused Madam Lau.

'That was a reward for serving in the victorious army in much danger and discomfort.'

'You are now a landlord yourself,' Madam Lau reminded him.

'That is different,' Ho replied.

'How?'

'Anyone can see that it is.'

I felt very much at home. It was just like a Court of Appeal in Hong Kong, with two members bickering over what each of them called a matter of principle and the presiding judge keeping quiet while they did so.

'Anything more to say?' asked Captain Fang, who had not given any indication of what he was thinking. I assumed that this meant either that he had made up his mind or that he was in a state of acute indecision. He was applying the same principles as I used.

The secretary announced that the court would inform the parties of its decision at a later date. I heard later that the defendant was told to pay over all he had received as rent to Poon or give him back his flat.

In Shanghai, I was received by Yung Sau Tze. He was generally known as Judge Yung, or as 'Comrade Judge' by party members who preferred the old rules. There were not many of them in Shanghai, which appeared to be prosperous and peopled by dissidents. Judge Yung was a round faced, cheerful man, who greeted me warmly when I visited him in his chambers. He spoke to me in English with an American accent.

'I am an odd animal,' he announced.

'You do not look like one,' I replied courteously.

'I read law in the United States, just after the Pacific War. When I came back, lawyers were not needed, for a very long time. So I earned my living running a restaurant. Fashions changed about five years ago. Somebody pulled out my file and found that I studied US law about 30 years ago. So I was told to give up my restaurant and be a judge instead.'

'Do you like it?'

'I do rather. It's better than having to be polite to the customers in a restaurant. Those who come here have to be pleasant to me. The change suits me.'

'Do you sometimes find the law a bit difficult, Judge?'

'I expect I would do, if there was much, but fortunately there is not. There is a Penal Code, which sets out the crimes, a Procedure Code, which tells you how to hear them, and that's about all.'

'Don't you look at other cases sometimes? You might do something quite different from a judge in Chunking.'

'I expect I often do. Does it matter?'

'Would it not be a good idea if you all did the same thing?'

'Like in America? There you have fifty sets of law reports and never make up your mind, because there is authority in the cases for most things.'

'Surely there must be some guidance, especially as a lot of the judges are not qualified in law at all,' I said.

'There are not many lawyers in China. So there isn't anyone trained to argue that there was a case decided quite differently in 1790. There are circulars from the Supreme Court, from time to time. They do state what has been done in the Supreme Court in a few of the cases which come before it.'

'What cases do you have this morning?'

'One murder and one corruption.'

'Both will plead not guilty, I suppose.'

'I don't think so. It's not usual for the police to bring a man to court unless he has already admitted that he did it.'

'Don't the police sometimes force a confession from an accused?'

'Certainly they do. Like any other police officer, they want to get a conviction. So I always ask the accused if he made his statement voluntarily. If he says he did not, I remand him in custody and try him again next month.'

'What if he still insists that a confession was forced out of him?'

'Then I see if there is enough evidence without the confession. There usually is. Shall we go in? Please sit on the bench with me. I'll tell them that you are the chief judge from Hong Kong and that you have come to hear how we do things here in a criminal trial.'

The first defendant was brought in. He bowed to the judge, who was wearing a black gown over his ordinary clothing. He looked impressive, without a wig. I wished that I did, with one.

'I've read the papers, Lee,' said Judge Yung. He now spoke in Shanghainese, which was translated for me. 'You are charged with murder. What do you say?'

'I killed him,' Lee agreed.

'Did you mean to?'

'Certainly I did. He was trying to rape my wife.'

'Did you tell the police this? it's not in your statement.'

'I told them,' replied Lee indignantly.

'Is this true?' Judge Yung asked the police officer who had brought in Lee.

'Of course not,' he replied. 'I recorded everything he said.'

'If you are telling the truth, Lee, you are guilty of killing under provocation, aren't you?'

'That's what I kept telling them.'

'How long have you been in prison, waiting trial?'

'I was arrested four years ago, Comrade Judge. They told me you were too busy to see me if I did not confess. So I gave in and did so.'

'I think you've been in prison long enough,' said Judge Yung. 'I'm going to give you four years' imprisonment.'

'That's far too much,' Lee protested.

'Including all the time you've been in custody already.'

'That was very courageous of you,' I suggested, as Lee left.

'I couldn't do anything else,' said Judge Yung. 'He was a good party member. I just hope he won't do it again. He's quite a violent man.'

The next defendant, named Wan, was brought in as Lee left, acknowledging the clapping at the back of the court.

'This man is a very wicked fellow.' Judge Yung shook his head. 'Wan, you are charged with corruption. What do you say?'

'He pleads guilty,' said the police officer. 'Don't you, Wan?' Wan nodded.

'I think we'd better let him reply, so that I can take it down. Is that true, Wan?'

Wan nodded. 'I'll record that as a plea of guilty. You'd better tell me what Wan did, Officer, for the benefit of those members of the public who have come today.'

'When the accounts were being checked at the party headquarters, it was discovered that 1,000 yuan was missing. After further investigation, we found that Wan had been taking money for several months.'

'That is appalling,' commented the judge. 'What have you got to say for yourself, Wan?'

'Please be merciful, Comrade Judge. I only did it because I cannot support my wife and eleven children on my salary.'

'Eleven children! You should be ashamed of yourself. A good cadre does not have more than two children.'

Wan was in tears. It was clear that he regretted the other nine.

'It is not so much the stealing,' went on the judge, 'nor the amount, nor the abuse of trust, but where you did this. It was at party headquarters. They were party funds.'

'I know,' agreed Wan. 'It was disgraceful. There is no excuse for what I did. I ask you to be kind to me.'

Judge Yung paused for a moment. He had a good sense of the dramatic.

'I am going to take a very unusual course,' he said. I shall not sentence you to death, which would be a proper reward for your wickedness.'

There was what sounded to me like a hiss of surprise from the public galleries.

'Because we have a guest from Hong Kong today, I have been authorized by the party to pass an unusual sentence on you.'

'No, no,' shouted Wan. I imagine that he expected to be burnt alive before he was executed.

'I am going to release you to your family. You'd better carry him out,' Judge Yung added. 'He seems to have collapsed.'

As I left the court, the audience clapped, as did Judge Yung behind me. I rather enjoyed this, as I had not been clapped since I made sixteen not out for my prep school against Heath Brow (prepares boys for the services), a school which we did not like, because the boys mostly had fathers in the navy and were snooty.

'When you go back to Hong Kong,' said the Judge as I left, 'you can tell them that the courts in China are not what they think. We do not treat criminals harshly, as you saw.'

I wonder why, as we went past one of the ground floor rooms, I saw a man who looked like Wan putting on a police officer's jacket.

Perhaps nobody was sure what to do with me. Whatever the reason, I was told to be in the lobby at ten o'clock, the day after I reached Canton, to be taken to the industrial fair. This was a late start, by Chinese standards. In the past, I had been told to be ready by half past seven, so that, for the first part of my programme, I was not fully awake. This was usually followed by a 'Western breakfast', as it was described in the menu at the hotel in Shanghai. In Canton, which I found easier to pronounce than Kwangzhou, I was given a room in the Tung Fang Hotel, where both the room and the food were Chinese.

I was greeted in the hotel lobby by my interpreter, Mr Tze, who was with me throughout my visit to Canton.

'You are, of course, interested in engines,' he told me as we left the hotel in a battered black car.

'Some more than others,' I replied.

I was not so sure of Mr Tze that I could tell him what I really believed about engines. I was careful always to be complimentary about what I was shown. This was not easy, as some of the things about which Mr Tze, and others, were enthusiastic were not of a high standard, according to Western requirements. I had to remind myself, several times, that China was a poor and overpopulated country. I had not realized how it could change in a few years.

'Shall I switch on the siren?' Mr Tze asked eagerly.

I nodded. He enjoyed the siren, which screamed from the car as we motored through the streets. The windows were covered in lace curtains, except the one beside the driver, who was able to see his offside wing mirror. The road was mainly occupied by cyclists, not by other cars. Most of them, unable to see who was inside our car, but realizing from the siren that it was an official one, hurriedly rode to the side of the road and stopped. Mr Tze sat chuckling at the back.

We were greeted at the entrance to the fair by a Mr Au, who introduced himself as the publicity manager for the fair.

'What would you like to see first?' he asked, beaming at me in a friendly manner through his thick glasses.

'Whatever you think best,' I replied. This seemed to be the right answer.

'These are parts,' he announced proudly, taking me to a large room.

'They look excellent, Mr Tze. What exactly do they fit?'

'Oil drills, of course.'

'Have you found oil?' I asked.

'Not actually found it. These parts can be used in machinery that makes holes for water, as well.'

'Which factory makes them?' I asked.

'The local factory for the Industrial State Corporation.'

'Is that a state corporation?'

'Certainly. We do not allow any capitalists to operate in China yet, though I expect the day will come.' He shook his head sadly as he took me into a nearby warehouse, full of towels and sheets.

'How do you fix the prices, Mr Au?'

'We find what the towels made in Japan, or Hong Kong or a European country, would cost. Then we charge about half.'

'Market forces, Mr Au?'

'Certainly not. It is only by charging less that we can be sure that we shall sell many towels.'

'What do you do if people don't buy your products?'

'Market then more cheaply.'

'Then you're bound to lose money, aren't you?'

'That is a capitalist outlook. What does it matter if we do? It's only an entry in a book. We have no shareholders in China, so we do not have to worry about them.'

'But what if one of the workers in one of your factories does not work well. Can you get rid of him?'

'Not for being a poor workman. We keep him in the factory, as we can't sack anyone – except for having unhealthy political thoughts, of course.'

'Is everyone paid the same?' Au nodded. 'What about incentives, to make them work a bit harder?'

'The incentive is already there. It is working for the motherland.'

'What if some of them have been ruined by the capitalist system? It's only just over the border? They might hope to get more pay if they work harder?'

'If we found anyone like that, we should have him put in prison for trying to spread ideas which are opposed to the state and for economic sabotage. Any other questions?'

I did not have any, even if I was attracted by the thought of someone asking for more pay being locked up for economic sabotage.

Some years later, I asked a Hong Kong entrepreneur who had established a factory in Szenchen inside China if he had any difficulty with his workers.

'At first,' he agreed. 'We had to carry a lot of dead wood, because we could not sack anyone. Then we paid large sums to the local party funds, so that those who were nominated by us could be transferred to other work.'

'Were the Chinese workers very productive?'

'Not in the beginning. Why bother, if you are paid the same amount whether you are good or bad? So we had to introduce incentives. We had some trouble over this, as the profit motive was not popular then.'

'How did you get round it?'

'By giving presents to workers who produced more than a specified quota. It was surprising what an effect the gift of a radio or a bicycle had. The final phase was to pay different wages. By then, China was full of capitalists and what we did was no longer disreputable.

I wrote a long report on my visit to China.

'Well done,' said the Political Adviser on the phone. 'You don't seem to have upset anyone. Even the journalists were happy, because they did not believe a word you said.'

Chapter 31

Another visit to China

The Political Adviser came to see me again in the summer of 1985.

'It does not look', he said in tones which seemed, to my rather sensitive ears, to indicate surprise, 'as if you managed to upset the Chinese, when you last went there three years ago.'

'I did my best,' I replied modestly. 'I said as little as possible.'

'I suppose that is why you have been asked to go back. The Supreme Court in Beijing will be your host, though I think it will be mainly sightseeing this time.'

'No meetings?'

'Come now, you can't expect to visit China without any meetings. This is supposed to be an official visit. You will be leading a delegation of Chinese judges from Hong Kong.'

'What about wives?'

They are included in the invitation. I hope you will let them all know that shrill cries of joy, at whatever they are shown, will be much appreciated by their hosts.'

'I do not think, P.A., that my wife is very good at that. She is Welsh and people from the valleys are only really happy when things go wrong. I went to a funeral in Cardiff. Everyone was very solemn until a man fell and broke his ankle. After that they were very cheerful.'

'Don't worry, the Chinese sense of humour is rather similar. Don't forget to delegate one of your group to break an ankle. It never fails if things get difficult.'

We were accommodated, for the Beijing part of our visit, in the Fragrant Hills Hotel, about twenty kilometres out of Beijing. The day began with what the hotel described as an English breakfast. This consisted of cornflakes, made in Switzerland, American muffins, Chinese tea, oranges from California and half cooked tinned frankfurters. There was, in addition, jam made in Taiwan, from which the caption had been removed. Instead, the words 'Made in the People's Republic of China' had been written on an attached sticky label.

On the first morning, the lift, in which one of the wives of the group was travelling, stopped between floors at the hotel. It took forty minutes to release her. This was made possible by officers of the fire brigade, who flooded the main hotel foyer with water before anyone could convince them that there was no fire. After turning off the hoses, the firemen attacked the lift shaft with blow lamps and axes. After a few minutes, the lift, now badly damaged, was lowered to the ground floor by hand and its door wedged open long enough for its occupants to leave it. No lift worked again in the hotel before we left, though this was only a few days.

'Everybody must use the stairs,' explained Mr Yiu, our interpreter. 'It is the fault of the beastly Japanese. The three wrestlers in the lift weighed a thousand pounds.'

'I thought', I said, 'that it was the Russians who were responsible for most of the shortcomings in China, not of course that there are any, rather than the Japanese?'

'Not so,' replied Mr Yiu firmly. 'Both are very wicked people, who tried to exploit China when China was weak and they were strong. Why,' he finished indignantly, 'the lift would be working if it were not for the Japanese. Wretched people!'

The following day I decided that I would like to lock my hotel room. It was a stupid ambition. I first spoke to the forbidding woman who sat in a booth at the end of a long corridor which led from my room to the lifts, now superseded by the stairs.

'Have you got the key for Room 252?' I asked her.

'Room 252 on next floor,' she said, confidently.

'It says 252 on my door,' I explained.

'All rooms have new number,' she replied.

'Why?' I asked.

'State policy,' she answered. 'This now floor one. You want Room 152 key.'

'Oh, all right, if you say so.'

'No key for Room 152,' she said, with a happy smile.

I could not make her change her mind.

'You ask manager,' she advised. 'Maybe he has a key. I have no key. So you have no key, ha ha.'

I asked Mr Yiu whether it would be possible to get a key to lock my room, telling him about the corridor woman's refusal. Mr Yiu shook his head.

'Every guest to this hotel has asked for a key, for the last two years. There are no keys. It is better to have no keys. Then if there is a fire everyone can get out of the room! Besides,' he added, 'if you cannot lock your room, you will not commit adultery.'

'I'm afraid that this is not likely to put anyone off,' I explained. 'If you move the beds out as well, this might have some effect.'

'There were some keys when the hotel opened,' Mr Yiu conceded. 'Then they were lost. I expect it was the Americans who took them. They are always taking back souvenirs. Anyway, it is not the hotel's fault that there are no keys.'

The meetings which we attended in Beijing, Sian and Canton followed the same general pattern. As our wives had been asked to come to China, they attended the meetings, though they were given uncomfortable chairs near the door and were not expected to say anything.

The Hong Kong delegation waited in an ante-room for a quarter of an hour before the agreed time. This made it clear to us that we were being received by senior Chinese officials, and that this was a privilege.

It is likely that we would, in each place, have been greeted by the second most senior official of whichever ministry in the area was unfortunate enough to have been chosen to look after us. The most senior official was reserved for the top level visitors. We were, however, given considerable face, in Chinese eyes, by being received by the second most senior official.

The receiving official would rise from the central chair, beaming happily. Hovering over his right shoulder was the interpreter, who translated everything into English for my benefit. The official often spoke admirable English himself, but custom required that Mandarin, or Cantonese in the South, should be spoken when any delegation of foreigners was received.

To the left of the official were the members of his party. I was introduced to them by the man who ushered us into the room. They all seemed to be called Chau or Li. They took no part in the proceedings, other than to smile throughout and nod their heads from time to time during the speeches. They did this when I spoke as well.

The members of the Hong Kong group passed along the line of Chinese officials, smiling and bowing as they went. They were shown to the empty chairs to the right of the chairman, whom I will call 'Big Li'.

In front of everyone was a small table, containing a cup of lukewarm Chinese tea. Big Li sipped from this, followed by the members of his group and the visitors. Big Li was handed a script by the interpreter and read from it. Wherever we went, his speech was more or less the same. I suppose that the Ministry of Foreign Affairs distributed copies, so that Big Li and other chairmen should not say anything unfortunate to visitors.

> It is my pleasure to welcome our guests and to hope that their stay in China will be interesting and rewarding. We shall, of course, do all we can to ensure that our distinguished visitors are comfortable and well looked after.
>
> China is a vast country, of great natural beauty, with many fine buildings and national monuments. It is prospering greatly as a result of the inspiring efforts of the Communist Party and the fulfilment of socialist ideals, under the guidance of Deng Xhau Ping, our great leader.
>
> If any of you should see anything in China which you think is capable of being improved, you must let us know, so that it can be put right.

Big Li sat down, handed the paper back to the interpreter, lit a strong smelling cigarette and nodded at me.

I read my reply, which had been cleared with the British Embassy in Beijing, to make sure that I did not upset Big Li or any of his colleagues. There had been a time in the past when every advance, even if it were backwards, was attributed to the genius of Chairman Mao, though this was no longer the case and it would have been worse than tactless to mention it.

The invitation to mention matters capable of improvement was not to be taken seriously. One delegation, when one of its members was injured by a fall of stones on the Great Wall, had suggested that it might be a good idea to repair it. The Chinese had refused to accept any responsibility for the injury, which was attributed to an American/Russian/Taiwanese plot to discredit China's national memorials.

> It is a great honour for the Hong Kong delegation to have been invited to China, which has for long been the focus of international attention and which everyone wishes to visit.
>
> We hope that our visit will do something to cement the happy relations between Hong Kong and the People's Republic of China, and in the years ahead Hong Kong will be as valuable to China as it is at present, when it becomes part of China and preserves its present way of life.

At the end of what I said, I was politely clapped. Once I was received in stony silence when I referred in error to the Republic of China, which was the term used by Taiwan. Although the interpreter refused to translate it, the audience heard the slip and did not regard it as an amusing mistake.

It was assumed that all those who visited the country would like to visit the Great Wall of China. This was modestly described by the Chinese themselves as a superb achievement.

No doubt it was, allowing for the primitive methods available at the time it was built. The fact that it was designed as a defence against invaders from outside, was never finished, and soon became redundant as China's frontiers moved west of it, were conveniently forgotten.

We were taken to a portion of the Great Wall which had been restored. Below it was a huddle of shacks, restaurants and temporary stores, designed to separate the tourist from his foreign currency. This was done with much aplomb by those Chinese who were allowed to sell souvenirs.

We ascended by a flight of badly worn stone steps to a watch-tower, from which a large stretch of land, heavily cultivated, could be seen to the west of the wall.

'This way, please,' shouted the guide, pointing at the crowd which was moving slowly towards me along the open portion of the wall. Nobody seemed to be going the other way.

I tried to follow him, as he forced his way along one side of the wall, uttering shrill cries in Mandarin. I asked him afterwards what he had said.

'I said "Make way. I have some foreigners with a disease",' he replied. 'Nobody got out of the way, so I expect the other people on the wall were foreigners too.'

'They looked Chinese to me.'

'They must have come from Canton or Chunking. Or they may have been Japanese or Korean. They look like Chinese, though they are really rather ugly.' The guide shuddered.

We had managed, with some difficulty, to force our way along one side of the wall, when I realized that the guide and I were alone. The rest of the party, which had been asked to stay close to the guide, had disappeared.

I turned back to tell the guide, whom I could not see. I was alone, surrounded by strange faces, all of them trying to get past me. I reminded myself that they were not hostile and that there was no need to be apprehensive as they came towards me. On reflection, I am obliged to admit that I was quite courageous – at least I was until the stranger gripped hold of my clothes and shouted at me.

'I'm terribly sorry,' I replied. 'I'm afraid I don't understand the language.'

This did not seem to be sufficient. The stranger shouted back at me. To my horror, tears began to run down his face. He pointed downwards towards his ankles. One was on the ground and one in the air. He continued to hold on to me and shout. As he did so, a small space opened behind us. I put one of his arms round my shoulders and slipped one of mine under his left arm. I was quite skilled at this, as I had twice come in second in the three-legged race at school. Indeed I should have won if my partner's knicker elastic had not let her down. I managed to regain the steps to the wall. I picked up the walking wounded and carried him down. He was an old man, who did not weigh much. He was still shouting when I laid him on the ground.

I discovered later that he had been shouting 'Make way for the English dog.' I suggested to the guide that he might find this a useful phrase in a crowd. He told me that he had already used it, slightly varied, with some success.

As I stood over the old man, and the latter was massaging his ankle, two men in khaki appeared and spoke to him, in what seemed to me to be a threatening manner. He scrambled to his feet and ran off. It was later explained to me that the police had been after him for some time and that he was a professional pickpocket, who had been very successful in removing tourists' wallets.

'Well,' my wife asked, as the old man disappeared, 'and where the hell have you been this time?'

'On the wall, of course,' I protested.

'Oh, really. And what wall was that?'

'We have come out this morning', I replied, in what I thought was a conciliatory tone, 'to see one of the wonders of the world, the Great Wall of China.'

'That does not explain why you went blasting off on your own with the guide, leaving the rest of us on our own on the wall with 20,000 strangers all trying to get off it.'

'You should have kept up.'

In the middle of this disagreement, which we were both enjoying, the guide reappeared, looking worried and dishevelled.

'I lost you,' he said. 'It was all my fault.'

He expected me to disagree with him. I let him down.

'There you are,' I said to my wife, with some pleasure. 'You can see it was not my fault at all.'

'I expect that you have all seen enough of the top of the Great Wall?' he enquired. 'It looks very good from down here,' he added hopefully. 'Would anyone like some refreshment?'

We spent another two days in Beijing, visiting the various monuments which are shown to visitors. Making the proper expressions

Tiananmen Square, 1985

of appreciation, we were shown the Ming Tombs, Mao's Mausoleum, the Forbidden City and Tiananmen Square.

We gave, as a small gesture of thanks to out hosts, a dinner in the Great Hall of the People. This was thought to have been something of a success, as none of the Hong Kong delegation drank too much or insulted the Chinese guests, unlike the last group of Russians entertained there, who were said to have done both.

We were then asked to be at the airport in Beijing, to be taken by plane to Sian, where we were to be shown the Terracotta Warriors. The plane was due to leave at three in the afternoon, so that we would arrive at Sian airport before dark. At four o'clock we were told that there had been a short delay. At five o'clock we were told that we would leave as soon as the necessary repairs had been carried out. At six, we were led out to the plane by our guide.

The plane had propellers. It was an aircraft donated by the Russians in 1954. It was out of date then. A man in stained overalls, who later was found to be the pilot, was trying to repair the windscreen wipers at the front of the cockpit.

It was soon apparent that there had been a serious overbooking. The plane had about sixty seats. These were already occupied, when we climbed aboard, using bent metal stairs from which one step was missing. The guide shouted at the passengers in front. They left without argument. I assume this had happened to them before.

The door to the plane was closed, with some difficulty. I searched for my seat belt. I found one end, but not the other. Next to me was my wife, in a reclining position.

'I expect that, before they take off, they will make you sit upright,' I explained.

'Good luck to them,' she replied. 'My seat back is broken and I can't move it. What about yours?'

'Well,' I said. 'I've got half a belt. What have you got?'

'You are very lucky. I have no belt at all.'

'I'm sure the air hostess will produce one when she comes round.'

'What air hostess?'

'There are a couple of ladies at the back, dressed in smocks. As they are not sitting down, I assume that's what they are.'

I looked back. Every seat was occupied. In addition, four women were squatting in the aisle, one of them attempting to calm an excited chicken.

An air hostess did not appear in the aisle before we took off. One of them spoke into a microphone at the back. As the loudspeaker system was not working, we did not hear what she said, though we should not have understood it even if we had heard it, as she only used Mandarin.

Half an hour after take-off, one of the air hostesses deposited a cardboard box in my lap. Inside it was a bun, filled with bean curd jam, a container of cold rice, a chicken's foot and two boiled sweets. The latter were excellent. The wrappers said 'FOX'S GLACEER MINT'. The spelling suggested that they were probably made in Hong Kong.

Soon afterwards, it became dark and began to rain. The door to the pilot's cabin opened and banged noisily. An air hostess went forward to deal with it. Before she shut the door, I noticed that the pilot was peering through the windscreen in front of him and shaking his head.

The guide spoke to the air hostess, when she returned to the cabin.

'There is a small trouble,' he announced. 'The windscreen wipers are not working and you can't repair them from inside. The radio is not working either. So the pilot has decided that he will land at the airport at Taiyun. We can go on to Sian in the morning.'

'How will they know that we are going to land at Taiyun?' I asked.

'Don't worry about that. We have ways of letting them know!' I did not ask what these were. I found out at Taiyun. The pilot opened one of his cabin windows slightly, poked a Verey pistol through it and fired a green flare at the ground. He circled the airport and landed.

We were led by the guide into the airport terminal. 'Please wait here', he announced, 'while we arrange for your overnight accommodation in Taiyun.'

It was about eight o'clock when he delivered this optimistic message. We waited in the lounge until about eleven, when he rushed in, smiling happily.

'We shall be staying in the Happy Blossom Hotel. It is a new hotel which is not yet open for business. The pilot says he can take off for Sian at seven o'clock tomorrow morning. He asks us to be here by half past five.

'Why must we be here so early?' I asked.

'Because of your luggage,' explained the guide. 'It has to be taken out to the plane and put on by hand. We are expecting trucks next year,' he added. 'Please follow me to the luxury bus which we have secured for your exclusive use.'

The bus, a fourteen-seater minibus, made in Japan, had not been used before. Plastic covers still adorned the seats.

'Put on specially for you,' my wife commented. 'They must have guessed that you make a mess wherever you go.'

Before I could reply suitably, the bus started with a jerk. The driver, directed by the guide, made his way into town in a series of jerks. He pulled up outside the Happy Blossom Hotel. In the reception area were two lights, which cast a sufficient glow to show that the reception desk itself was empty.

'The first six rooms on the ground floor are empty,' the guide said. 'I have not been able to find the keys.'

I took the first room on the left, at the prompting of my wife.

'Let's be close to the exit when the fire alarms go off,' she said.

'What makes you think there are any?'

'I don't suppose there are. But if there were, if they were working and if someone remembers to switch them on, I'd like to get out.'

'Nonsense,' I replied. 'You're heavily insured. Please don't be selfish. It would be better if you did not survive.'

The bedroom was spacious. The bed was comfortable. The paint pots and brushes stood neatly in the corner. On the bed was a pile of dirty bedclothes, still in their covers. There were no clean sheets, blankets or covers. What there was kept us warm throughout the night, which was now getting short. It was nearly midnight and we should have to get up at five if we were to reach the airport on time.

The toilet contained water; however, it did not pull and had been used by the workmen for various sanitary purposes. We added to their contributions and slept soundly until awakened by the guide at four thirty. He had served for a time with the Chinese People's

Liberation Army and believed that the only way of ensuring that people arrived on time was to get them to a place an hour before they were meant to be there.

We were taken back to the airport, where we arrived soon after five o'clock in the morning. At seven o'clock, we were informed that the plane was not yet ready to take off, as it had to be repaired by a mechanic, who had not yet arrived.

At eight o'clock we were given a bowl of congee and a cup of Chinese tea. With this came a rich cake. The guide had heard that it was my wife's birthday. Somehow, he had managed to conjure up something to celebrate the day. She was very touched.

'You see,' she said, 'somebody has remembered it is my birthday.'

'But I did,' I protested. 'I sang "Happy birthday" to you at the hotel!'

'Is that what that dreadful noise was? I thought you were trying to clear your throat.'

The plane did not leave Taiyun until eleven in the morning. After a short flight, uneventful except for the woman who tried to light a stove in the gangway to warm her Chinese tea, we arrived at Sian about noon.

We were met at the airport by another guide, who led us to a restaurant. Here we were given an excellent lunch. At the end of this, my wife was presented with a birthday cake by the new guide, who had organized this hurriedly on having been told of the occasion by the other guide.

We were put in the severe, rectangular 'guest house' built by the Russians some years before. The more comfortable hotel was the place for tourists, but guests of the Government continued to be accommodated in what had previously been the best appointed place.

The guest house was, in spite of a somewhat grim and unfriendly concrete exterior, more comfortable inside than was expected. There was a reception desk, in which a bearded woman, of uncertain age and temper, viewed every visitor with a suspicious eye. As I looked like a foreigner, and probably had a right to be there, she let me past with no more than a sneer. The guide, however, was required to produce his identity card and pass each time he sought to enter the guest house.

The dining room was large and the food served there was adequate. The bedroom was large and spacious. There was no comfortable chair, but this was so throughout China. Either Chinese bottoms were different or it was considered to be decadent to be comfortable.

Leading off the bedroom was a large bathroom. In it, one of the two light bulbs was broken. The other hung from the ceiling by a frayed cord. I had not bathed since the night before we left Beijing. There was a good supply of hot water. I filled the bath and undressed. As I started to climb into it, my wife screamed.

'Oh dear. Have you seen another cockroach?' For some reason, she found cockroaches frightening only when she was pregnant. The rest of the time, she had no difficulty in dealing with anything that crawled, including myself.

'Don't get into the bath!'

'But I'm dirty.'

'Everyone knows that. If you get into the bath, you'll be sorry. It's full of broken glass.'

I peered hard at the water. Without my spectacles I could not see much.

'Looks all right to me.'

'Well, it's not. Now I've warned you, it won't be my fault if you cut your bottom to ribbons.'

I let out the water. I could still see nothing, but decided that she should be humoured. As the last of the water flowed out, the exit was surrounded by broken glass.

'How did that get there, I wonder? It's not the light bulb that doesn't work. Perhaps the previous occupants did it?'

'If so, why put the bits in the bath?'

'You'd better report it when we go down for dinner.'

I told the guide what had happened. He burst into laughter, for the first time for two days. He was genuinely amused. Before we went to the dining room, he informed the woman behind the desk. She was bent double with laughter.

It was a good dinner, at which a number of toasts were drunk to the advancement of China and to the prosperity of Hong Kong. I proposed one myself to the improvement in China of civil aviation, which was greeted with cries of approval by the guides. I did not drink any of the Chinese brandy myself, explaining that I had a dreadful ulcer and that my doctor had told me that I must not drink. This excuse was acceptable as a reason why I could not take much brandy. The dinner was completed with another birthday cake and a further celebration of my wife's birthday. She joined in the singing, the only sign that the twelve brandies which she had drunk had had any effect on her at all.

When we reached the bedroom, it was full of people. One of the guides, who had escorted us to the room, explained that the woman at the desk had come, because the broken glass had been found in an area which she was supposed to control; the guest house manager and the room cleaner were there because it had happened in the hotel; and there were four or five policemen, one of whom was sweeping the glass into an envelope while the rest were arguing. The argument continued for about an hour. I was asked three times to repeat my story of the glass in the bath. Eventually, everyone left the room.

'Well, I shall remember my 30th birthday,' she said. 'I've eaten three birthday cakes, been got out of bed at four thirty, flown in a plane which had been rescued from a junkyard and saved my husband from losing his knackers. And I'm pregnant.'

The guide knocked on the door and re-entered the room.

'I thought you would like to know that the hotel manager has expressed his deep regret that such a thing should have happened in his guest house. The police officers asked me to say that they will vigorously pursue the perpetrators of this wicked crime against the visitors of the state.'

'It was only a bit of glass,' I protested.

'I am sure you would like to know that the room cleaner has been arrested by the police.'

'What will happen to him?'

'The penalty for economic sabotage is death. The police told me that they were short on the quota for this year.'

'Please tell them not to execute the cleaner on my behalf.'

'Thank you. I will let them know. They will be happy that you do not wish to be revenged on the cleaner.'

Two days later, we flew from Sian to Canton. We only had to wait three hours for an aeroplane this time, as it was in excellent mechanical condition. Apparently there was difficulty in finding a pilot. The one who was supposed to fly the plane had been arrested for activities against the state, as he had crash-landed some months before. Another pilot was found who had been trained on a different model. As it was made in the same year as ours, it was thought to be close enough. We stayed only a day in Canton, before taking the train which ran from there to Kowloon.

'At least I will be able to say what I really think. I've been charming to everyone for the last ten days, whether I agreed with them or not,' said my wife.

'A splendid performance. I hardly recognized you. More than once, you actually agreed with me.'

'Don't worry, please. I shall not do that again.'

'I'm afraid you will have to be dishonest a bit longer. There is a press conference at Kowloon station.'

'Surely nobody is likely to be very interested in us?'

'It depends. A lot of people are interested in the mainland, now that we know Hong Kong is to revert to China in 1997. But if there is a more interesting visitor to Hong Kong, they will be at Kai Tak, asking him questions he can't answer.'

I was led into the press room at Kowloon by a press officer. The rest of the delegation dispersed. Only my wife was left. She sat on a chair beside me, looking beautiful, dressed elegantly and made up for the occasion. She had spent most of the journey from the bridge at Lo Wu into Hong Kong in the lavatory. It was the first time for ten days that she had made up her face.

'First of all,' announced the press officer, 'the Chief Justice will make a statement about his visit to China. Then you can ask him questions. One at a time please. He has to leave here in thirty minutes.'

I made a short statement on how warm the welcome was in China, how well we were entertained wherever we went, and how this augured well for the future prosperity of Hong Kong when it reverted to China. I found that I believed what I was saying. I had been trained in the Colonial Secretariat in Hong Kong, as well as in other colonies, to tell 'white lies' with conviction, when this was necessary.

As I finished my short statement, a number of reporters came forward, some with tape recorders and others with microphones, which were thrust towards me. I was asked a number of questions. I answered those which did not seem too awkward.

'Why did your delegation go to China?'

'Because we were asked.'

'What about judges? Are the expatriate ones going to stay on after 1997?'

'We were told that they would be very welcome.'

'What about the Final Court of Appeal, which is to replace the Privy Council? Was anything said about this?'

'In the meeting which we had in Beijing with the Vice-President of the Chinese Supreme Court, he said that he could see no objection to it.'

'Did you see any trials? Is it true that 15,000 people were executed for crimes last year?'

'We did not see any trials. We went to China to be entertained. The only legal business we did was in Canton. Where did you get your figure of 15,000 from?'

'It was in a hand-out from the NCNA.'

'Then you'd better ask them if they've got it right.'

'What was the legal business which you did in Canton?' I was relieved that I was not asked if I thought the 15,000 had been given a fair trial.

'It was about the service of Canton documents in Hong Kong. I don't suppose you'd be very interested in that.'

'Does it mean that, if I am accused of a crime in Canton, you can arrest me here and force me back across the border into China?'

'Certainly not. This only applies to civil cases. It seemed to us to be reasonable for those over the border to be able to use our courts here to serve a witness summons on somebody in Hong Kong.'

'Why is it reasonable? Will it work both ways?'

'There are a lot of enterprises over the border in which the real owner is a Hong Kong businessman. If anyone in China has a claim against the business, it is surely sensible for the summons to be served here by a Hong Kong court.'

'You said it would work both ways?'

'That's right. If a party to a Hong Kong civil claim wants to call a witness who lives in China, the Canton court will make sure that he knows about the case.'

Nothing had been done to bring this agreement into force before I left. Perhaps it has now.

'Your visit must have cost a lot of money.'

'The People's Republic of China was most generous. It must have been very expensive for China, which is not a rich country.'

'I mean for Hong Kong. Five judges have been out of court for nearly two weeks. Will they still get paid?'

'I hope so. If you are really asking whether the visit, which certainly cost Hong Kong a great deal, indirectly if not directly, was worth the expense, I am quite sure that it was. Such a visit is a good omen for your future.'

I still believe that it was.

Chapter 32
Notable achievements

It would be wrong to assume that I occupied the post of Colonial Secretary of Hong Kong without several important achievements. Those who regard my tenure of this office as a wasteland, and there seem to be a surprising number of them, clearly did not take into account the many advances made during this period, from later 1973 until late 1978. Among these was the change of title of Colonial Secretary to Chief Secretary.

I tested this important alteration on Michael Clinton, the Deputy Colonial Secretary, a clever, pleasant man, who had insisted that he did not want to be the Colonial Secretary, as he should have been.

'How would you feel if I changed my title?' I asked him.

'Would it involve changing your initials? To Permanent Secretary or something like that?'

'Certainly not. That would be going too far. I thought of changing Colonial Secretary to Chief Secretary.'

'Why?'

'It is more in accordance with modern thought, Michael. Colonies are no longer fashionable.'

'I thought the laws had lots of reference to the Colony?'

'That is different,' I replied firmly. 'Besides, I will do something about them in time.'

'Well, if you really want to know what I think, I am sure it is a rotten idea, even worse than your proposal to save electricity.'

This was an unfair reference to my courageous reaction to the sharp increase in oil prices and electricity costs. To reduce the Government's consumption, I had ordered that the air conditioning should be switched off everywhere. How was I to know that this would be the hottest summer for twenty years and that it was not possible to open windows in most offices?

'I note your reservations, Michael. What would you say to a sub-committee?'

'Waste of time,' he replied. 'If it recommends what you want to do, you'll do it. If it says something else, you'll give it what you call "further consideration", which means that you'll put the report in the third drawer on the right in your desk and try to forget about it.'

'You've been in my drawers again!' I protested.

'You asked me to put a paper on the reorganization of the medical services in a safe place. Your third drawer is already full, by the way.'

'They recommended a flying doctor service with two helicopters. We can't afford that.'

'Hong Kong has plenty of money,' he retorted. 'There has been a budget surplus for the last five years.'

'You make it sound sinful!'

'Nobody else has a surplus. Besides,' he added, 'you are afraid of the Financial Secretary!'

'Nonsense,' I replied. 'We get on splendidly. He does his job and tells me to get lost if I make a suggestion to him. I do my job and he tells me how to carry it out.'

'What would he say to a change of name?'

'I'd rather not ask him. He'd probably say it didn't matter, as the job that matters is his and he ought to be called Chancellor.'

'I wonder why he was not appointed as C.S.,' Michael commented. 'Not, of course,' he added quickly, 'that he would have done it as well as you.'

'He is not popular in London among the politicians, because he says what he thinks rather forcefully, including his views on the economic mess he thinks Britain has got itself into.'

'You think so too, don't you?'

'If I have any opinion on things I don't understand, I try to keep my mouth shut. Whom shall we have as a sub-committee?'

'It depends what you want it to say in its report.'

'I wouldn't think of telling it what to do. Indeed, I will leave it to you to decide whom to appoint.'

Michael Clinton did not hurry. He did not share my view that the change would be important psychologically. Over the next few months he assembled a committee of those heads of departments and secretaries who had displeased him. About a year after I had spoken to him, I received a report. This recommended, in a long and convoluted sentence containing at least two double negatives, that nothing should be done. It was a public service report, of which I would usually have been proud, containing a careful dissection of a number of issues and a measure of unintelligible but weighty conclusions. Unhappily, it did not accord with my wishes. I therefore took the statesmanlike decision to ignore it and press ahead with the reform. Henceforth, the post was that of Chief Secretary.

A year or so after I had taken office as C.S., the Financial Secretary, who carried the English hyphenated name of Haddon-Cave but had been educated in Australia, where he had acquired a sense of humour and directness, passed to me a file about the Supreme Court.

'The C.J. is asking for a new Supreme Court. We can't afford it. Perhaps the Jockey Club would stump up after it has finished paying for its own amusement park. Please do not encourage him.'

Some years before, Sir Michael Hogan had decided that he did not want a new Supreme Court and that he would prefer the existing one to be further divided. I drew the attention of the incumbent Chief Justice to this. He phoned. I pretended to be out until my secretary told me that it was time I spoke to him, as she had tried her full range of untruths on his secretary without success.

'How are the frogs?' I began, hoping that this would ingratiate me with him, as model ones were his main interest.

'I have not phoned about them. It is about your letter.'

'Alas, it's the shortage of money, Geoffrey. Otherwise we would be happy to meet you. What a pity one of your predecessors wanted to stay where you are.'

'I am sure that he was right in the 1960s, but there is much more work and we can't divide up the present building any further.'

He was following the accepted practice. This was to blame your predecessor for whatever went wrong in the first year or so following your appointment. After that, you did not blame him but indicated, with an expression of regret, that you were still suffering from decisions taken in the past which were no doubt correct at the time but had been outmoded by later events.

'What about a committee?' I enquired.

'There is one, Roberts. It thinks we should have a new building.'

'Who was on it?'

'Members of the judiciary, of course.'

'Oh dear,' I replied. 'You'll have to put some other people on it, if you want its report to be taken seriously.'

'That would be compromising the independence of the judiciary,' he replied in tones which suggested that I should know better. It was a useful phrase, employed by a judge whenever he wanted something. I used it myself later, whenever I needed a washer changing.

'Oh, I quite agree, C.J. But the F.S. says we are short of money this year. It's the oil crisis, you know.'

'That was last year,' he protested.

'Yes, but its effects will be with us for a long time.' I was still referring to this some years later, whenever I was obliged to refuse some entirely reasonable expenditure, but could think of no other excuse.

'What do you suggest, C.S.?'

'Another committee, chaired by an outsider.'

'That would undermine the constitutional position of the judges!'

'I daresay. But it is the only way of getting anything.'

'I agree under protest.'

I still hoped, in spite of the fact that, as C.S., I appeared to be responsible for a chain of disasters, that I would be able to succeed the C.J. when he retired. I therefore established a neutral committee, with myself as chairman. The members included a Public Works Department architect whose job it would be to design a new courthouse, a judge who would sit in it and a member of the Bar who would appear in it.

We were able to show, by judicious use of statistics, some of them taken from the 1930s, that the volume of work had increased to such an extent that the present building could no longer accommodate all the judges, and that a new courthouse was essential.

There were two possible sites, one in the centre of town and another on the site of an abandoned ammunition store at the front of the Victoria Barracks area, which had been occupied by the services since the 1840s. The Bar representative argued vigorously for the area in the centre, on which a bus terminal was later constructed. It would have been much closer to his chambers than the ammunition store. He insisted that he was merely representing the views of the legal profession.

Some months later, I sent a report to the F.S., with a unanimous recommendation that a new courthouse should be built in the barracks. In my covering letter, I hoped that the necessary funds could be found. I had by then ceased using the word 'money', which was vulgar and triggered an adverse reaction.

'A very convincing report,' the F.S. commented when I entered his office a fortnight later to see how his back was. This gave him some pain and helped him to maintain that appearance of ill humour which is expected of a good F.S.

'I tried so hard to prevent the committee from suggesting a new building,' I said.

'I can see that from the report. At least this committee only had one judge on it. So I suppose we shall have to find the funds from somewhere. It will, of course, mean that we shan't be able to pay any orphans' allowance for another year.'

'As they have managed without one for the past hundred years, I suppose another year won't matter.'

'If you insist on putting judges before orphans, that is a matter for you. I only provide the funds. You decide the priority.'

A new Supreme Court was designed, built and occupied in 1984, shortly before the F.S., who had by then become Chief Secretary, left Hong Kong.

'What a stroke of luck that the committee was in favour of this building,' the C.S. said, gazing round the hall, 'though I don't recall anything about marble.'

'I am afraid that there was a cost overrun. You know what it is with these Government contracts.'

Early in 1976, I had occasion to look at the Letters Patent. These provided, with the Royal Instructions to the Governor, the Constitution of Hong Kong. Embedded in these Letters were articles governing the retirement of judges. One of them provided for the Chief Justice to retire at 62. This was in accordance with a circular issued by the Colonial Office in the 1930s, when it was assumed that judges would either have drunk themselves to death by that age or, if not, would no longer be effective. I mentioned the matter to the Governor.

'This means', I explained, 'that if I don't go in May I can't go at all. And you will be stuck with me until I retire.'

'Good lord!' he replied.

'Or I could go across as C.J. in May and you would have to appoint a new C.S.'

'I can't do that yet.'

'Oh? Why not?'

'Because one of the possible men is doing an excellent job where he is, and the other has upset the ministers in London and will have to wait until we get a change of government.'

'There is another possible answer. You could extend the C.J.'s retiring age to 65. That would mean that I could succeed the present holder in 1979. The drawback is that I would occupy this post for another three years.'

'I suppose that is possible, Denys. The protests against your appointment seem to have died down.'

'What about the other judges?' I asked. 'They won't like the idea of the C.J. being given an older age of retirement than theirs.'

'Let's say they all must retire at 62, but can apply for an extension to 65?'

'They won't like that. They will complain that it is yet another example of interference with the judiciary.'

'But they will ask for the extension.'

'It will have to be offered to them.'

The Governor nodded. He was used to dealing in a similar way with the Chinese. Having first discovered whether, if asked, they would agree to do something, he would then arrange for them to be asked.

The Foreign Office did not approve the changes to the Letters Patent until a few days before the C.J. was due to retire.

When I had occupied the C.S.'s office for a couple of years, Mr Plinth, the secret service man, came to see me, closing the door behind him in a furtive way.

'You are overlooked,' he hissed out of the corner of his mouth.

'Are you having trouble with your teeth, Mr Plinth?'

'Certainly not. I am just being cautious. We do not know if this room is bugged.'

'I have it swept regularly,' I replied.

'That's not enough. What have you done about the directional laser beam?' I had to confess that I had done nothing, as I had not heard of it before.

'You are vulnerable to a beam from the Bank of China. Have a look for yourself.'

I looked out of the small window behind my chair. The Bank of China, which was one of the principal buildings occupied by the officials of the Chinese People's Government stationed in Hong Kong, was a couple of hundred yards away.

'I don't see anything, Mr Plinth.'

'You wouldn't. If the Communists had a secret device in the top floor, or on the roof, they could point it at your office and find out what you are doing!'

'I don't think I do anything most of the time!'

'Anyone on the roof with a high powered rifle could take you out easily.'

'Ah, that's different. What do you want me to do?'

'No need for you to do anything. I will arrange for a couple of men to put in some bulletproof glass, which will protect you against being assassinated and will stop the Communists listening to you all day.'

'I'm glad we have the priorities right, Mr Plinth.'

'We will return with your glass tomorrow.'

When he did so, the new window was too large. My old one was simply dismantled by striking it with a hammer, so that some of the glass fell into the gardens below.

A week later, Mr Plinth returned with two men and another window. Mr Plinth told me, in answer to my question, that they could speak if necessary and denied that he had removed their tongues so that they were unable to report what they had heard.

This time the window seemed to be the correct size, until it fell into the garden. Mr Plinth returned with a replacement three days later. He watched as my window was fitted again.

'You are safe from murder and eavesdropping,' he told me proudly. 'Just call me if anything goes wrong.'

I thanked him for his kindness in installing such an expensive piece of equipment. I had already received four claims from persons who alleged that they had been cut by falling glass.

I handed over my office a couple of years later to my successor. Before I did so, the current Mr Plinth examined it, to see if anything needed to be done. He was impressed by my window, and asked why I had put it in the wrong way round.

'You mean that the Bank could find out what was going on in here, if anything was?'

'That's right. But you could not see the Bank. Very clever, sir, if I may say so. Sort of double bluff, I expect.'

Ex. Co. had advised that Hong Kong should build an underground railway, which would run along the north coast of Kowloon on two separate lines covering much of the New Territories. Tenders were invited for its construction. The most attractive of these was a quotation from a large Japanese firm, which submitted a sum for the whole line, though it was understood that much of it would be undertaken by sub-contractors.

On the instruction of the Governor, I asked the member of the tender board, who attended Ex. Co., if the firm could guarantee that the Mass Transit Railway, as it was called, would be built for a fixed price, even if the expected profits would be eroded by inflation. I was assured that the price would remain in any event. On that basis, Ex. Co. awarded the contract to the Japanese firm.

Early the following year, when inflation during the past two years had reached a total of about 30 per cent, the Japanese firm withdrew from the contract, on the ground that it could no longer expect to make a profit. The Governor was annoyed. He had been assured that the firm would continue in any event.

'I think the time has come to call in the Japanese Consul,' he said.

'What for?' I asked. 'Is it to congratulate him on a Japanese firm's breach of contract?'

'Certainly not. It's good Foreign Office practice, if you don't like what the national of another country has done, to call in its Ambassador and protest.'

'Can you usc foul language?'

'Certainly not. It is a diplomatic protest. The worst you can say is that Her Majesty's Government views with grave concern the conduct of X and expects that appropriate steps will be taken to put matters right.'

'Does it work?'

'Not often. It used to be very effective, when we had a large navy. I thought it would be a good idea if you told the Japanese Consul what the Hong Kong Government thinks about this withdrawal.'

'I don't suppose he can do anything.'

'Of course he can't. That's not the point of the protest. You let them see that you are upset.'

I asked the Japanese Consul if he would come and see me. The appointment was postponed, so that he could go on leave first. He came to my office with a box of cigars, which he handed to me with a formal bow.

'For Chinese New Year,' he said. I did not remind him that this had taken place four months before.

'Please sit down, Mr Consul.' I had forgotten his name, which was long. I had written it down but lost the paper.

'I expect you want to tell me that the Hong Kong Government is upset about the Mass Transit Railway?'

'That is so, Mr Matsukama.' I had found the piece of paper, which was upside down on my desk with a note to buy more toffees scrawled on it.

'It is a grave embarrassment to my Government. I know that we Japanese are not yet popular here.'

'Yes, but –'

'It is only a month since the mass grave of the victims of Japan's militarism was found at South Bay.'

'Yes, but –'

'I know how long it takes for people here to forget the Japanese occupation. If the skeletons can be identified, we shall be ready to pay a proper compensation to the families.'

'I did not want to talk about them, Mr Matsukama.'

'Please do not apologize, Mr Roberts. I know you are under pressure yourself. Now about the Mass Transit Railway, which is, I realize, of much less importance than the grave. My government has spoken severely to the firm, which agreed to a fixed price.'

'A bad show,' I contributed.

'It is not in accordance with Japanese honour to withdraw from a contract.'

'I'm very pleased to hear that, so –'

'Only in exceptional circumstances would a Japanese, when he has given his word, consider withdrawing.'

'Do you mean that the firm would like to cancel its withdrawal?'

'There has been terrible inflation in Hong Kong, so that the firm could only make a huge loss. You would not expect that, I am sure.'

'Why not?'

'I knew you would agree,' replied the Consul. 'I have the authority of my Government to say that it deeply regrets the inconvenience and disappointment you must feel, because your railway is no longer to be built by the Japanese.'

'I say, look here, Mr Matusukiki.'

'Matsukama, though I assure you it does not matter. If only we could interfere, we would do so, but you will understand that we cannot. We are a free enterprise economy, though we have not, of course, yet achieved your own remarkable success.' He bowed over the desk.

'Yes, but –,' I began.

'Alas, if only we had been able to build your railway. And how unwise to offer a fixed price in a time of acute inflation.'

I agreed. Mr Matsukama left my office in a flurry of bows.

'Well,' the Governor asked the next morning, 'did you give the Japanese Consul a rough time?'

'Rather,' I replied. 'I told him how upset you were. By the time I had finished with him, he was apologizing.'

'Good. I must use you for another hatchet job.'

One of the last things done by Sir Hugh Norman-Walker, before he left Hong Kong, was to ensure that those who had joined the public service before a specified date should remain eligible, on retirement, to a sea passage to their country of origin. Sir Hugh travelled home on a container ship, as no other passenger vessel was due to visit Hong Kong for several weeks. I had benefited from Sir Hugh's refusal, in spite of Treasury insistence, to give away a privilege which he valued. He must have been a brave man, as well as being an admirable C.S.

I had arranged to sail home on the *Canberra*, occupying a cabin which I could not afford, because my wife reminded me (as she had already pointed out on several previous occasions) that I was spineless, weak and allowed the Treasury to walk all over me.

She greeted me, a month or so before we were due to go, with some unhappy news.

'I've been rung up,' she began.

'Not another heavy breather? It must be someone from the Legal Department again.'

She ignored me, apart from a sniff. 'T.V.B. have phoned. They want to do a programme about you before you go.'

'Another carefully prepared spontaneous statement? I'm rather good at that!'

'They want to do an hour on what you have achieved in your quarter of a century here. I told them it would have to be a very short programme.'

'That's not fair!'

'You just tell me how they are going to pad it out. They can just about manage a minute a year – so long as the camera takes some lingering shots of your houses and of the places where you were supposed to work.'

'I could say that I found a young wife here.' I thought this might placate her.

'We can't have an hour TV show based on the story of how a dirty old man decided to go straight for once.'

'What about Henry, our son, then?' I asked.

'I suppose that disproves the stories about you being impotent. I mean personally as well as officially.'

'Well, I delivered some splendid judgments.'

'Splendid! Everybody has been trying to distinguish them ever since. The facts were different is the polite way of saying the judge must have been off his rocker.'

'Do you think anyone will remember that I was S.G. and A.G. once upon a time?'

'It depends on what you did.'

'I drafted lots of laws.'

'They got rid of most of them, when I was in the A.G.'s chambers.'

'I was a great success in the social magazines. I was in the 'Top Ten Bachelors' three times, you know.'

'What did you have to pay for that?'

'And I recommended, when I was A.G., that the Government should have both an ICAC and ombudsmen. They've got both now.'

'Not when you were A.G. Since then someone else has recommended them. And what did you do as C.S.?'

'I learned to play scales with two hands, when I went for my music lessons.'

'I meant in your official capacity.'

'Apart from changing the title of my post, which was something of a triumph, I learned how not to give an unconditional answer to anything. I taught all the secretaries to do the same. It's been very useful since the treaty with China.'

'I expect you ought to have some credit for that.'

'Certainly not. I had nothing to do with it at all.'

'That does not usually stop you.'

'It does, of course, depend on how the treaty works. If it goes well, I shall modestly claim to have played a leading role. If it does not, I shall insist that I was not concerned with it at all.'

My most notable achievement in Hong Kong was to find Fiona, who will continue to put up with me for the years to come. When our son Henry was born, she appointed as godparents and guardians two of her best friends, Cheng Huan and Gilbert Rodway, both of whom had very successful practices in Hong Kong. They have kept me in touch with it over the years.

I hope that Hong Kong will continue to grow and flourish, as it did during my twenty-five years there. I wish the people of Hong Kong every happiness and prosperity.

Henry Roberts

INDEX